Gossip a

Routledge Studies in Management, Organizations, and Society

This series presents innovative work grounded in new realities, addressing issues crucial to an understanding of the contemporary world. This is the world of organised societies, where boundaries between formal and informal, public and private, local and global organizations have been displaced or have vanished, along with other nineteenth century dichotomies and oppositions. Management, apart from becoming a specialized profession for a growing number of people, is an everyday activity for most members of modern societies.

Similarly, at the level of enquiry, culture and technology, and literature and economics, can no longer be conceived as isolated intellectual fields; conventional canons and established mainstreams are contested. Management, Organization and Society addresses these contemporary dynamics of transformation in a manner that transcends disciplinary boundaries, with books that will appeal to researchers, student and practitioners alike.

Gossip and Organizations

Kathryn Waddington

Routledge
Taylor & Francis Group
NEW YORK   LONDON

First published 2012
by Routledge
711 Third Avenue, New York, NY 10017

Simultaneously published in the UK
by Routledge
2 Park Square, Milton Park, Abingdon, Oxon OX14 4RN

*Routledge is an imprint of the Taylor & Francis Group,
an informa business*

© 2012 Taylor & Francis

First issued in paperback 2014

Library of Congress Cataloging-in-Publication Data

Waddington, Kathryn.
   Gossip and organizations / by Kathryn Waddington.
      p. cm. — (Routledge studies in management, organizations, and
society ; 20)
   Includes bibliographical references and index.
   1. Communication in organizations.   2. Gossip.   3. Corporate culture.
4. Organizational behavior.   I. Title.
   HD30.3.W33 2012
   650.01'4—dc23
   2011052506

ISBN13: 978-0-415-41785-3 (hbk)
ISBN13: 978-1-138-01831-0 (pbk)

Typeset in Sabon
by IBT Global.

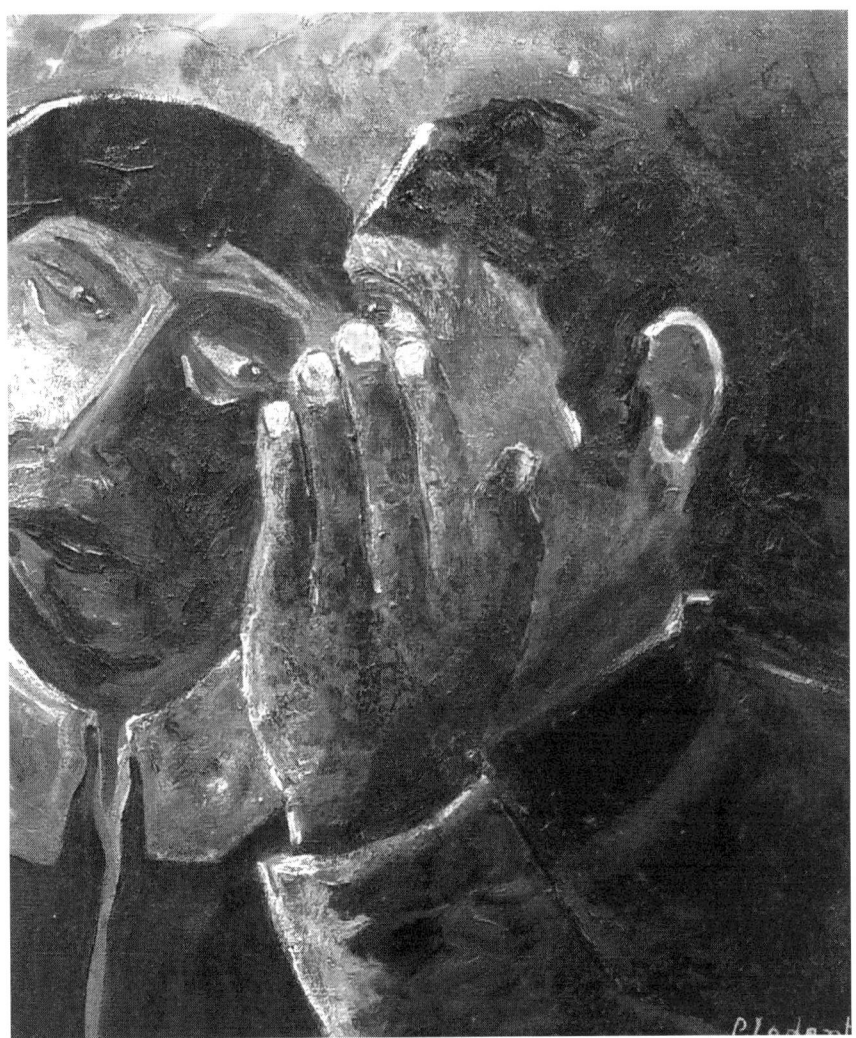

Frontispiece *Gossip* © Copyright Pol Ledent.

Dedicated to my Dad

Reg Croft (1920–2009)

Contents

Figures and Tables

FIGURES

TABLES

Foreword

Gossip is a much maligned phenomenon. It is especially problematic when applied to organizations and organizational processes. 'Celebrity gossip' is often seen as interesting and entertaining, but 'organizational gossip' is generally perceived to be something which should be ignored or eschewed.

Arguably, one of the main reasons why gossip gets such a 'bad press' in organizations is because it is constituted through informal and unsanctioned interaction. Key organizational stakeholders tend to find this form of 'unofficial discourse' both disconcerting and threatening on the basis that it is almost impossible to meaningfully regulate and control. Hence, from the manager's perspective, gossip at best operates as superfluous interference or 'noise' in organizational settings. At worst, it questions legitimate goals and actions, and potentially undermines formal authority. More simply, managers typically do not like gossip because it implicitly challenges their power.

The propensity of managers to ignore or downplay the role and status of gossip in organizational settings is perhaps unsurprising. However, the fact that academics have tended to overlook this inescapable facet of organizational life is far more difficult to fathom. If one looks at mainstream organization theory and organizational behaviour textbooks, gossip is rarely mentioned let alone properly discussed (see, for example, Fincham & Rhodes, 2005; Mullins, 2002). It would be easy to attribute this systemic oversight to an inclination to primarily focus upon the more formal and more tangible aspects of organizing (e.g., leadership, organizational structure, and job design). Yet, other less formal aspects of organizing do nevertheless receive attention (e.g. organizational culture, norms, and politics).

It is disappointing that organizational scholars have generally failed to acknowledge and engage with gossip, but what is even more difficult to explain is why those with cognate specialist interests, such as organizational discourse, management communications, and work and interaction studies, have also neglected the topic. For instance, if one thumbs through *The New Handbook of Organization Communication* (Jablin & Putnam, 2001) or *The Handbook of Organizational Discourse* (Grant, Hardy, Oswick, & Putnam, 2004), gossip in organizations is not covered.

Overall, it is evident that gossip in organizations is both underplayed and undervalued by practitioners and under-researched by academics. It is against this backdrop that this book provides a timely contribution. It offers a robust, thorough, and thought-provoking examination of organizational gossip. In particular, it does three important things. First, it offers a rich, nuanced, and contextualized account of the nature and genealogy of gossip in organizations. In doing so, it draws together and skilfully synthesizes the limited body of work on the topic.

Second, this monograph persuasively challenges conventional wisdom and dismantles the taken-for-granted assumption that gossip should be seen as peripheral or parasitic in organizations. In this regard, the book resonates with François Cooren's seminal contribution within organizational communication where he posits that the field has tended to focus on the 'communicating properties of organizations' at the expense of considering the 'organizing properties of communication' (Cooren, 2001). Here Kathryn Waddington employs a similarly compelling process of inversion and posits that gossip is not merely an impediment to organizing or an unintended consequence of organizing. It is a form of organizing. Hence, as with other forms of discourse through which reality is socially constructed and negotiated (Berger & Luckmann, 1967), gossip organizes perceptions, shapes actions, and impacts upon material outcomes.

Finally, the sophisticated and innovative analysis of gossip as an integral and inescapable feature of organizations and organizing provided in this volume builds a solid platform for the further exploration of this under-researched facet of organizational life. More specifically, potential avenues of inquiry are encouraged and facilitated through the articulation of a framework for future theorizing and an agenda for future research.

This is an excellent book. It makes a very significant contribution to our understanding of organizational gossip.

Cliff Oswick
Cass Business School, City University London

Preface

This book has its origins in my doctoral research in psychology (University of London), which explored the role of gossip in nursing and healthcare organizations. Gossip is a complex and ubiquitous phenomenon—widely found and variously practiced—and the interdisciplinary nature of the field of gossip is well understood. Gossip as a social phenomenon has been extensively explored from within the traditions of anthropology, history, linguistics, gender studies, psychology, and sociology. However, despite Noon and Delbridge's (1993) seminal paper: 'News from behind my hand: Gossip in organizations', its examination from within management and organization studies, has been minimal. The sparse literature has polarized around arguments that regard gossip as problematic for managers and organizations, and those which are a little more circumspect, if not positive, in their conclusions. In the absence of empirical research into organizational gossip, the arguments in previous management and organization studies literature have been, at best, speculative. In the popular management/human resources (HR) literature the arguments have been based largely on value-laden assumptions, stereotypical perspectives, or anecdote. There has, until relatively recently, been a distinct lack of a substantive evidence-base in the field of organizational gossip. Gossip has been under-valued, under-researched, overlooked, and neglected as a topic worthy of serious theoretical attention. This book seeks to redress this imbalance.

The book has been written with two main audiences in mind. As a monograph, the first are clearly scholars and academics interested in the interdisciplinary field of gossip and organizations, which, as we will see, touches many other extant areas of inquiry such as and emotion, identity, power, and sensemaking. The second main audience are managers and leaders looking for an evidence-based approach to better understand, and, more importantly perhaps, use to better effect, the everyday phenomenon of gossip. The book will also be of interest to a wider audience of graduate students, practitioners, consultants, and other readers looking for innovative and imaginative thinking and perspectives that challenge mainstream assumptions about gossip in the workplace. The book introduces a new theorizing framework, which synthesizes interdisciplinary perspectives to guide future research, theoretical development, and critical reflection in the field of organizational gossip.

A central argument of the book is that gossip is an important constitutive organizing process. Rather than being seen solely as problematic individual behaviour, the book repositions gossip as organizational communication and knowledge. This is not to absolve or cleanse gossip of its negative and harmful dark side; rather, it is to argue that there are also a number of other sides and perspectives with which to understand gossip. Notably, the book introduces a *visual* dimension to gossip. In other words it argues that gossip also embodies non-verbal and material, nonhuman elements. Gossip crosses a number of domains in organization studies, especially those which focus on work and organizational psychology, communication, and discourse. There is increasing interest in the 'communicative constitution of organization' (CCO) perspective, and the book uses empirical materials to illustrate how gossip makes a contribution to this growing area of organizational scholarship. The theoretical perspectives and ideas advanced in *Gossip and Organizations* also have the potential to make a contribution to the growing field of positive organizational scholarship.

The nature of the topic—gossip—has influenced the way the book is written. I have tried to avoid the gratuitously complex language which can creep in to academic texts. Such texts are not always a pleasure to read. I have therefore blended academic analysis and empirical and reflexive materials with a liberal sprinkling of metaphor to try to capture the spirit of gossip. I have enjoyed writing this book; I hope you enjoy reading it.

Acknowledgements

This book has been 'forthcoming' for some time. It has no doubt been gossiped about by those who have asked out of interest, curiosity, or exasperation 'Is it finished yet?' Many people have contributed to its starting and finishing, and there are a number I would like to thank in particular for their assistance. First are the managers and practitioners who were the research participants in my doctoral research, and Clive Fletcher who was a supportive and pragmatic PhD supervisor. Grant Michelson contributed to the initial idea for the book; he and Ad van Iterson have become my 'comrades in gossip.' Their input, and gossip, has sharpened my thinking and arguments. The ideas in the book have also benefitted from comments on earlier drafts of chapters, and also conversations with: Heather Canary, Kevin Daniels, Liz Ellis, Piers Myers, Cliff Oswick, Jo Silvester, David Sims, Dave Snowden, Philippa Sully, Annie Topping . . . but there are, as always, many more people I could thank. Ian Croft and Pamela Sawyer have provided much needed reality checks, and Hannah Waddington helped with the illustrations. Eleanor Chan at IBT/Hamilton provided careful and timely help with page composition. In addition, I acknowledge the thorough professionalism—and patience—of the editorial team at Routledge. The book started under the guidance of Terry Clague and Sarah Hastings, and ended with Laura Stearns and Stacy Noto. Finally, I would like to thank Belgian artist Pol Ledent for permission to use *Gossip* in the frontispiece of the book. His work can be viewed in full and in colour at: www.ledent-gallery.be

1 Introduction

Our globe discovers its hidden virtues, not only in heroes and arch-angels, but in gossips and nurses.

—Ralph Waldo Emerson, *Representative Men*, 1860

This book is about gossip and organizations, organizing and gossip, and the hidden virtues of gossip. The central tenet is that gossip is a valuable but under-studied phenomenon worthy of further inquiry and scholarship. This is a contentious assertion perhaps, given that gossip has a less-than-positive history and reputation. However, its ubiquitous nature and pervasiveness suggest that gossip, as a form of communication, is also constitutive of organization. Many organizing processes occur, at least in part, through gossip. Therefore, this introductory chapter seeks from the outset to develop the argument that gossip is not inconsequential, nor without purpose, and that it plays a significant role in contemporary organizations and workplaces. The chapter raises questions about why it is important to have a better understanding of who gossips to whom about what, and about how and where gossip happens. These questions, and some answers, are more fully developed in later chapters. In addition to illustrating the significance of gossip, this chapter also begins to outline some of the potential problems, and pragmatic solutions, for researchers. This includes definitions, and ethical and methodological issues.

Gossip is at the very core of society and the human social relationships and networks it sustains. Gossip featured in the ancient Greek *Agora*, an open political and commercial space, and in middle-class English Regency society as described in Jane Austen's (1775–1817) novels. Today it is found in global internet celebrity and media gossip and in everyday talk at work. Gossip can be seen as a political strategy, a source of power and pleasure, and for writers of fiction, a plot device. When people talk about the details of daily lives it is gossip, yet when novelists such as Austen write about such detail, it is literature. Ironically perhaps, when writing about gossip is based upon empirical material and claims that 'communication is constitutive of organizing' (Putnam, Nicotera, & McPhee, 2009, p. 2), as this book is, it is academic scholarship. The book is written with academic and practitioner audiences in mind, and I am mindful from the outset that this is a challenge. The book's primary audience are scholars interested in the inter-disciplinary field of organizational gossip, which as we will see touches many extant area of inquiry such as sensemaking, identity, power, and emotion. The second audience are senior leaders, managers, and others, looking for evidence-based approaches to help them understand and use to better effect the everyday phenomenon of gossip. I hope that both audiences find fresh ways of thinking about gossip and organizations which challenge traditional views and assumptions.

The title of the book could have been *Gossip in Organizations* because it draws, in part, upon empirical material and insights from my own doctoral research into gossip in nursing and healthcare organizations, but it isn't. Taking a narrow focus on gossip *in* organizations would be to ignore its role in the *constitution of* organizations and overlook its relevance as an organizing process. Gossip is much more than a simply a communicative variable to be measured and manipulated within an organizational container. I move beyond this and adopt a wider perspective, and claim that organizational gossip is a relational, reflexive communicative process through which individuals engage in sensemaking and knowing. In making this claim, *Gossip and Organizations* contributes to what has recently been called the CCO perspective (communicative constitution of organization). The CCO approach aims to address how 'complex communication processes constitute both organizing and organization and how these processes and outcomes reflexively shape communication' (Putnam & Nicotera, 2010, p. 159).

WRITING AND THINKING ABOUT GOSSIP

The nature of the topic, in other words gossip, has influenced the way I have written the book. Writing found in work and organizational psychology, management and organization studies often uses dull, obscure, and pretentious language, and is seen to have little practitioner relevance (Gelade, 2006; Grey & Sinclair, 2006). Gratuitously complex language can be irritating to read, resulting in gossip amongst academics about texts and journal articles which are written in such a way. Arguably this might also be described in terms of 'peer review,' illustrating the importance of context when describing and differentiating evaluative talk and text. Acknowledging, therefore, the 'chatty' and familiar nature of that which is constituted and experienced as gossip, I have tried deliberately to reflect *some* of this in my writing about gossip (see also Waddington, 2010). At various points in the book, I reflexively (re)consider some of the issues and empirical material I have encountered by critically reflecting upon incidents, insights, and metaphors. These reflections are not necessarily in any chronological order, and in some instances for reasons of confidentiality, some names have been changed and some details have been altered. Empirical material is used here in the manner advocated by Alvesson and Sköldberg (2009). That is, as an argument which seeks to '*make a case for a particular way of understanding social reality, in the context of a never-ending debate*' (Alvesson

& Sköldberg, 2009, p. 304, original emphasis). In other words, I am using empirical material to inspire new ideas and theorizing about gossip, organization and organizing, rather than as unequivocal and clear-cut data.

The overarching intention in including such reflective and reflexive material is to develop a wider thinking and analysis of gossip as a complex, equivocal, and ambiguous phenomenon. In doing so, I have adopted the kind of emphasis that Alvesson and Sköldberg (2009, p. 313) refer to as R-reflexivity:

> R-reflexivity is about developing and adding something; the person engaged in R-reflexivity is in the construction rather than the demolition industry. It means bringing in issues of alternate paradigms, root metaphors, perspectives, vocabularies, lines of interpretation, political values and representations; re-balancing and reframing voices in order to interrogate and vary data in a more fundamental way.

R-reflexivity is differentiated from D-reflexivity thus:

> D-reflexivity practices challenge orthodox understandings by pointing out the limitations of, and uncertainties behind, the manufactured unity and coherence of texts, as well as the way that conformism, institutional domination, and academic and business fashion may account for the production of particular knowledge. (p. 313)

In practice, there are no absolute distinctions, and the border between the two kinds of reflexive emphasis is fluid. Creation of a dialectic between R- and D-reflexivity allows for movement between the various positions that each represent, acknowledging *multiple reflexivities*. The overarching intention is to stimulate thoughtful and creative challenges to conventional thinking and set out new ideas and directions for future research. The book, therefore, calls into question gendered and managerialist assumptions and thinking which have often uncritically viewed gossip as trivial women's talk, or dangerous discourse. It introduces new assumptions and thinking which seek to construct fresh understandings of gossip and organizational life.

REFLEXIVITY AND GOSSIP

Reflexivity is a contested term, used variously to acknowledge the role, influence, positioning, subjectivity and visibility of the researcher in the processes of research, knowledge generation, and theory building (Alvesson & Sköldberg, 2009; May, T. with Perry, 2011; Weick, 1999). *Gossip and Organizations* draws, in part, upon original empirical material from my doctoral research in psychology into the characteristics and functions of gossip in healthcare organizations (see Appendix A for summary, and also Waddington, 2005a; 2005b; 2005c; Waddington & Fletcher, 2005). It is pertinent at this point therefore to begin to articulate my own reflexive position. That is, 'the self-conscious acknowledgement by authors of their own immersion in an historically contingent and invariably institutional-ized set of knowledge-producing practices' (Ybema et al., 2009, p. 315).

REFLECTION 1: WITNESS TO GOSSIP

When practising as a nurse in acute hospital settings in the early stages of my career I watched, listened, and also participated in gossip. It happens everywhere and not just in healthcare organizations. My academic curiosity was later sparked when gossip of a different nature and in a different con-text appeared later as 'data' in research I was undertaking into perceptions of organizational culture in a university. The organizational literature at the time in the early 1990s yielded little theoretical or empirical work that addressed gossip 'head on' and this eventually (because at first I was put off by gossip's dismal reputation) led to doctoral research in psychology into gossip in nursing and healthcare organizations. So my reflexive position has its roots in several institutionalized sets of knowledge-producing practice perspectives: Organiza-tional psychology, nursing, hospitals and universities.

Reflection 1 is the 'back story' to the book. It is included as point of ref-erence from which my reflexive and inter-disciplinary choices and actions variously depart, disconnect, return, revise, and re-integrate. Researching a relatively unconventional topic such as gossip from the relatively conven-tional starting point and perspective of psychology has involved crossing disciplinary boundaries and paradigms. Such inter-disciplinary scholar-ship also involves 'crossing words' when different vocabularies, paradigms, and perspectives collide. I contend that this is a good thing, promoting an open-minded approach, intellectual flexibility, and creativity (Wadding-ton, 2011). Nevertheless, as T. May with Perry (2011) observe, reflexive researchers may find that it is sometimes easier to critically challenge their own disciplinary assumptions, power, and identity than it is to challenge institutionalized knowledge-producing practices.

Similarities can be drawn between crossing disciplinary boundaries, institutionalized or otherwise, and Jörg Bergmann's notion of gossipers as 'border-runners':

> Gossipers are border-runners who, in their exciting excursions into the zones of the improper, do not simply ignore the boundaries of the domains of virtue and vice, but recognise and disdain them at the same time—must recognise them in fact, in order to be able to disdain them. This is precisely what gives gossip its equivocal character. (Bergmann, 1993, p. 118)

Healthcare organizations and the applied field of organizational psychology have provided me with a starting point from which to develop an empirical and theoretical analysis and understanding of gossip and organizations. Communication is crucial in healthcare organizations. It plays a vital role in the delivery of high quality care, ensuring patient safety, and promoting the development of effective relationships between patients and healthcare professionals. Communication is also crucial to establishing and maintaining effective professional and interprofessional relationships between nurses, doctors, allied health professionals, and social workers. Communication in healthcare organizations is simultaneously formal and structured, as well as informal, unplanned, and opportunistic (Becker, 2007). Healthcare organizations provide a fertile information-rich environment and context for the communicative study of gossip, but obviously this is not the only place nor perspective where gossip can be found.

Gossip features peripherally in literature relating to storytelling, mergers and acquisitions, and complexity (e.g., Boje, 2008; Brown, Denning, Groh, & Prusak, 2005; Moeller & Brady, 2007; Stacey, 2001; 2010). Empirical work is scant, and psychology is but one starting point from which to empirically investigate gossip, or indeed any other, organizational phenomenon. There are obvious limitations to using just one frame of reference. As an applied disciplinary field, organizational psychology is still relatively under-theorized, characterized by much 'micro-theory,' and a limited amount of overarching and integrative conceptual work (van Knippenberg, 2011, p. 3). In order to address these limitations the conceptual analysis of gossip and organizations needs to be positioned in a larger literature and context. I therefore draw upon ideas and theories from other disciplines and fields including sociology, anthropology, ethics, and communication studies to advance the theorizing of gossip and organization. My intention is to identify synergies and challenges within an overall framework of reflexive inquiry because:

> reflexive inquiry *can* offer valuable insights into organizational studies and practice by stimulating a critical exploration of how we constitute knowledge and enact our own practices as researchers. In doing so, it raises possibilities for different forms of inquiry and new ways of understanding experience. (Cunliffe, 2003, p. 999, original emphasis)

Reflexive inquiry is underpinned by a number of principles, or higher order contexts, that frame meaning and guide action (Alvesson & Sköldberg, 2009; May, T. with Perry, 2011; Miettinen, Samra-Fredericks, & Yanow, 2009). Oliver (2005) identifies five principles which are '*systemic, constructionist, critical, appreciative,* and *complex*' (p. 4, original emphasis). Clearly these principles are not mutually exclusive. As Oliver notes, each principle overlaps and interweaves with the others to provide a theoretical and ethical framework for reflexive inquiry practices. However, it is worth briefly highlighting each one individually to differentiate the value of each as a practice lens with which to examine gossip and organizations.

1. *Systemic Principle:* this is about patterns, used here to denote forms of feeling, thinking, and action that become enacted and embedded as stories in disciplinary cultures, relationships and identities.
2. *Constructionist Principle:* this asserts that we share the everyday world of inquiry and scholarship with others, there is concern and engagement with the detail of language, reflexive practice is shaped by the contexts and cultures in which researchers work and talk.
3. *Critical Principle:* the construction and enactment of power is made visible through inquiry and sensemaking, the development of reflexive positioning encourages mindfulness and critical co-production of knowledge.
4. *Appreciative Principle:* this positions self and others with care, vulnerability, and empathy and encourages an appreciation that meaning and action are open to multiple interpretations, which are partial, contextual, and unstable.
5. *Complex Principle:* this adopts the position that we are all members of complex networks and systems inviting us to find strategies and language that go beyond prediction, control and regularity, and find value in so-called negative and difficult experiences.

The above principles are introduced here as orienting points, and will be further developed and interwoven throughout the book. They are blended with reflexive constructs drawn from Cunliffe (2003), which challenge researchers and readers to: (i) question our intellectual suppositions; (ii) recognize that research is a reflexive narrative comprising participant stories which interconnect with researcher stories in some way; (iii) examine and explore researcher-participant relationships and their impact on knowledge; (iv) acknowledge the constitutive nature of our research conversations; and (v) construct emerging practical theories rather than objective truth.

A reflexive inquiry position is thus constituted in terms of *relationships*, in which researchers construct and co-create knowledge through critical engagement with themselves, research participants, their readers and epistemological communities (Doucet, 2008). Reflexivity occurs at the interfaces in these relationships, and also across levels of interpretation and interaction with empirical material and underlying meanings, power, and contexts. Doucet (2008, p.73) uses the provocative metaphor of 'gossamer walls' (which is drawn from Anne Michaels's (1998) novel *Fugitive Pieces*) to explore aspects of reflexivity and the construction of relational knowing. Michaels's novel narrates the relationship between Jakob, a Holocaust survivor, and the ghost of his sister Bella, captured in the imagery of a gossamer wall. In the novel the image is used metaphorically to represent both the sense of separation and connection and also the fragile space between them. However Doucet argues that personal, political, intellectual, and theoretical 'ghosts' can also appear in social science work. Consideration of these metaphorical 'ghosts' can help to widen current discussions of reflexivity in the social and organizational sciences.

I argue that the illusive imagery of ghosts and gossamer walls allows for further consideration of the 'ghosts of paradigms past.' For instance, the lingering influence of orthodox assumptions in organization studies which have previously negated or neglected organizational gossip. The imagery of gossamer walls also resonates powerfully with the elusive nature of gossip and the spaces it occupies. Gossamer is a gauze fabric with an extremely fine texture (http://webster-online-dictionary.org) and the metaphor of gossamer walls combines this sheerness and transparency with the notion of fragile boundaries which 'provides for creative ways of conceptualizing reflexivity in temporal and spatial terms [and] the *constantly shifting degrees of transparency and obscurity, connection and separation* that recur in the multiple relations that constitute reflexive research and knowing'(Doucet, 2008, p. 73, emphasis added).

The *spatial* quality of reflexivity is important, as it implies different sets of distant and close relationships. Similarly, T. May with Perry (2011) differentiates between endogenous and referential reflexivity. The former is expressed in terms of relations between researchers and their disciplinary communities, the latter in terms of relations between researchers and research respondents. The movement between, and meeting of, these two forms of reflexivity is dependent upon the notion of 'epistemic permeability' between disciplines, and the metaphor of gossamer walls is highly pertinent here. The movement from endogenous to referential reflexivity is characterized 'as one from reflexivity *within* actions to reflexivity *upon* actions, enabling connections to be made between individuals and the social conditions of which they are a part (May, T. with Perry, 2011, p. 86, original emphasis). The metaphor of gossamer walls, with its combination of the sheerness of gossamer and the solidity of walls, offers a challenging, but imaginative, way to think about the ambiguous nature of reflexivity and reflexivities. The metaphor also chimes with the shifting degrees of transparency, obscurity, connection, and separation between gossip and other fields of inquiry and organizational phenomena, which are considered next.

GOSSIP: LINKS AND GAPS

Gossip touches many fields of inquiry, and what is known about gossip permeates many disciplines, for example psychology, anthropology, sociology, and social history (e.g., Capp, 2003; Foster, 2004; Gluckman, 1963; Tebbut, 1995). This is both a strength and limitation. The strength lies in the wide appeal that gossip holds for a number of academic and practitioner communities. For instance, there is growing evidence that gossip is highly relevant to many organizing processes and practices such as organizational culture, ethics, emotion, sensemaking, and change (e.g., Ernst, 2003; Hallett, Harger & Eder, 2009; Michelson, van Iterson, & Waddington, 2010; Mills, 2010; van Iterson, Waddington, & Michelson, 2011; Waddington, 2005b; Waddington & Michelson, 2007). The limitation is that without clear articulation of disciplinary positions, boundaries and reflexivities, the emerging field of organizational gossip risks epistemic drift becoming neither one thing nor the other in terms of knowledge claims.

Alternatively, gossip may be seen as a fashionable 'new toy' with indistinct conceptual underpinnings for established fields, such as storytelling or organizational discourse, to play with but not treat seriously. Without strong theorizing and research, the field of organizational gossip also risks being hi-jacked by 'conceptual cowboys' seeking to capitalize on its popularity. Gossip risks being marketed as an eye-catching faddish 'solution' to fixing a multitude of organizational problems, but without a sound evidence-base. There are insights and lessons to be learned here from other fields such as emotion, which has rapidly expanded over the last twenty years or so into one of the most popular and popularized areas of organizational scholarship. At some extremes there are claims that emotion encompasses every phenomenon across organization and management studies (Elfenbein, 2007). There are two important lessons. The first is to articulate clear conceptual boundaries, because for gossip to mean anything, it cannot mean everything. The second is to integrate the inter-disciplinary roots of gossip into a theoretically sound, coherent whole.

Gossip bears a relationship to a number of other communicative and conversational phenomena, such as chatting, rumour, myths, legends and storytelling (Banks-Wallace, 2002; Brown et al., 2005; DiFonzo & Bordia, 2007; Gabriel, 1995; Jones, D., 1980; Sunstein, 2009; Talbot, 2010). DiFonzo and Bordia (2007), who have paid particular attention to rumour, argue that the differences between these phenomena can be understood in terms of their contexts, content and group function. For example:

- *Rumour:* occurs in ambiguous or threatening events or situations, its content is largely instrumentally relevant information statements that are unverified and its function is to make sense of ambiguity and manage threat/potential threat;
- *Gossip:* the context here is one of social network building, structuring or maintaining; content is summarized as evaluative statements about individuals' private lives, and its function is to entertain, supply social information, and establish, change, or maintain group membership, group power structure, or group norms;
- *Storytelling:* the depiction of an event or series of events that is generally, but not always, encompassed by time and space. Like gossip, storytelling is used to preserve and communicate core characteristics of

a culture. Stories vary in form (see urban legends below), and reflect individuals' experiences as they see (or want to see) and remember them, and their 'truth' may be selective;

- *Urban legends:* are a form of modern folklore; stories of humorous, unusual or horrible events, often told with a sense of exaggeration, but which persist because they address long standing questions and fears, and propagate moral values and virtues within a culture;
- *Chatting:* is friendly talk for its own sake, for example about the weather, and like gossip, is informal communication involving mutual self-disclosure and commentary upon particular incidents and experiences.

Gossip does not always fit neatly into conceptual categories. It is equivocal, ambiguous, slippery, and highly resistant to paradigmatic summing up. This creates a tension between the disparate nature of gossip and the need for conceptual clarity in research and theorizing. In essence, gossip is informal evaluative talk between at least two people that may be spoken (most common), written (less common) or visual. Notably, the visual and non-verbal characteristics of gossip are frequently overlooked in the literature. However, a hastily closed office door, a knowing look exchanged during a meeting, little huddles of people in public places such as corridors and canteens, graffiti, and communally displayed cartoons in the workplace are all visual signifiers and materialities of gossip.

Although I contend that gossip is a type of informal evaluative organizational communication, it can also occur in formal communicative contexts (see Mills, 2010). Meetings (as outlined above) and material images such as pictures used in the ubiquitous PowerPoint presentation are examples. Formal communicative contexts and settings are often interspersed between informal 'unmanaged spaces', such as travel time, refreshment breaks, interruptions and gaps in proceedings. Therefore, it is not necessarily helpful to consider informal and formal organizational communication as mutually exclusive systems and processes. As Becker (2007) noted, communication in healthcare teams is particularly important, yet much of this communication is, in reality, informal, unplanned, and opportunistic. Informal and formal communication processes, networks and relationships influence and inform each other in a complementary manner, and this is particularly pertinent in risk and crisis management (Borodzicz, 2005).

Gossip is therefore perhaps better conceptualized in terms of 'communication at the margins,' because as Adkins (2002, p. 216) asserts, '[g] ossip can demonstrate the value of ideas and talk on the margins.' The margins, or borders, may be formal-informal, public-private, intra- inter-organizational, as well as intra- inter-disciplinary. Additionally, gossip is often variously described in the literature as critical and uncritical, positive and negative, information sharing and judgemental, blame and praise gossip, good gossip and bad gossip (Michelson et al., 2010). However, it is important to note that these are not intended to be seen as separate, polarized discourses. As Fitzgerald, Oliver, and Hoxsey (2010, citing Weick, 2003) observe, such a view can obscure unknowable complexities, such as accidents or chance, which can result in unintended outcomes and organizational failure. Rather, by advancing the notion of gossip as communication at the margins it can be variously positioned on both sides of metaphorical gossamer walls, which are porous, moveable, transgressable, and transparent.

Although a trend for disciplinary repositioning of gossip as valuable organizational discourse is becoming evident in some of the organization studies literature, its negative reputation and heritage lingers. Gossip is still historically and stereotypically associated with negative value-laden assumptions; it is seen as inauthentic discourse and pejorative, superficial women's talk (Emler, 1994; Heidegger, 1962; Jones, D., 1980; Tebbutt, 1995). Are these assumptions some of the metaphorical 'ghosts' which have haunted the field? Such assumptions have no doubt proved somewhat of a challenge for researchers and scholars in the past. We now need to look beyond such negative assumptions, and see what *really* lies beneath the surface manifestations of organizational gossip. Gossip has had a plausible presence in anthropology, sociology, social, and evolutionary psychology (e.g., DiFonzo & Bordia, 2007; Dunbar, 1992; 1996; 2004; Eder & Enke, 1991; Elias & Scotson, 1965; Gluckman, 1963; Kniffin & Wilson, 2005; Rosnow & Fine, 1976). It is now undergoing a degree of selective rehabilitation in psychology, organization, and communication studies, and arguably some of the ghosts are now being laid to rest.

Some early signs of growth in the field of organizational gossip are beginning to show. For instance, the second edition of the *Handbook of Organizational Culture and Climate* (Ashkanasy, Wilderom, & Peterson, 2011a) now includes a chapter on the role of gossip in organizational culture (van Iterson et al., 2011), where previously there was none. There have also been Special Issues of the *Review of General Psychology* (e.g., Baumeister, Zhang, & Vohs, 2004; Bloom, 2004; Foster, 2004), and more recently *Group and Organization Management* (e.g., Grosser et al., 2010; Kniffin & Wilson, 2010; Mills, 2010). As Ashkanasy, Wilderom, and Peterson (2011b) comment, pervasive change has symbolized the first decade of the 21st century, and it exists at every level of ontology. A consequence of this pervasive change is that 'old ways of viewing phenomena [such as gossip] become outmoded, and new paradigms must be sought' (Ashkanasy et al., 2011b, p. 8).

Nevertheless, some significant gaps remain, and gossip is absent in the substantive literature relating to organizational communication and discourse. For example, both *The Sage Handbook of Organizational Discourse* (Grant, Hardy, Oswick, & Putnam, 2004) and the more recent *Organizational Discourse Studies* (Grant, Hardy, & Putnam, 2011) contain no explicit material on gossip. Neither does gossip appear in *Engaging*

Organizational Communication Theory and Research (May, S. & Mumby, 2005a) nor in *The New Handbook of Organizational Communication* (Jablin & Putnam, 2001). The more recent *Communication and Organizational Knowledge: Contemporary Issues for Theory and Practice* (Canary & McPhee, 2011a) is also silent with regard to gossip, as is the practitioner-focused text *The IABC Handbook of Organizational Communication* (Gillis, 2006). These texts are given simply as illustrative examples that describe fields where one might logically expect to find gossip. These fields are selective, and scholars often have to necessarily pick and choose amongst many perspectives. However, looking to a future based on innovative scholarship, this will require 'a dialectic attention to, and understanding of, what is visible and *invisible*, spoken and *unspoken*, and present and *absent* with regard to organizational communication theory and research' (May, S. & Mumby, 2005b, p.280, emphasis added). Gossip is now emerging as a compelling area of inquiry for work and organizational psychologists, discursive scholars and those interested in organizational communication and knowledge.

WHY GOSSIP IS IMPORTANT

Gossip is a ubiquitous aspect of organizational and social life, but is also something that has traditionally been ignored, marginalized, demonised, or trivialized. It is, however, remarkably resilient, and as we have seen is currently a (re)emerging area of scholarship within the social and organizational sciences. Up until fairly recently the negative attributes have tended to overshadow the positive, but the picture is changing. The social and communicative context of gossip is also changing. Research undertaken in the field of mobile telecommunications suggested that mobile phone gossip and text messaging has replaced the face-to-face 'natural' communication patterns of pre-industrial times (Fox, 2001). Whilst acknowledging that a British mobile phone network commissioned this research at a time of increasing competition in the industry, its conclusions, which are theoretically informed by evolutionary psychology, are pertinent. In other words, language evolved to enable people to exchange social information, and people like to gossip (Dunbar, 1996).

The last decade or so has witnessed a remarkable growth in social networking sites such as Facebook and Twitter, image and video sharing websites such as YouTube and Flickr and increasingly sophisticated mobile phone technology. Web 2.0 technologies such as blogs, wikis, and Really Simple Syndication (RSS) feeds are now part of the fabric of everyday life. Web 3.0 technologies, the third generation of internet-based services are growing fast. Individuals and organizations are becoming increasingly aware of both the enabling *and* constraining role and consequences of technology and digitalization in many social and organizational processes

(Canary & McPhee, 2011a; Flanagin & Bator, 2011; Greenfield, 2009). One of the consequences is a change in the way we communicate and relate to each other both inside and outside of the workplace. However, whereas there has been a parallel growth in information technology research, scholarly research on the social consequences has had a slower start (Harrington & Bielby, 1995; Ivester, 2011; Tufecki, 2008). The creation of intelligent networked organizations and teams now means that the people may rarely see others with whom they work. In a virtual world of cyberspace, different forms of gossip via email and the internet have replaced some of the opportunities and spaces for face-to-face gossip. Arguably an unanticipated consequence of digitalized networked societies, economies, and organizations is that gossip, which was always present 'in the background,' is now thrust into the foreground as the spaces it previously occupied disappear.

In today's organizations, the opportunities and spaces for face-to-face gossip are also shifting and changing in other ways beyond the virtual. For example, the creation of open-plan office spaces in the Treasury Building of the UK government entailed the removal of seven miles of internal walls (Dale & Burrell, 2008). This effectively dismantled the original 'corridors of power' (and the juxtaposed 'power of corridors') where power *and* gossip circulate (Hurdley, 2010a; 2010b; van Iterson & Clegg, 2008). As the spaces of organization and the organization of space shift, so do the 'unmanaged spaces' where gossip and power flow. In addition to its relationship to power, gossip can also be, controversially perhaps, re-presented as knowledge (Adkins, 2002; Ayim, 1994). Code (1994) warns against reclaiming gossip-as-knowledge within traditional objective scientific paradigms and modes of inquiry, which would, she contends obscure its power as disorderly discourse. Shotter (1989; 2008) claims that social order is constructed and sustained only within the context of the relatively *disorderly*. That is, the kind of everyday activities and interactions, such as gossip, which are often dismissed as a trivial waste of time. This is not a new argument. Cooren and Fairhurst (2009) and Latour (2007) note the relatively recent rediscovery and vindication of the French sociologist Gabriel Tarde (1843–1904) who advocated a bottom up perspective to explain social order. In *Les lois sociales* (1999, translated by Cooren & Fairhurst, 2009) Tarde commented:

It is precisely because everything, in the world of facts, goes from the small to the big, that, in the world of ideas, inverted mirror of the first, everything goes from the big to the small and, by progress of analysis, lastly reaches the elementary facts, which are truly explicated. (Cooren & Fairhurst, 2009, p. 125)

Therefore I contend that gossip can be re-presented as a process of realizing organizational knowledge and knowing, embodied in everyday conversational practices and relationships. A practice-perspective evokes the idea of 'knowledge as being rooted in an extended pattern of interconnected activities that only when taken in its living and pulsating entirety constitutes the site of knowing' (Nicolini, 2011, p. 602). Furthermore, as Shumate (2011) argues, knowledge management practice and research should encompass a range of informal and network organizing which occurs 'beyond traditional organizational boundaries and structures' (p. 204). This is surely an open invitation for scholars and researchers interested in gossip and knowledge management to collaborate? An awareness of the precursors, predictors, and power of gossip is relevant to a deeper understanding of knowledge management and much important work and innovation relies upon informal networks and processes (Taminiau, Smit, & de Lange, 2009). This is what might be termed the 'other side' of knowledge work, involving individuals and processes working outside of the formal 'knowledge-worker' status and scope.

Knowledge management is crucial to competitive success, and is influenced by the ways people interact, and how forms of knowledge, including gossip, flows among and through individuals and technology. Foresight is also an important factor in the creation of new opportunities and competitive advantage and has been described as 'a refined sensitivity for detecting and disclosing invisible, inarticulate or unconscious societal motives, aspirations and preferences' (Chia, 2004, p. 22). Such motives, aspirations, and preferences may be manifested in and through gossip. Furthermore, when things go wrong, foresight is necessary in order to prevent organizational failures and scandals from happening again. Organizations alleged with corruptible behaviour during the past decade include Enron, World-Com, Global Crossing, Tyco, the Federal Bureau of Investigators, Merck, Halliburton, and the U.S. Army (Richardson & McGlynn, 2011). Organizations and public services are constantly challenged to demonstrate that they *really have* 'learned lessons' from failure and subsequent costly public inquiries (e.g., Colin Thomé, 2009; van Iterson & Clegg, 2008; Weick & Sutcliffe, 2007).

Suitable and subtle approaches need to be found to detect, describe, and understand the complex and ephemeral phenomenon of gossip. However, this is not necessarily easy or straightforward. There are challenges and controversies which make the study of gossip, organizing, and organization a problematic, but not impossible task, and these are considered next.

PROBLEMS AND PRAGMATICS

The problems associated with studying gossip are predominantly associated with definitions, methods, and ethics. In addition, until relatively recently, gossip has been a bit of a taboo topic. Gossip is variously defined linguistically as a noun (a gossip/the gossip) and a verb (to gossip). Furthermore, different disciplines often fail to agree upon definitions and methodological approaches (Noon & Delbridge, 1993). Noon (2001) has speculated that the ethical problems associated with gossip, such as privacy, the rights of absent third parties who are the subject of gossip, and eavesdropping without consent may render it unresearchable. I contend that the problems and difficulties inherent in researching gossip can be overcome by adopting a pragmatic approach, which:

- Acknowledges but also *challenges* the existence of problematic issues;
- Looks for *new ways* of approaching definitions, concepts and methods;
- Espouses *inter-disciplinary principles*, rather than rigid disciplinary practices; and
- Explicitly *includes ethics* as both procedural and reflexive elements of the research process.

Others have approached the problem of definition by proposing that gossip is best thought of as a prototypical category, using terms like 'usually,' 'typically,' and 'often' when referring to the attributes or characteristics of gossip. Prototypical categories exhibit vague boundaries:

> The prototypical category has neither clear-cut and definite boundaries nor an equal degree of membership. Some items are so similar to or so different from the prototype that we have no doubt about their inclusion or exclusion; with other items the degree of similarity makes it difficult or impossible to say for sure whether they belong or not. (Ben-Ze'ev, 1994, p. 11)

Thinking about gossip as a prototypical category reframes vagueness as a *feature of*, rather than a *problem with* gossip. Furthermore, the notion of vagueness as a defining feature is not just attributable to gossip. Vagueness and ambiguity are features of many other terms such as 'market,' 'firm,' 'rational,' 'competitive,' 'price,' 'optimal,' 'efficient,' and 'equilibrium,' as well of everyday conversational and organizational realities (Klaes, 2004; Kurtz & Snowden, 2007; Shotter, 2008). It could also be the case that ontological vagueness may simply reflect a young and emergent field of inquiry. As Michelson et al. (2010) argue, a degree of flexibility is needed, but with some agreement as to the core elements of gossip such as evaluative talk (written or spoken) occuring between at least two persons about an absent third person/s. Such agreement is necessary to enable accumulation of research findings across studies, but a more nuanced approach is needed when studying gossip from different perspectives and contexts. For example, from the viewpoint of the person being gossiped about, the ethical consequences of gossip or whether gossip is face to face, virtual or visual and so on.

Some of the inherent problems of studying gossip are found in the American writer E. B. White's observation that 'analyzing humor is like dissecting a frog. Few people are interested and the frog dies of it' (cited in van Iterson et al., 2011, p. 385). Something similar may be said of gossip; in other words, you don't necessarily have to kill it to understand it. Overly academic analyses of gossip and gossiping can result in dead descriptions, and disengagement on the part of readers. Gossip is vibrant and vivid, simultaneously alluring, amusing, disorderly, dangerous, and difficult to catch using traditional academic approaches. Laboratory and experimental studies have questionable relevance, and dissecting gossip for the sake of scrutinizing the phenomenon is a pointless exercise. The uniqueness, authenticity, and idiosyncratic nature of gossip can very easily become obscured by methodological and ethical constraints. What remains after such dissection is meaningless abstraction served up as academic leftovers for publication. The ambiguous and subterranean nature of gossip is such that it lends itself more easily to metaphorical comparisons in order to better explain its nature, role and place in organizations. Better, that is, than killing it in order to understand it.

GOSSIP AND METAPHOR

A number of metaphors are interwoven throughout the book, which may initially sometimes appear contradictory. However, the metaphorical landscape is constituted in a way which is consistent with the complexity of organizational gossip. Metaphor is the 'understanding and experiencing one kind of thing in terms of another' (Lakoff & Johnson, 1980, p. 5). The use and analysis of metaphors is a well established approach in psychotherapy, linguistics, and organization studies (Cornelissen, Oswick, Christensen & Phillips, 2008; Heracleous & Jacobs, 2008; Kolb, 2008; Moser, 2007). The aim in introducing metaphor here is twofold. Firstly, to provide imagery and concepts which will ultimately lead to the articulation of a framework for theorizing and reflecting upon organizational gossip. Secondly, to stimulate fresh ways of thinking about the practice of theorizing.Theories can be developed by using metaphors which, when 'projected' onto organizational reality, or observations of organizational reality, can describe and explain aspects of that reality. As Cornelissen et al. (2008, p. 9) argue:

> Much if not all work on organization theory and theory-building has such a 'projection' focus on metaphor, because the purpose of much theorizing is essentially to identify and abstract 'second-order' constructs which, when related to or projected onto empirical settings, describe and explain the 'first-order' lived experiences of people within organizations.

Cornelissen (2006a) asserts that metaphors provide theorists and researchers with vocabularies and images to represent and express organizational phenomena which are complex and abstract. Metaphorical language, he suggests, 'sets up a creative and often novel correlation of two concepts or ideas which forces us to make *semantic leaps* to create an understanding of the information that comes off it (p. 1584, original emphasis). The point in working with metaphors therefore is to introduce concepts which facilitate critical reflection, and 'help us resist the temptation to get stuck in a favourite position' (Alvesson & Sköldberg, 2009, p. 312). The metaphors of gossamer walls and border-runners have been introduced in order to avoid getting stuck in a preferred disciplinary position. In particular, these two metaphors are used to conceptualize reflexive inter-disciplinary knowledge/s and the elusive nature and spatial aspects of gossip. Metaphors provide another way of looking at things, of simultaneously seeing the good, the bad, the positive, the negative, the traditions that limit growth, and also the opportunities for new ideas and knowledge.

CONCLUSION

One of the intentions of the book is to provoke thought and advance theorizing about gossip, organizing and organizations. This chapter has introduced a core assumption, namely that gossip can be conceptualized as organizational communication and knowledge. It is pertinent at this point to reiterate two distinctive arguments advanced in the book. First, I argue that gossip can be understood within the *communicative constitution of organization* (CCO) perspective, and that organizations and organizing processes occur, at least in part, through gossip and gossiping. Second, I argue that gossip is a form of evaluative talk which can be verbal, written, or *visual*. Gossip is an important, but hitherto neglected, area for management and organizational research, organizational discourse research, and organizational communication research. The key task of the book is to move gossip from being a largely invisible, neglected human interpersonal process, to becoming a *visible* and valued constitutive organizing process. Another distinctive quality of the book is the way in which gossip features as a central rather than peripheral, or as discussed above, absent theme. The chapters which follow address topics and fields of inquiry which will be familiar to organizational scholars, researchers, and practitioners, but from a fresh perspective which foregrounds gossip. This fresh perspective seeks to illustrate how an understanding of the meaning and purpose of gossip can inform these more familiar aspects of organizational life.

HOW THE BOOK IS ORGANIZED

The chapters which follow draw upon empirical material from my own research to develop the arguments, themes and issues introduced here. Analytical depth, theoretical and conceptual insights are extended through the use of an inter-disciplinary approach and the principles of reflexive inquiry. I have selectively incorporated my own reflective and reflexive material and insights as short sections of text and narrative. For simplicity, these are identified as sequentially numbered 'Reflections,' but this does not represent or imply a chronological order. Chronological order is linear and orderly. Gossip is disorderly, disruptive and digressive. In the chapters which follow I explore further the role of gossip and organizations, and the communicative processes of organizing and gossip, in order to reveal the hidden virtues of gossip. The chapters can be read as discrete entities in their own right, and in whatever order readers find useful or interesting. There is an internal coherence to the book, which cumulates in the creation of a theorizing framework. Together, Chapters 2 and 3 provide the broad conceptual, theoretical, and ethical underpinnings of the book. Individually, Chapters 4 to 7 draw upon empirical and theoretical materials to illustrate, respectively, issues surrounding gossip and emotion, identity, power and politics, sensemaking and management. Collectively, Chapters 1 to 7 also constitute the conceptual components and boundary conditions of the theorizing framework, which is articulated more fully in Chapter 8, the concluding chapter.

2   Organizing Gossip

Talk is at the heart of all organizations

—Boden (1994, p. 1)

The role of language and conversation dominate a range of societal institutions, structures, and practices including organizations. Despite this dominance, the visible and measurable elements of working life have largely been privileged in research endeavours, whereas the more subterranean and hidden phenomena, such as gossip, are often neglected. As Putnam et al. (2009) note, for decades organizational communication scholars have claimed that '*organizations are communicatively constituted*' (p.1, original emphasis). Organizations are quite literally talked into existence on a day-to-day basis as well as over time, and they are always 'in process.' This process is represented in various elements including textual forms (such as procedures, protocols and documents) artefacts (such as uniforms and architecture) and human interaction (Cooren & Fairhurst, 2009). However gossip, which as day-to-day communication that includes visual and non-verbal elements, has been overlooked as a way of understanding organization as it happens. This chapter, therefore, looks at the significance of gossip as a constitutive organizing process, and its role in the communicative constitution of organization (CCO) perspective.

Starting with a brief history of gossip, the chapter shows that there is little consensus on what gossip is and how different disciplines treat gossip. The foundations of a framework for organizing gossip are more firmly established, drawing upon wider theoretical perspectives of organizational communication and knowledge. As I said in Chapter 1, and have argued elsewhere (Waddington, 2010), it is not always helpful to talk and write about gossip using obscure language which can irritate, confuse, and alienate others. So I have tried, as much as possible, to drop the heavy tools and academic trappings of complex language which make it 'difficult to talk about how communication constitutes organizations' (Putnam & Nicotera, 2009, p. xi, citing Weick, 2002). This is not easy. Organizational communication and knowledge are large fields, full of big ideas and big words. The CCO part of the field in particular has been described as 'ontologically audacious [and] analytically ambitious'(Reed, 2010, p. 121), and newcomers to the field may find themselves in need of a translator. Fortunately, Ashcraft, Kuhn, and Cooren (2009), Putnam and Nicotera (2009), and Cooren, Kuhn, Cornelissen, and Clark (2011) have all done an excellent job of deciphering the current field of organizational communication studies and CCO theorizing. Interested readers are directed to their work for more detailed coverage of the issues and debates than is provided here. The overarching aims in this chapter are to:

1. Explore the concept of gossip as constitutive of organizational communication and knowledge; and
2. Establish foundations for the theorizing framework which is further developed in subsequent chapters throughout the book.

A BRIEF HISTORY OF GOSSIP

Seminal literature relating to gossip in the social and organizational sciences has been reviewed elsewhere, and is not reproduced in depth here (see Baumeister et al., 2004; Bergmann, 1993; DiFonzo & Bordia, 2007; Foster, 2004; Goodman & Ben-Ze'ev, 1994; Michelson et al., 2010; Noon & Delbridge, 1993; van Iterson et al., 2011). Wilkes (2002) and Collins (2007) also provide useful commentaries about gossip and scandal in the media and politics. Although this book is about gossip and organizations, not celebrity, political, or media gossip, the latter provide a background and context within which to understand organizational gossip. The internet is saturated with gossip. We are force-fed a diet of media/celebrity gossip and scandal in tabloid newspapers, gossip columns, reality TV, soaps, and radio programmes, whether we like it or not. Gossip is part of the soundtrack to our lives inside and outside of organizations. But gossip often gets 'bad press' in organizations and it is necessary to consider the history of gossip in a little more detail here, in order to understand why.

Historically and linguistically, the term 'gossip' originates from *godsib,* meaning the godparent of one's child or parent of one's godchildren, and referring to a relationship of close friendship. Usage of *godsib* can be traced back as far as 1014. Middle English removed the 'd' and *gossib* took on the meaning of godparent, drinking companion, and being a friend of. Use of the term 'gossip' to mean idle talk, trifling or groundless rumour, tittle-tattle, easy, unrestrained talk or writing, especially about persons or social incidents can be traced back as far as 1811. The verb 'to gossip' dates to the early seventeenth century (http://www.webstersonline-dictionary.org). The term 'gossip' was also used to describe the woman who attended birth with a midwife who was sent out following the birth to make the event known to others (Tebbutt, 1995). The Middle Ages seemed a particularly gossipy time, and censure of gossip flourished, largely influenced by Judeo-Christian writings warning against slander, and the association of gossip with transgressions such as sloth, malice, envy, and deceit (Schein, 1994).

In medieval society, gossip was seen as something intrinsically evil or bad, with well-documented punishments, designed to discourage the activity of gossiping, and to publicly chastise and humiliate the gossip. Emler (1994) for example, describes how gossip was both disapproved of and punished by public shaming, wearing of masks of torture with tongue spikes and burning. These punishments were most often given to women, and accusations of witchcraft were not uncommon, as Stewart and Strathern's (2004, p. xii) anthropological analysis of witchcraft, gossip, and rumour illustrates:

> Historically, in small-scale or community-level contexts, gossip about neighbors, always tinged with hostility arising from specific incidents of conflict and misfortune, or jealousy and resentment of the fortunes of others, has led to the accusations of witchcraft . . . Often the malign powers attributed to those who are socially weak can be interpreted as resulting from a fear that the weak will try to take revenge on the strong.

D. Jones's (1980) classic analysis of women's oral culture defines gossip as a way of talking between women in their roles as women, arguing that the wider theme of gossip is always personal experience. Tebbutt (1995) notes that the exclusion of men in women's talk in working class neighbourhoods was threatening, and moral injunctions against gossip served to separate and isolate women. To some extent, the physical environments and spaces in which men and women historically worked also contributed to gossip being seen, and heard, as women's talk. Figure 2.1 is a photograph of my grandmother Daisy (bottom right), taken when she worked in domestic service in the North East of England in the early part of the last century.

Chatter, gossip, knowledge of family secrets, and scandals were an implicit part of the 'upstairs downstairs' nature of the work of household servants (Richardson, 2010). In contrast, Figure 2.2 is a photograph of my grandfather, Edwin (standing in the foreground) at work in the Central Marine Engine Works in Hartlepool in the 1940s.

The photograph in Figure 2.2 shows very noisy, hot, and dangerous work. Verbal workplace gossip and talk was impossible in such environments, but happened through non-verbal, visual means and in less visible settings, such as the working men's club (Woolford, 2002). Women also worked in noisy, hot, and dangerous environments such as weaving sheds and cotton mills, where lip reading was not uncommon. On the whole however, in working class neighbourhoods women's gossip historically occurred in more visible places, whilst men's gossip took place in less visible settings (Tebbutt, 1995).

Figure 2.1 Women at work in domestic service.

Similarly in a Spanish rural community, women were observed gossiping in the marketplace, whereas men gossiped in less visible settings of taverns and barbershops (Gilmore, 1978). There are many associated derogatory terms for women's talk such as nag, bitch, and, obviously, gossip. Such terms are not necessarily used when describing men's talk. However, it is not that men do not talk in this way; rather it is either called something else, for example 'chewing the fat' (Green, 1998). Over time I have come across many euphemisms for the activity of gossiping, which appear in day-to-day workplace conversations such as 'briefing' 'debriefing', 'feeding back' and 'catching up'.

Figure 2.2   Men at work in the shipbuilding industry.

Less pejorative terms describing people who gossip include 'good listener', 'has good people skills' and 'knows how to network'.

Terms such as 'word of mouth' and 'informal interaction' feature in academic papers (e.g., Fayard & Weeks, 2007; Zinko, Ferris, Humphrey, Meyer, & Aime, 2012) albeit not as frequently as terms such as 'discourse' or 'interpersonal'. Gossip's historical 'dark side' leaves traces of the 'talk-that-cannot-be-named', and has cast a shadow over gossip as 'stigmatized speech' and pejorative women's talk. The view of gossip as primarily an activity undertaken by women is misplaced, and although legalized sanctions have disappeared over time, its negative reputation remains as an enduring legacy (Emler, 1994; Schein, 1994).

There is a discrepancy between the 'collective public denunciation and the collective private practising of gossip' (Bergmann, 1993, p. 21). This is the paradox of gossip. It occurs everywhere, in many forms across history and across cultures, yet there are numerous social sanctions against it. It has a questionable legitimacy as a public discourse. Popular opinion of gossip is inclined to be fairly low on a scale of worthy, profound, or significant human action, with an associated reputation of trivial, superficial and idle talk. This leads to a second paradox associated with 'common sense' understandings of gossip; if gossip really is so unimportant, trivial, vacuous, and idle, why is it also threatening, and why is it so violently condemned? (Emler, 1994). Arguably there is a third paradox of gossip, which is that in order to be useful, gossip *has to be* publically condemned, and occur 'below the radar'. Attempts to sanitize or legitimize gossip as sanctioned talk may simply eradicate its value and utility. What is important then is to find ways of uncovering and understanding the *processes and flows* of gossip as it circulates around and between organizations.

The public face of gossip and the widespread stereotypes, perceptions, and definitions can be problematic for researchers. As Bloom (2004) comments, many researchers, at least implicitly, give up on gossip as it is *normally* understood and defined. 'To gossip' is simply to engage in the activity of relating gossip, and popular notions of gossip refer to informal chatty talk or people who habitually reveal often sensationalized and unsubstantiated information about social incidents and other people. Such definitions are unsatisfactory for organizational research purposes because they fail to address a wider range of theoretical perspectives and contexts. As we have already seen, gossip is frequently associated with pejorative assumptions and negative evaluations, but as Foster (2004) demonstrates, most researchers who claim to study gossip also include positive and neutral evaluations. In terms of organizational theory, gossip is also problematic because of the multiplicity of theoretical underpinnings, which perceive gossip differently. Different authors in different disciplinary traditions have rarely agreed upon what constitutes a definition of gossip. This is further compounded by gossip's relationship to a number of other communicative and conversational phenomena, such as chatting, rumour, and storytelling (see Chapter 1).

The literature surrounding gossip is indicative of the need to contain 'unruly contamination' (Rogoff, 2003, p. 269, citing Derrida). Thus, it is no coincidence that 'dishing the dirt' is a colloquial term for gossip. Clegg and van Iterson (2009) regard formal organization as a 'self-regulating system that constantly refines its boundaries, and gossip is the *dirt that trickles in and out of these boundaries*, illegitimate, formally disdained and often destructive' (p. 275, emphasis added). Before we can properly explore gossip as a constitutive organizing process, it is necessary to look a little more deeply at gossip's own constitutive elements and diverse theoretical understandings.

ORGANIZING GOSSIP

Putnam et al. (2009) note that typically, definitions highlight the formation, composition or making of something, as well as providing a description of the phenomenon that is constituted. In the past, disciplines such as anthropology, sociology, psychology, and communication studies have failed to agree upon definitions, concepts and consequences of gossip. For example, Gluckman's (1963) highly influential anthropological study of gossip and scandal was one of the first to emphasize the virtues of gossip in creating group morale, establishing and vindicating norms and values and maintaining the unity of social groups. From a social psychology perspective, Fine and Rosnow (1978) identified three main social functions served by gossip: information, influence, and entertainment. Bergmann's (1993) sociological analysis of gossip draws upon Simmelian constructs to understand the central relational structure of the gossip triad (gossiper, listener/respondent, and target). Secrecy, as a constitutive element of social relationships, is implicit in Bergmann's analysis. Not only do participants know something about each other, but they also keep secrets too. An evolutionary perspective (e.g., Anderson, Seigel, Bliss-Moreau, & Barrett, 2011; Dunbar, 1996; Kniffin & Wilson, 2005; 2010) suggests our penchant for gossip, in its many guises, reveals a deeply ingrained interest in the lives and behaviour of other people which has played a role in our survival chances.

The theoretical diversity of definition and purpose is such that gossip can veer from an all-encompassing exchange of social information and knowledge, to evaluative talk between at least two persons about an absent third party. Gossip has many different forms, variously described in terms such as good, bad, critical, uncritical, healing, blame, and praise (Bergmann, 1993; Goodman & Ben-Ze'ev, 1994; Soeters & van Iterson, 2002; Spacks, 1985; Taylor, G., 1994). Therefore, as discussed in Chapter 1, gossip is best seen as a multi-faceted prototypical category. Prototypical categories have vague boundaries, and this is nicely illustrated by the fictional story of the 'most-most' from Saul Bellow's novel *Herzog* (cited in Waddington, 2010). The novel follows five days in the life of Moses Herzog, a failed academic whose wife has recently left him for his best friend; a not uncommon topic of gossip in real life. The story of the 'most-most' is about a club in New York whose members are people who represent the most of every type, such as the hairiest bald man, the baldest hairy man, and so on. Every Saturday night there is a competition to tell them apart, and the person who can differentiate between the hairiest bald man and the baldest hairy man gets a prize.

The philosophical thinking behind the story of the 'most-most' lies in the Greek *phalakros* paradox, attributed to Eubulides of Miletus, a contemporary of Aristotle (Hyde, 2008). There is no sharp boundary demarcating the category of bald men; no precise number of hairs separating the bald from the hairy. Some people are clearly bald, others are clearly hairy, and in between there are a variety of borderline cases. So it is with gossip. Some evaluative talk at work is clearly gossip—for example, the conversations often prefaced by 'Have you heard. . .?' followed by disclosure of information about a colleague's departure or a competitor organization's downfall. Evaluative talk is also necessary for strategic planning and is part of everyday managerial and professional discourse, discussion and decision making. Context is therefore an important aspect to take into consideration when thinking about borderline cases. For example, Nevo, Nevo, and Derech-Zehavi (1994) point out the striking resemblances between gossip, and the way that psychologists discuss client material at case conferences. The differentiating feature here is that the latter occurs within a theoretical framework for professional and therapeutic reasons. Gossip does not necessarily have such an explicit or formalized purpose, but it can still occur in formalized settings and be blended with other communicative genres and practices such as rumour and storytelling (e.g., see Boje, 2008; Mills, 2010).

I have approached the thorny issue of defining organizational gossip by describing it in terms of constituent attributes with coalescent properties. Put more simply, gossip has a number of inherent characteristics which unite in various combinations, patterns, blends, and flows. Gossip is informal evaluative talk about individuals/issues/groups in and about organizations between at least two people which may be spoken (most common), written (less common), or visual. Although a little cumbersome, this composite sets out constitutive components of gossip drawn from different disciplinary perspectives. It also offers an explicitly *organizational* perspective by identifying talk which is 'about individuals/issues/groups in and about organizations.' This is an important distinction which addresses the question raised by Schoeneborn (2011), which is what is it within a CCO framework that makes communication *organizational*? What is also notable and novel in the composite definition is the inclusion of visual and non-verbal attributes of organizational gossip. The composite builds upon the dimensions of gossip which were used in research into gossip in nursing and healthcare organizations (see Appendix A, Table A.1). For instance, when participants were asked to comment upon these dimensions of gossip, and also upon their wider experiences, a number commented upon non-verbal aspects of gossip:

> Yes, although I thought they were quite accurate—but a lot of gossip here goes on in the canteen and you can pick it up by watching peoples' body language, that was missing.

There is an intimacy of being huddled around a table with a drink [after work], it's collusion, but it opens up conversation in a situation because there is less opportunity to do so at work.

Additionally, Wolf's (1997) account of the New York underground art scene in the 1960s makes the argument that pictures can be acts of 'visual gossip' (p. 33). Visual gossip in this sense is a means of displaying artistic identities, and constituting 'in groups' of viewers who are 'in the know' (see also Elias & Scotson, 1965; Fletcher, P., 2009). Thinking conceptually about organizational gossip in a visual sense may seem counterintuitive at first. However, thinking about gossip in a visual sense, and use of terms such as composite and coalescence, honour the essence of gossip as a diverse, non-linear phenomenon. Finally, thinking about gossip in a visual sense provides metaphors which can help us find new and creative ways of thinking about gossip as constitutive communication.

VISUAL METAPHORS

Clegg and van Iterson (2009) draw upon the metaphor of 'figure and ground,' suggesting that '[g]ossip buzzes in the background, as a part of the grounds of everyday organizational life, repositioning its figures' (p. 278). This metaphor is highly pertinent to the consideration of gossip as communication which is constitutive of organization and organizing. In other words, background conversations provide the ground underneath the constructed reality of organizational experience.

In Chapter 1, I argued that the ambiguous and subterranean nature of gossip is such that it seems to lend itself easily to metaphorical comparisons. Furthermore, as Cornelissen et al. (2008) contend, theories can be developed by using metaphors which, when projected onto organizational reality, or observations of organizational reality, can describe and explain aspects of that reality. Pursuing the figure and ground artistic metaphor a little further, the organizational reality constituted in background conversations is not necessarily that which the conversationalists would choose to paint. That is, the organization as constituted in gossip as communication may differ from the formal organization as constituted in corporate communication. Clegg and van Iterson's (2009) use of the figure and ground metaphor helps us understand the organizational dynamics of gossip, and is reproduced in some detail below:

But in life, unlike most art, the ground against which the figures are set can be experienced and felt as if it were the earth moving under the feet, because the figures not only inhabit that ground but also remake it. If one were of a punning disposition, one could say that they remember that ground—often in different terms from those of its designers. The ground is 're-membered' through the 'back ground' conversations in which they share and remake the formally constituted ground. Picasso's *Les Demoiselles d'Avignon* is a case in point, a representation in the cubist style of a bordello scene—to many the first twentieth-century painting—which problematizes the established figure–ground hierarchy by placing an equal relevance on each—in fact, by letting them interplay, even leading to figure–ground reversals. In a static medium—the painting—it captures the relativity and dynamics of movement through cubist conventions. With Picasso, we see figure and ground as existing in dialectical tension that is constantly in movement—even if we can freeze it in a painting or a paper. (p. 279)

The figure and ground metaphor for gossip can also be developed further still to incorporate perspectives from psychology and visual science about figure-ground perception. It is clearly not my intention here to apply the neuroscience of brain function to the idea of gossip as a cognitive process. But given the recent interest in organizational and social neuroscience (e.g., Becker, Cropanzano, & Sanfey, 2011), this is probably only a matter of time. Rather, I will seek to draw *metaphorical* similarities between the perception of visual information and the perception of gossip as an organizing process. This is not an easy task, but I will try.

Visual perception is 'the process of acquiring knowledge about environmental objects and events by extracting information from the light they emit or reflect' (Palmer, 1999, p. 5). Metaphorically, gossip can be seen as the process of *acquiring knowledge* about organizational *objects* and *events* by extracting information about the 'light' they emit or *reflect*. In Waddington (2010), the spookfish was used as an organizing metaphor to illustrate how attention to everyday talk can illuminate our understanding of gossip. The spookfish, which lives in very deep water, has highly specialized eyes, each with two parts to cope with very low light levels. In effect, it has four eyes. The upward looking part of the eye uses a conventional lens to focus light onto the retina. The downward looking part comprises many reflective light crystals, which collectively make up a composite mirror. The two eyes looking up are sensitive to the small amount of sunlight that filters down to the ocean's depths, the two looking down act as mirrors to detect bioluminescent and reflective objects from below. This unique anatomy improves the spookfish's ability to detect prey and spot predators in all directions. The deep-sea is a hostile environment. There are big fish with big teeth lurking in its gloomy depths, and organizations are not that different.

The spookfish provides an intriguing organizing metaphor to better understand gossip for two key reasons which have both theoretical and practical importance:

The spookfish's eyes have a 'conventional' lens and the ability to reflect light particles using its second set of eyes as mirrors. Similarly, our theoretical understanding of organizational gossip can be enhanced by using 'conventional' disciplinary lenses, as well as developing reflective and reflexive research practices that allow us to develop a multi-perspective 'composite mirror' on gossip. Secondly, the spookfish metaphor helps us to understand experiences of organizational gossip and its potential to help make sense of our environment through attending to multiple small sources of informal information. (Waddington, 2010, p. 314)

The field of visual science and figure-ground perception have also provided many well known images and illusions such as the ambiguous 'face-vase illusion' devised by Danish psychologist Edgar Rubin around 1915. The image can be perceived as both a vase or as the profiles of two human faces gazing at one another (see Figure 2.3).

Figure 2.3   An example of Rubin's 'face-vase' illusion. © Hannah Waddington.

Illusions such as Figure 2.3 seem to suggest that visual perception is fallible and cannot be considered to be an accurate representation of reality. This is a clearly a mistake. It is also a mistake to think that gossip is a fallible representation of organizational reality. On the contrary, I contend that gossip is constitutive of organizations and organizing. Furthermore, I suggest that repositioning gossip as organizational communication and knowledge can help us to better understand ways in which organizations are constituted. One way of achieving this understanding is to adopt a practice perspective to organizational knowledge which:

> locates knowing both in the doings and sayings and in the body, artefacts, habits, and preoccupations that populate the life of organizational members. In this way, the idea of practice as the site of knowing offers a vastly richer picture of both knowing and organising. It is one in which materiality, spaces, time, the body, affectivity, interests, and preoccupations are given prominence and explanatory power. (Nicolini, 2011, p. 617)

The idea of practice as the site of knowing is an important consideration in repositioning of gossip as a process of realizing organizational knowledge and way of knowing. Additionally, reorienting towards a CCO approach as discussed in more detail below, foregrounds communication as a conceptual and explanatory construct in theorizing gossip. The next section begins to develop a framework for organizing gossip which draws upon wider theoretical perspectives and principles in organizational communication and knowledge in order to assist its conceptual repositioning.

DEVELOPING A FRAMEWORK FOR CONCEPTUAL REPOSITIONING

A central argument of the book is that gossip should be seen and heard as a form of organizational communication and organizing. Influenced by works such as Weick's (1979) *The Social Psychology of Organizing* and Cooren's (2000) *The Organizing Property of Communication,* organizational communication scholars have long claimed that communication is an important building block of organizing and organization. This constitutive principle in organizational communication studies emphasizes the process of organizing. So rather than being discrete entities or 'things,' organizations 'emerge' in acts of communication or are 'constituted' by communication. The constitutive principle marks a sharp contrast to the notion of 'organization as container,' and models of communication which emphasize linear creation and transmission of a 'message' from sender to receiver and back again. Organizational communication, and therefore gossip, is much more than information processing and social interaction. Gossip cannot simply be reduced to a variable which is measured and manipulated inside an organizational container.

The theoretical roots of the claim that communication is constitutive of organizations and organizing are varied. They include, in no particular order, systems theory, phenomenology, ethnomethodology, critical discourse analysis, conversational analysis; structuration theory, narrative theory, and critical theory (Putnam et al., 2009). What links these theoretically eclectic roots is a shared emphasis on the influential effect of language and speech on social coordination and sensemaking. Put more simply, this view depicts organizations as *being* communication. Others have advanced the concept of 'firms *as being* knowledge; [and that] knowing is among the fundaments of organization' (McPhee, Canary, & Iverson, 2011, p. 304, original emphasis). However many analyses of organizational knowledge have given communication a peripheral role. Arguably gossip, which is a ubiquitous form of informal talk and information, is a potentially valuable organizing concept with which to better understand organizational communication *and* knowledge processes. This works both ways, and theoretical perspectives from organizational communication and knowledge also provide frameworks for organizing gossip.

Organizational communication and knowledge are advanced here as boundary conditions for the theorizing framework which is developed throughout the book. Van de Ven's (2007) approach to engaged scholarship and theory building provides some guiding principles. Canary and McPhee's (2011a) use of Glaser's (1978) grounded theory model of the 'six Cs' (context, conditions, causes, covariances, contingencies, and consequences), also has value in clarifying the relations among constructs in theory building. As we have seen above, the concept of organizing and a communicative perspective in general are strongly processual. Furthermore, Michelson et al.(2010) demonstrate that the characteristics and features of gossip lean strongly towards a process-oriented approach. A process orientation is therefore central to developing a better understanding of gossip and organizations, organizing, and gossip and uncovering the hidden virtues of gossip.

It is evident that gossip is under-researched in organization studies for a number of reasons. First, it lies outside of existing theoretical and frameworks and paradigms, which have historically privileged more easily observable and measurable phenomena. This is another example of gossip occuring 'below the radar'. Second, it is ethically and empirically a difficult phenomenon to capture 'in situ' in the workplace. Third, its history and reputation as tainted talk has kept it hidden from view. That said, other less tangible aspects of organizing such as organizational discourse, culture and politics have received attention (e.g., Ashkanasy, Wilderom, & Peterson, 2011a; Hartley, Fletcher, Wilton, Woodman, & Ungemach, 2007; Grant et al., 2004). Gossip is undoubtedly tainted talk, but as Mary Douglas's (1966) seminal *Purity and Danger* argues, 'there is no such thing as dirt, no single item is dirty apart from a particular system of classification in which it *does not fit*' (p. xvii, emphasis added). It is important to state that in advancing a theoretical framework for organizing gossip, it is not my intention to make gossip *fit* a narrowly defined classification system. Nor is it my intention to 'conceptually cleanse' gossip of its negative constitutive components. Maliciousness, idleness and the potential to harm are all intrinsic aspects of gossip, which are addressed more fully in Chapter 3.

GOSSIP AS COMMUNICATION AND KNOWLEDGE

Gossip, communication, and knowledge are complex micro- and macro-organizing processes. Because of the many 'turns' and 're-turns' in organizational studies, there is now a dizzying array of conceptual approaches and frameworks with which to think about gossip as communication and knowledge (e.g., see Ashcraft et al., 2009; Brown & Duguid, 2001; Canary & McPhee, 2011a; 2011b; Christensen & Cornelissen, 2011; Kuhn & Jackson, 2008; May, S. & Mumby, 2005a; Miettinen et al., 2009; Schreyögg & Geiger, 2007). The task now is to explore further the concept of gossip as constitutive of organizational communication and knowledge, because knowledge it is something that people do together, not something that people possess in their heads.

Whereas the term organizational knowledge has only been in widespread use for twenty years or so, interest in the field has been emerging over a longer period of time. A frequently cited definition is:

> Knowledge is a flux mix of framed experiences, values, contextual information, and expert insight that provides a framework for evaluating and incorporating new experiences and information. It originates and is applied in the minds of knowers. In organizations, it often becomes embedded not only in documents or repositories but also in organizational routines, processes, practices, and norms. (Davenport & Pruzak, 1998, cited in Greenhalgh, 2010, pp. 494–495)

An enduring notion is that organizational knowledge can be created and described in terms of tacit and explicit dimensions, based largely upon seminal works by Nonaka (1994) and Polanyi (1966). This approach suggests that tacit knowledge is unarticulated and tied to the senses, movement skills, physical experiences and intuition. Explicit knowledge on the other hand can be articulated and captured in drawings and writing, and the concept of knowledge conversion explains how tacit and explicit knowledge interact along a continuum. The broad aim of Nonaka's organizational knowledge creation theory was to explain the nature of knowledge assets and strategies for managing them, and the dynamic processes of organizational knowledge creation (Nonaka & von Krogh,

2009). Although considerable academic work has extended organizational knowledge creation theory, conceptualizing tacit and explicit knowledge as opposite ends of a continuum loses sight of Polanyi's assertion that *'we can know more than we can tell'* (1966, p. 4, original emphasis). Tacit knowledge cannot be 'converted' and knowing as a process, rather than knowledge as a resource or 'entity,' is both tacit *and* explicit. With regard to gossip, I assert that *we can tell more than we think we know*. It is through the processes of *telling and attending to* gossip that we can begin to address the practical question of how organizational knowledges and ways of knowing emerge in practice.

McPhee et al. (2011) stress the importance of organizational communication as a means of teasing out the connections between tacit and explicit knowledge. They argue that:

> Tacit knowledge cannot be "converted" to explicit knowledge any more than the image on one side of a coin can be converted to the image on the other side. Both sides of a coin are necessary for it to maintain its integrity and identification as a token of exchange. (p. 305)

Rather than thinking in terms of knowledge conversion, it is more appropriate to think in terms of *knowledge as conversation*, constructed in and through communicative processes. This approach to knowledge moves the focus away from the explicit/tacit philosophical debate and transcends a purely cognitive view of knowledge as that which lies 'within' a person (Myers, 2011). Furthermore, as Leonardi (2011) notes within a global organizational context, different cultures have distinct conceptualizations and perceptions of what counts as knowledge and unique beliefs about where knowledge lies. Therefore, a more complete understanding of organizational knowledge needs to account for unarticulated, culturally bound knowledge and theoretical, codified, concept based knowledge.

Canary (2011) also provides a practice oriented perspective view of organizational knowledge which transcends the explicit/tacit divide. Her study adopted Blackler's (1995) typology of embrained, embodied, encultured, embedded, and encoded knowledge to examine the types of knowledge developed and used in interpreting and implementing policy in an educational setting. Knowledge typologies have been constructed and used to ascertain if different types of organization create, use and privilege certain types of knowledge over others (see Canary, 2011, for other examples). Blackler's (1995) typology is used here to ascertain its relevance and applicability for theorizing gossip as a situated social process. Table 2.1 outlines a gossip-as-knowledge typology based upon Blackler's five categories of knowledge, and how they can be mapped on to empirical and conceptual studies of organizational gossip.

Table 2.1   Gossip-as-Knowledge Typology (adapted from Blackler, 1995)

Gossip-as-embrained knowledge	Lies within the individual, is dependent on conceptual skills and cognitive abilities, a form of intuitive knowing linked with 'gut feelings', expert practice and creativity (see Waddington 2010)
Gossip-as-embodied knowledge	Developed in action, knowledge of 'how' to go about activities, how things 'really work' in informal/unmanaged organizational structures and spaces (see Waddington and Michelson 2007)
Gossip-as-encultured knowledge	Knowledge grounded in shared understandings, meanings and stories, is also constitutive of organizational culture (see van Iterson et al. 2011)
Gossip-as-embedded knowledge	Residing in system rules, roles and relationships, is submerged in taken-for-granted routines, and also experienced as sensemaking and social exchange (see Mills 2010)
Gossip-as-encoded knowledge	Information conveyed in signs and symbols, under-represented and under-researched visual/non-verbal gossip, for example found in graffiti, cartoons on notice boards, or in gestures and glances

The gossip-as-knowledge typology in Table 2.1 offers an alternative to the explicit/tacit divide and allows us to think differently about where and how knowledge carried in/through gossip may be situated. This represents a continuum embracing knowledge embedded in sensemaking conversations which is embodied in 'unmanaged spaces,' and embrained as intuitive knowledge based on 'gut feelings' (Mills, 2010; Waddington & Michelson, 2007; Waddington, 2010). The typology also includes knowledge encultured and encoded in stories and material aspects of organizational culture (van Iterson et al., 2011). Blackler (1995) does not necessarily treat knowledge as constituted in *interaction*, and this represents a limitation of this model for thinking about gossip as organizational knowledge. Typologies such as Blackler's thus provide a partial understanding, but have the advantage of moving thinking away from the tacit/explicit divide and notions of 'knowledge conversion.'

One the one hand, the gossip-as-knowledge typology in Table 2.1 illustrates different types of knowledge, and this is important to developing insights into the role of organizational systems and contexts. On the other hand however, the typology fails to capture the nature of gossip as a diffuse and transient form of communication which spreads across organizational boundaries, disappearing, reappearing, and mutating. The typology therefore also illustrates the *problem* of attempting to categorize gossip using existing classification systems which tend to 'tidy up' or sanitize the phenomenon. The everyday nature of gossip as it is experienced, in other words informal, chatty, dangerous, and unpredictable, can become obscured by rigid classification systems. However CCO theorizing, and thinking about gossip in processual terms of communication flows, offer more promising perspectives for the future scholarship of gossip and organizations.

GOSSIP AND THE COMMUNICATIVE CONSTITUTION OF ORGANIZATION

CCO theories and the view that organizations are communicatively constituted represent a growing area of inquiry and scholarship. The CCO (sometimes interchangeably referred to as 'communication constitutes organization', or 'communication is constitutive of organizing') perspective, or question, has its origins in the transdisciplinary field of organizational communication (Putnam & Nicotera, 2009; 2010). The central CCO claim is that organizations exist principally through communication processes and flows which interconnect. Organizations are quite literally talked into existence on a day-to-day basis as well as over time. CCO is a field in organization and management studies which is proving to be of considerable interest. A recent special topic forum in *Management Communication Quarterly* (e.g., Bisel, 2010; Putnam & Nicotera, 2010; Reed, 2010; Sillince, 2010) provides a critical analysis of the implications of the CCO approach. *Organization Studies* has also recently published a special issue on the CCO approach (e.g., Cooren et al., 2011; Stohl & Stohl, 2011; Taylor, J. R., 2011). Canary and McPhee's (2011) *Communication and Organizational Knowledge: Contemporary Issues for Theory and Practice* also gives a comprehensive overview of theory, research, frameworks, and models for future research and practice.

The CCO field is generally considered to have three main 'schools of theorizing' but it is beyond the scope of the chapter, and indeed the book, to address them all in detail. There is the Montreal School, represented by James R. Taylor, François Cooren and colleagues, and the lesser known body of work inspired by Luhmann's (1995) general theory of social systems (see Ashcraft et al., 2009; Cooren, Taylor & Van Every, 2006; Cooren et al., 2011; Schoeneborn, 2011). The third approach which is addressed in more detail here is McPhee and Zaug's (2000; 2009) 'four flows'model. The four flows model represents a 'set of criteria that provide a means to assess the adequacy of any theory of the constitution of organization in communication' (Taylor, J. R., 2009, p. 181). The model is therefore used as a sounding board for the arguments and ideas developed in the book. In particular, in Chapters 5 and 6, the four flows model is used to revisit empirical materials and analyse the relationships and connections between gossip, identity and power. In the final chapter I use the wider premises of CCO scholarship to gauge the relevance of theorizing framework developed in the book. I take as a starting point the general claim that:

> if communication is indeed constitutive of organization, it cannot be considered to be simply one of the many factors involved in organizing, and it cannot be merely the vehicle for the expression of pre-existing 'realities'; rather, it is the means by which organizations are established, composed, designed, and sustained. (Cooren et al., 2011, p. 1150)

McPhee and Zaug's structuration influenced model identifies communication processes that constitute organization, and its analytical starting point is the individual and her/his reflexive capacity (Cooren & Fairhurst, 2009). Four fundamentally different processes, or flows, of organizational communication are identified. These flows represent ways in which an organization enacts and maintains relations towards its members, itself, its internal subgroups and processes, and other organizations. The four flows have been more broadly defined, and applied, by McPhee and Zaug (2000; 2009), McPhee and Iverson (2009) and Browning, Greene, Sitkin, Sutcliffe and Obstfeld (2009). The flows are defined as follows.

1. *Membership negotiation*: by which organizations draw distinctions between their own members and non-members and includes processes of socialization, identification and self positioning activities. Membership negotiation asks the question: 'Who are we?'
2. *Organizational self-structuring*: this distinguishes organizations from other social groupings, often referring to formal managerial control activities, governance structures, organizational policies and procedures. Self-structuring asks the question: 'What rules do we operate by?'
3. *Activity coordination*: relates to the manifest purpose of the organization reflected in multiple processes and attitudes towards the organization regarding how work does, or doesn't, get done. Activity coordination asks the question: 'What work are we doing together?'
4. *Institutional positioning*: is where the organization's status is continuously negotiated in interaction with stakeholders and other institutions. Institutional positioning asks the question: 'What external forces provide legitimacy, and what kinds of communication are necessary to please them?'

Browning et al. (2009) use examples from observations of a U.S. Air Force maintenance squadron to show that whereas the four flows are conceptually separate, they can easily drift quickly into each other's space. This suggests that understanding the overlap in communication flows is important in understanding the model.

The four flows model was originally published in 2000, and reprinted in 2009. In an afterword McPhee, writing in 2009, notes that the original article, which was written in opposition of the assumption that there should be a single process of CCO, drew a degree of attention that was, at least to him, surprising. However, whereas there was a broad consensus that many different sorts of organizational communication have constitutive force, 'the implied theoretical question, whether the strongest account provides just one model, or a small number of different but related models, or an unruly plethora of accidentally constituted processes, still hasn't generated much debate' (McPhee & Zaug, 2009, p.45). Arguably it might all be a matter of timing. The four flows model, although not initially generating much debate, now chimes with the current 'turn' in contemporary organizational knowledge and communication theory. In Reflection 2 below I consider whether gossip is also something whose 'turn' has now come.

The CCO approach is now receiving considerable theoretical attention, and the four flows model has been proposed as a framework for examining other CCO theories, processes and their underlying assumptions (Putnam & Nicotera, 2009; Taylor, 2009). Notably, Putnam et al. (2009) suggest that the main reason for examining different orientations to CCO is theoretical, 'we say that communication is constitutive of organizations *without fully understanding what this means, conceptually or empirically*' (p. 5, emphasis added). Therefore, the view that organizations are communicatively constituted represents an approach which is not without challenge and critique.

REFLECTION 2: THINKING ABOUT GOSSIP AS AN IDEA WHOSE TIME HAS COME?

Looking back over what I have written so far in this chapter, I seem to have acquired the habit of italicizing words and I think I might also be 'ing-ing' more. The use of 'organization-as-verb' rather than 'organization-as-noun' is pervasive in the CCO field. The activity of 'verbing' is contagious. But gossip does this all by itself. Gossip is a verb and a noun, an activity and an entity. What's more, as an entity, 'the gossip' can be an individual—often prefixed by terms such as 'insatiable,' 'dreadful' or 'terrible'—as well as information or content as in: 'What's the gossip?' Gossip embodies a person, a process and a product. Maybe its 'turn' has come quite simply in the guise of the communicative constitution of organization?

Cooren and Fairhurst (2009) have challenged the role of agency in McPhee and Zaug's model, arguing that the model vacillates between human and organizational agency. They also argue that the model does not adequately explain, analytically, or practically, the connections between the flows. In addition, Schoeneborn (2011) identifies three key questions emerging within the current CCO debate. The first question is, quite simply, what makes communication organizational? The second is, if organizations are defined in terms of something as ephemeral as communication, how are they stabilized over time? The third is, what differentiates organizations from other social phenomena such as networks and communities? Schoeneborn therefore suggests that the four flows model is probably better seen as a soft set of criteria, rather than a precise definition of what makes communication organizational.

I would argue that use of the term 'flow' in the model is also potentially problematic. The four flows are analytically distinct, and seen as being 'different in their *main direction* and in their contribution to organizational constitution' (McPhee & Zaug, 2009, p. 44, emphasis added). The notion of direction implies a dynamic not dissimilar to the way that 'flow' has been used in knowledge management thinking:

> To the extent that organizational knowledge does not exist in the form needed for application or at the place and time required to enable work performance, then it must flow from how it exists and where it is located to how and where it is needed. This is the concept [of] knowledge flows. (Nissan 2006, cited in Bratianu, 2011, p. 163)

Bratianu's (2011) analysis of dominant metaphors in knowledge management thinking illustrates that mechanical models of knowledge flows, such as Nissan's, imagine knowledge as a fluid, and organization as a field of forces. These metaphors have limited value when considering gossip as constitutive of organizational communication and knowledge, mainly because they are based on concepts of linearity. Gossip is anything but linear. As Michelson et al. (2010) note, the beginning and end points of gossip are not always easily identifiable. Gossip about an issue, person, or organization can temporarily disappear, but then resurface elsewhere in time and space.

The notion of a 'main direction' of flow therefore represents a potentially significant weakness for the relevance of the four flows model for future organizational theories of gossip. On the other hand, there is also scope for organizational gossip research and theorizing to make a significant contribution to future directions for CCO work. The four flows model provides a springboard for CCO theory building, and empirical studies of the model are just beginning. Furthermore, studies which have used the four flows model are showing 'significant promise' (Ashcraft et al., 2009, p. 19). There is scope for the four flows model to contribute to the theoretical argument that gossip is a constitutive organizing process and example of CCO thinking. Putnam and Nicotera (2010, p. 163) therefore offer the following suggestions which provide valuable guidance for future research:

1. Clarify and distinguish the senses in which the term *organization* refers to process, entity, and/or entity from a process view;
2. Clarify what the four flows signify as a condition or prototype of CCO;
3. Unpack authority and legitimacy as they become naturalized in and through CCO; and
4. Attend to materiality, such as objects, physical sites, and bodies, by showing how the material shapes communication and knowledge practices in political ways.

The flows (membership negotiation, organizational self-structuring, activity coordination, institutional positioning) constitute organizations and organizing by establishing boundaries, linking members together, shaping operations, and adapting interaction. There are two important ongoing questions. The first is how does a communicative constitution of organization perspective shape understandings of the organization's embeddedness in social contexts? The second is how does gossip as a particular communicative process produce and reproduce social structures which constitute an organization? The first question is beginning to be answered (e.g., Browning et al., 2009; McPhee & Iverson, 2009; Stohl & Stohl, 2011); the second is partially answered in this book, particularly in Chapters 5 and 6, where I examine how gossip-related empirical materials might elaborate and enhance McPhee and Zaug's model.

CONCLUSION

This chapter represents the conceptual core of the book. Rather than seeing gossip as an impediment to organizing, or as an unintended consequence of organizing, it has re-presented gossip as a constitutive organizing process. In exploring gossip as constitutive of organizational communication and knowledge, I have established boundary conditions for theorizing gossip. This marks the first stage in the development of a framework for the conceptual repositioning of gossip. The framework incorporates ethics, emotion, identity, power, and sensemaking. These concepts are drawn firstly from empirical and theoretical studies of gossip, and secondly from research themes and intellectual developments in CCO scholarship.

However, in developing this framework for the conceptual repositioning of gossip it is not my intention to make gossip 'fit' into a particular way of thinking. Neither is it my intention to conceptually cleanse gossip of its negative constitutive components. The new ways of thinking and knowing about gossip presented here are not imperatives, but are an attempt to counterbalance gossip's negative reputation and legacy. Nevertheless, maliciousness, idleness, and the potential to harm remain as intrinsic aspects of gossip. These issues are addressed more extensively in the next chapter.

3   Gossip and Ethics

Oh! gossip is charming! History is merely gossip. But scandal is gossip made tedious by morality.

—Oscar Wilde, *Lady Windermere's Fan*, Act III, 1892

Gossip has been generally discredited or condemned in the public domain as being a corrosive and pejorative discourse, particularly where it is considered disproportionate or improper. The reality however is that there is widespread interest and participation in gossip. In other words, as discussed in the previous chapter, there is a discrepancy between collective public censure and collective private—or not so private now, given the ubiquitous reach and public visibility of the internet—practicing of gossip. This is one of the many paradoxes of gossip. It is a ubiquitous social, organizational, and digital phenomenon, yet there are numerous sanctions against it. This paradox is reflected in such statements as 'You didn't hear this from me, but did you know...?' or 'I'm not one to gossip, but.....'. People seem keen to talk about gossip, yet also seek to distance themselves from being associated with gossiping and being seen as a gossip.

This chapter addresses the negative reputation of gossip as something which is morally repugnant by exploring the ethics and taboo-like nature of gossip and organizations. It addresses two inter-related questions:

1. Can gossip be justified in an ethical and moral sense, and if it can, under what circumstances is gossip acceptable?
2. What are the ethical issues surrounding the collection of gossip-related data?

It is beyond the scope and intention of this chapter to enter into detailed debate and discussion of ethical theories and abstract rules. Gossip does not lend itself easily to the analytical philosophical approach of definition and deduction. The core argument advanced here is that although not without considerable challenges and problems, gossip is not always taboo. It can also be acceptable, and indeed valuable, informal talk and an example of everyday ethics in practice. As Gotsis and Kortezi (2010) argue, in the real world, organizational practices are contextual, 'agents are concerned with both *consequences* and duties, but subject to *social relations* and *context*' (p. 506, emphasis added). This view resonates with the claim that gossip is constitutive of organizational communication and knowledge advanced in the previous chapter. However, a claim such as this is meaningless unless it can lead to the development of coherent theories of gossip and organizing. Therefore, this chapter also addresses some of the *practical* aspects and ethical challenges of researching gossip and organizations.

Researchers need to be mindful of the moral and ethical issues at stake when collecting and interpreting gossip-related data. These include attention to the rights of absent third parties who may either be unaware that they are the subject of gossip, or unaware that they are (indirectly) involved in research. I will give examples of how these ethical issues have been addressed in practice. In particular, I argue that this involves paying attention to the aspects of reflexivity which explicitly acknowledge the ethical dilemmas which permeate the research process and impact upon the creation of knowledge (Guillemin & Gillam, 2004).

In order to preserve confidentiality in the reflexive and empirical materials used in this chapter (and also throughout the book), unless individuals have given permission to use their name/s, the following strategies have been adopted: (i) altering specific characteristics and using pseudonyms; (ii) limiting the description of specific characteristics; (iii) obfuscating case detail by adding extraneous material; and (iv) using composites (American Psychological Association, 2010). So, some names have been changed and some details have been altered, but without adversely altering meaning or intention. Rather than using gender specific 'she/he' and 'hers/his,' I use 'they' and 'their' unless otherwise indicated. The chapter begins with further consideration of how the historical and gendered nature of gossip as pejorative, women's talk has resulted in tensions and taboo. This is followed by moral and philosophical considerations as to what constitutes the 'good,' the 'bad,' and the 'toxic' attributes and types of gossip. It also addresses methodological considerations and identifies some ways forward to address the real world challenges of researching organizational gossip.

TENSIONS AND TABOO

The conceptual repositioning of gossip as organizational communication and knowledge is not entirely unproblematic. The way that knowledge is seen and used is influenced by its relevance, legitimacy, and accessibility. There are tensions between epistemologies which are inclusive of narrative and anecdote, and more traditional approaches. In the fields of evidence-based management and organizational science, healthcare and policy, hierarchies of evidence are found (Contandriopoulos, Lemire, Denis, & Remblay, 2010; Rousseau, Manning, & Denyer, 2008). In these fields, knowledge which has been assimilated and generated using systematic reviews and controlled experiments has *traditionally* taken precedence over knowledge collected using narrative and anecdote. Narrative and anecdote are generally taboo topics and the bottom of hierarchies of evidence. Contandriopoulos et al. (2010) consider knowledge existing in two forms: (i) individually, that is inside people's heads, largely experimental, uncontested, and translated into practice (or not) through human will and agency; and (ii) collectively, in other words socially shared and embedded organizationally, with a more diffuse effect upon individual actions and outcomes. Importantly, they argue that in the field of healthcare and policy, knowledge exchange research needs to move from an individual level to an organizational and policy level. Or as Greenhalgh (2010, p. 492) put it '[t]he road to enlightenment on these meso- and macro-dimensions of knowledge exchange is not paved exclusively with controlled experiments.'

Contandriopoulos et al.'s (2010) review of knowledge exchange interventions at the organizational and policymaking levels has significant implications for the arguments developed in this book. I contend that the understanding of gossip needs to move from an individual level to an organizational level of analysis. However, the complexity of gossip is such that a range of inter-disciplinary psycho-social-cultural perspectives is necessary to account for human interactions and relationships at multiple levels. The framework which is articulated in Chapter 8, synthesizes these perspectives to guide future research, theory, and practice. Following Van de Ven (2007, p. 112, original emphasis) '[a]theory is an explanation of relationships among concepts or events within a set of boundary conditions.' Organizational communication and knowledge are the boundary conditions, and ethics, which is the focus of this chapter, is one of the core concepts of the theorizing framework.

There are other tensions in the gossip-as-knowledge claim which resonate with tensions found in feminist epistemology. Given the historical and gendered stereotypes of gossip as women's talk these tensions need to be aired and then dispelled. Adkins (2002) contends that gender-based arguments and explanations reproduce the outdated view that narrative knowledge, although valuable, is trivial. Trivial that is, when compared to the 'real thing' produced by logical positivism. Gender-based arguments and explanations ignore the wider role of social practices of narratives in the construction of knowledge, and I concur with Adkins, in seeking to:

> perform a historical resuscitation on narratives of gossip in particular, not simply so that we can appreciate the ways in which the *practice of gossip is not limited to women*, but so that we can turn this analysis towards epistemology writ large. In other words, if gossip for knowledge purposes is more widely and analytically practised

than we traditionally take it to be, perhaps the split between 'really' authoritative knowledge and women's knowledge is equally illusory. Therefore, the only way to have an integrated theory of knowledge is to see that these 'women's ways of knowing' are simply part of how *all humans come to knowledge.* (Adkins, 2002, p. 215, emphasis added)

One of the aims of *Gossip and Organizations* is to dispel the myth that 'women gossip, men talk.' However, in dispelling this myth I am not seeking to re-write history. As discussed in the previous chapter, in Early Modern England (i.e., the sixteenth, seventeenth, and eighteenth centuries) the word 'gossip' referred to midwives and companions in childbirth, and was also used as a term for women-friends generally (http://www.websters-online-dictionary.org). Patriarchy, social class, and women's powerlessness have all contributed to the historical legacy of gossip as women's talk (Capp, 2003; Jones, D., 1980; Tebbutt, 1995). Yet men in Early Modern England also gossiped, most notably Samuel Pepys, who has been described as 'the insatiable gossip, the keen observer, and the historian' (Hallam Moorhouse, 1909/2008, p. 41).

Undoubtedly then, men and women do engage in gossip, although the content, context and characteristics may differ. For example, Levin and Arluke's (1985) study using unobtrusive observers in a university cafeteria found that gossip accounted for 68% of the conversation. Levin and Arluke found that male and female gossip did not differ with regard to tone. In other words both men and women made positive and negative references to other people. However, women were more likely to gossip about friends and family, whereas men were more likely to gossip about celebrities and sports figures. Other studies of naturally occurring conversations using ethnographic approaches and diary records also demonstrate both men and women's engagement in gossip (e.g., Dunbar, 1992; Dunbar, Duncan, & Marriott, 1997; Emler, 1994; Kniffin & Wilson, 2005; 2010). Notably Kniffin and Wilson's work illustrates the role of gossip in two strongly male-orientated domains of competitive university rowing teams and cattle ranching communities. Adopting a transdisciplinary evolutionary approach they found that workplace gossip serves positive functions when organizational rewards—measured in context specific currencies—are allocated fairly at the level of small-scale groups.

Having demonstrated that the practice of gossip is not limited to women, and that gossip and gossiping are integral to how all humans come to knowledge I will not dwell any further *conceptually* upon gossip as women's talk. However gossip's historical legacy is still evident, as outlined in the following reflection on interviewing men about their experiences of gossip.

REFLECTION 3: 'NOW I'M NOT ONE TO GOSSIP, BUT . . .'

This was a phrase I heard many times, more often from men, when I was researching gossip. It resonates with the phrase 'I'm not a feminist but . . .' often used as a qualifying remark by women to distance themselves from negative stereotypes associated with feminism or being labeled as an angry, extremist man-hater. Men would also say things like 'I'm not sure how much help I can be with your research . . .' and yet were very willing to participate. Interestingly men's interviews lasted longer on average than women's. Being the topic of a doctoral research study seemed to give gossip a different status and credibility. It legitimized a taboo topic and behaviour, and interviews created a safe space for participants to be able to talk openly about their day-to-day experiences of what might be seen as tainted talk.

Taboo

Taboo derives from the Tongan *tabu* and the more general Polynesian term *tapu* meaning 'not allowed.' A taboo is a strong social prohibition or ban against words, objects, actions, discussions, or people that are considered undesirable or offensive by a group, culture, society, or community (http://www.websters-online-dictionary.org). Taboos result in social embarrassment and shame, are a form of control, and a manifestation of power and power relations. Taboos can be widely applied to different items or objects, both animate and inanimate. The concept of taboo has received considerable attention in anthropology, psychology, and sociology, but has been largely overlooked in organization studies. There are some notable exceptions, for example Martin (1990) discussed a series of sexual organizational taboos to illustrate on-going gender discrimination. More recently, Hofstede, Hofstede, and Minkov (2010) observe that in intercultural encounters, jokes and irony are taboo until individuals are absolutely sure of the other culture's assumptions regarding humour. What is considered taboo will clearly vary among different national and organizational contexts, and the list of taboo topics or items is potentially limitless. Nevertheless, it can be assumed that taboos will operate in all social settings, including organizations. Gossip has largely been a taboo topic in organizations, both in research and in practice.

The neglect of gossip can be explored in more depth by thinking about it as a socially disapproved, taboo, or 'tainted topic' in organizational studies (MacLean, Anteby, Hudson, & Rudolph, 2006). This could be potentially troubling for researchers, as stigma associated with tainted topics such as gossip can also lead to the phenomenon of guilt by association. In other words, the negative connotations and social disapproval of gossip get split off and projected on to others (Gabriel, 1999; MacLean et al., 2006). That is, participants, colleagues, editors, and readers might in some way, intentionally or unintentionally, shift the stigma associated with negative or bad gossip onto researchers. On the other hand, this is not necessarily problematic. In interviews, for example, a space can be opened up when the researcher holds the boundaries of the stigma and taboo associated with gossip. This creates a safe space where participants are 'allowed,' and enabled, to talk about and reflect upon gossip-related incidents and events (see Reflection 3 above). Nevertheless gossip has retained a stigmatized status in terms of both the activity of gossiping and the person who gossips. The ethical reasons behind the stigma and taboo of gossip are discussed in the following section, which addresses the widespread moral and philosophical condemnation of gossip in more detail.

MORAL AND PHILOSOPHICAL CONSIDERATIONS: THE GOOD, THE BAD, AND THE TOXIC

Gossip represents a transgression of the private/public boundary and there are a number of ethical issues to consider relating to human rights, freedom of speech, privacy, harm, and morality. Consideration of such a range of issues ultimately leads to the ethical question: Is gossip a good thing or a bad thing? Westacott's (2000; 2012) ethical analysis of gossip reveals many positive aspects of gossip which are often overlooked. Yet there are also many social norms and religious laws that condemn and prohibit gossip (Aziz, 2010; Glinert, Loewenthal, & Goldblatt, 2003; Stewart & Strathern, 2004).

In Buddhism, for example, the prohibition of gossip is seen as a central tenet of the faith, with the mandate that people should refrain from harsh words and frivolous talk. Similarly, Judaism is intensely aware of the power of speech and of the harm that can be done through words spoken without a constructive purpose (known in Hebrew as *lashon hara*). Talking negatively about people is seen as sinful, even if it is recounting factual information, and demeaning for the speaker and the subject of the gossip. Christian theology also eschews gossip as sinful idle talk, associating people who gossip, also referred to as backbiters, with sins which include sexual immorality and murder. Whilst in Islam, gossip is likened to eating the flesh of a dead brother, and seen as something that should be walked away from or renounced. All of these theological perspectives share a view of gossip as a moral problem, as something to be avoided at all costs.

From a philosophical perspective, Heidegger (1962) condemned gossip as inauthentic discourse, and dismissed it as being far too trivial to aid genuine understanding of the more profound aspects of human existence. He contended that gossiping:

[S]preads in wider circles and takes on an authoritative nature. Things are so because one says so. Idle talk is constituted in this gossiping and passing the word along, a process by which its initial lack of grounds to stand on [Bodenständigkeit] increases to complete groundlessness [Bodenlosigkeit]. (Heidegger, 1962, p. 212)

Heidegger's assumption that gossip is a groundless process is seemingly at odds with the numerous sanctions against it. If gossip really is groundless inauthentic discourse, where do its dangerous properties come from? There is surely a contextual element to the authenticity or otherwise of gossip? Gossip has evolved across cultures and societies, ritualized as a form of social interaction whose value lies in the sense of relatedness it imparts, rather than in the words or content (Dunbar, 1996; Gluckman, 1963). Although Heidegger's condemnation of gossip features in earlier gossip-related literature (e.g., Ben-Ze'ev, 1994; Jaeger et al., 1998; Laing, 1993), more recently his dismissal of gossip as inauthentic discourse has had diminishing impact. Indeed it could be argued that the process of gossiping is, in itself, authentic. In other words, to what extent does authenticity lie with the telling, the teller and the relational and contextual aspects of their interaction with the listener? This is an interesting and relatively unexplored question, with scope as a potential area for future work.

Other distinguished thinkers, including Aristotle and Kierkegaard, also expressed an abhorrence of gossip as frivolous (rather than real) talk, with its content seen as largely insignificant (Leach, 1995; 2000). Eleanor Roosevelt is alleged to have commented: 'Great minds discuss great ideas. Average minds discuss events. Small minds discuss people.' Such normative points of view against gossip condemn it as a mode of meaningless talk based upon individual and personal values, rather than public or social values. Clearly condemnation of gossip is justifiable in some circumstances, and three particular types of gossip have been judged as morally reprehensible, or *bad*: (i) gossip as a breach of confidence; (ii) gossip that the speaker knows to be false; and (iii) gossip that is unduly invasive (Leach, 1995). More broadly, coercive, destructive, deceptive, intrusive, secretive, and manipulative-exploitative types of communication activities have been identified as unethical (Jones, E., Watson, Gardner, & Gallois, 2004, citing Redding, 1996). Morally reprehensible gossip represents transgressions of trust, truth and privacy. There is no doubt then that gossip has an appalling reputation, and has been subject to widespread and enduring disapproval and censure, which in some circumstances and contexts is entirely justified.

Conversely however, gossip is also an inherently democratic process, acting as a resource for moral understanding and freedom of speech. Writing in the aptly titled *Good Gossip* (Goodman & Ben-Ze'ev, 1994, Ben-Ze'ev 1994) contends that typically gossip is a relaxing, interesting, and pleasurable activity. Prohibition of gossip on moral grounds is, he suggests, not necessarily justified because such prohibition focuses on extreme and non-typical cases. Prohibition and censure of gossip reinforces the negative stereotypes, perception, and reputation of gossip. Reinforcement promotes distortion and misunderstanding. The positive attributes of gossip and its intrinsic value as an activity that is easygoing and enjoyable are often ignored. Therefore, it can be argued that the view of gossip as a 'moral problem' is flawed by misrepresentation of the potential to harm. Ben-Ze'ev makes the analogy with eating. Even though excessive eating is harmful, this does not imply an intrinsic evil in eating. Therefore, even though excessive and distorted gossip is harmful, this does not establish or validate the intrinsic malicious nature of the majority of gossip. In some circumstances and contexts gossip is indeed *good*.

Other commentators have made metaphorical food related comparisons between gossip and rumour. For example, DiFonzo, Bordia, and Rosnow (1994) draw comparisons between gossip as something tasty, to be savoured and enjoyed, and rumour as a crumb or scrap of food hungrily devoured amidst an information famine. This is also an apt metaphor if we think about the language used to describe gossip and people who gossip excessively, such as *'juicy,'* and *'insatiable.'* People use metaphorical terms such as *'it left a bad taste in my mouth'* after hearing unwanted negative gossip about another person. Pursuing the food metaphor a little further then, it is also possible to binge on gossip, suffer the consequences of scarcity and malnutrition, and also savour the pleasures of gossip. Importantly, Aristotle's philosophy of ethics and virtue is relevant to the understanding of gossip and organizations. For Aristotle, the virtuous habit of action is always an intermediate state between the opposed vices of excess and deficiency (Ben-Ze'ev, 1994). Too much and too little are wrong, but the right kind of action lies somewhere in between. So it is, I would argue, with gossip. The decision to engage in the communicative practice of gossiping (or not) is therefore an ethical one, as is the decision regarding what to do next with knowledge gained through gossip.

Emler (1994) was an early advocate for 'good gossip' arguing for its rehabilitation as intelligent action:

> Successful gossip requires delicate judgements about what precisely to say to whom, how to say it and what to hold back. It also involves skill in extracting disclosures from others. If we recognize its many functions and its often high level of sophistication, we then may begin to appreciate the sheer scale of the intellectual achievement competent gossip represents. (p. 138)

Arguably the harmful and 'bad' aspects of gossip have overshadowed the 'good,' and it is time for a more complete evaluation of the subject. This is not to paint an overly optimistic picture, nor is it to deny the negative aspects of gossip, which when taken to extremes can become *toxic*. The notion of toxicity in the workplace is most frequently associated with emotion, leadership and bullying (e.g., Boddy, 2011; Frost, 2003; Gallos, 2008; Lipman-Blumen, 2005; Mark, 2005). As Gallos (2008) notes, the term toxic is a strong and evocative one, and its power as a concept, rather like gossip, lies in its pervasiveness. Toxic gossip is a harmful and extreme type of malicious, untrue, and negative gossip. Toxic gossip is part of a wider pattern of toxic diffusion, venting of strong emotions, stories about the circumstances that evoked them, accusations and attacks on colleagues.

The concept of toxic gossip is largely unresearched, and is introduced here as a potential topic for further discussion, critical debate, definition and empirical work. It represents the 'dark side of gossip' (Waddington, 2005b, p. 43) which refers to collusive, dysfunctional processes, which are detrimental to healthy social and organizational relationships. The dark side of gossip has an emotional undertow of anger, frustration, resentment, and hatred, as the following extract from an interview with a Clinical Nurse Specialist (CNS) reveals:

> I think the most interesting part of going to a conference is what goes on outside the lecture hall, and we all know that's where the real work gets done, and that's also where the gossip takes place. [So] there's nothing like a few glasses of wine for people to start to talk. And if they're looking across the room at somebody they've always hated, then it's inevitable that someone will say something, and so the process starts and it could be harmless, or poisonous. (CNS 7)

Toxic gossip can also be re-interpreted as a form of organizational violence and violation in and around organizations. Bosson, Johnson, Niederhoffer, and Swann (2006) suggest that there is some value in conceptualizing gossip as a form of 'indirect aggression that can have harmful consequences for gossipers and gossipees alike' (p. 148). The potential for gossip to harm must not be underestimated nor overlooked. Nor should organizational gossip be subject to conceptual cleansing of its dangerous dark side, nor uncoupled from its moral legacy of 'evil tongues.' However, gossip's moral legacy has undoubtedly contributed to the failure to see its positive attributes, and the neglect of gossip as an organizing process.

THE NEGLECT OF GOSSIP AS AN ORGANIZING PROCESS

This book argues that gossip is central to many organizing processes and dynamics surrounding communication, knowledge, ethics, emotion, identity, power, and sensemaking. Yet gossip is largely absent from empirical research and theoretical developments in these areas. Gossip has been infrequently researched as a topic in its own right. It is as if gossip has been ignored or written out of the organization studies and management literature, and arguably this neglect can be attributed to its miserable reputation as pejorative, trivial discourse. Gossip has been cast as 'tainted talk.'

Thinking about gossip as tainted talk involves exploration of the challenges facing researchers working with socially disapproved, dangerous and sensitive topics. These challenges are not new, and neither are they solely restricted to gossip research. The ethical, methodological and practical issues involved in researching such topics have also been comprehensively addressed elsewhere (e.g., Lee, 1993, 1995; MacLean et al., 2006; Nilan, 2002; Van Maanen, 1988). Key themes to note are: (i) shifting researcher subject positions of insider/outsider; (ii) gaining access to research sites; (iii) trust; and (iv) potentially idiosyncratic ethical dilemmas, all of which are highly pertinent for organizational researchers and scholars of gossip.

The following extract from another interview with a CNS illustrates an idiosyncratic ethical dilemma. Namely 'Do I call it gossip research?' I did, because if I didn't I was arguably reinforcing the notion of gossip as 'tainted talk', or 'talk-that-cannot-be-named.' But that was not always the case when I began my research, as the extract below shows. I sought reflexive feedback from participants about their perceptions of gossip as research topic:

> *CNS:* One thing that did strike me is why use the term gossip? Because it does have quite negative connotations doesn't it?
>
> *KW:* It does, yes, and when I first started doing this research I found myself talking about networks and informal communication, but quickly realized that at the end of the day gossip is something that happens, people come back from holiday and ask 'What's the gossip?' or they say. . .[CNS laughs and interrupts]
>
> *CNS:* Yeah, they don't say [heavy emphasis] 'close the door, let's informally network. . . .'

The above interview extract, and associated issues of reflexive research practice, are discussed more extensively in Waddington (2010). For the purposes of this chapter, the extract reveals a dissonance between the stigma associated with the term gossip, and the need to 'say it as it is.' There are threats to researchers' integrity if they mislead participants as to the true nature of their research. Gabriel (2000) advises, with regard to storytelling, that researchers should not engage in deception and subterfuge. Yet as Alvesson and Ashcraft (2011, p. 73) point out 'gate keepers and interviewees may be less likely to grant access to researchers overtly espousing a critical lens and investigating the underside of organizational life.' Potential participants may be disinclined to talk about or admit to gossiping because of its reputation, and what it may reveal about them and/or their organization. Indeed one participant asked me *'have you been given my name because they* [the hospital manager who had facilitated my research access] *think I gossip a lot?'* The negative connotations and stereotypes of gossip that (currently) persist might therefore hamper access to research sites and informants. There are particular issues relating to access to research sites and the nature of the topic. One solution to the potential problems surrounding access to informants *and* gossip in, around and about organizations is to ensure that the research agenda is not a hidden agenda. Research needs to be both theoretically and practically relevant, and one way of achieving this, as argued earlier, is to locate gossip in the communicative constitution of organization field.

ETHICS AND CCO RESEARCH

Chapter 2 examined the significance of gossip as a constitutive organizing process and example of CCO thinking. The issue of agency is central to the organizing role of communication, particularly to scholars of the Montreal School (Cooren et al., 2006). Analytically, the contemporary debates regarding the role of agency in CCO thinking are quite complex and can only be briefly addressed here. A pragmatic approach has been adopted, and the main focus is the *ethical* implications and broad principles for gossip-related research.

Agency implies a human agent endowed with properties of consciousness and purpose, power, and iteration and repetitiveness, which Robichaud (2006, p. 103, citing Giddens, 1984) refers to as the 'internalist view.' This view speaks to the ethics of gossip and gossiping and allows us to question and examine motives behind gossip, power dynamics and habitual *patterns* of gossip. But this is not enough. We also need to question and examine the *relational* context of Bergmann's (1993) gossip triad of gossiper, recipient and third party/target of gossip (or 'gossipee'). This is embodied in the 'externalist view' (Robichaud, 2006, p. 105, citing Latour, 1994) whereby the agent, or actor, does not remain the same throughout, and nor do other actors who are involved. This also speaks to the ethical *consequences* of gossip discussed above in relation to its potential to do harm or good. Robichaud also relies heavily on the relational ontology of Charles Sanders Peirce to transcend the tensions between internalist and externalist theories of agency. Put simply (if that is possible), '[o]rganizing is constituted through a plurality of agencies' (Robichaud, 2006, p. 113).

If organizing is constituted through a plurality of agencies, this raises the question of whether a plurality of approaches to ethics is necessary. A detailed answer to this question is beyond the scope of the chapter. I do not have the space, nor the skill, to answer it fully. A simpler answer is to include the perspective of virtue ethics as a method of approaching practical ethical situations and contexts. The ethical analysis and discussion so far in this chapter have considered the phenomenon of gossip as something which can be seen as good, bad, or toxic. The discussion so far has been largely based on ethical approaches which emphasize duties or rules (deontology), and the consequences of actions (consequentialism). Virtue ethics on the other hand is based on Aristotelian views which foreground virtue and character, rather than emphasizing universal principles and rules (Walker & Ivanhoe, 2009).

Virtue ethics shifts our gaze away from ethical prohibitions of gossip and its consequences, to a focus upon the individual who gossips and the ethical conduct of the researcher. I am approaching organizational gossip as an example of everday ethics in practice because, as Gotsis & Kortezi (2010) argue:

> First and foremost, virtue ethicists tend to view organizational activities as practices embedded in a specific context: it is the latter, not abstract rules or universal principles, which shapes morality in business. Virtues obtain social or interpersonal dimensions as distinct qualities of individuals who share and deeply respect others' viewpoint and attitudes, thus, demonstrating *civic virtue*. (p. 507, original emphasis)

Civic virtue is the cultivation of aspects of personal living that are claimed to be important for the success of the individual, the community, or other groups. In organizations, civic virtue has been defined as prosocial behaviours associated with information gathering and exercising influence, which are intended to contribute positively to the organization (Graham & Van Dyne, 2006). This also, I would argue, extends to the communicative constitution of organization. Gossip is 'soft information', in other words information that is typically expressed as talk, instinct, gut feeling, or vision. This is in contrast to 'hard information,' typically expressed as data, statistics and reports (Vidal & Möller, 2007). It has been suggested that the way that institutions and public bodies approach 'soft information,' such as gossip, rumour, and innuendo can be seen as part of their wider social and ethical responsibilities (Department of Health, 2005). Arguably openness to organizational research into gossip is also part of institutional social and ethical responsibility, particularly given the recent string of high profile business scandals, financial crises, and healthcare organizational failures (e.g., see Brenkert, 2010; The Mid Staffordshire NHS Foundation Trust Inquiry, 2010). These issues are addressed more fully in Chapters 6 and 7, which consider, amongst other things, power, politics, and the management of gossip as an indicator and forewarning of organizational failure.

When researching gossip as communicative organizing as it occurs in institutional settings, researchers need to consider how their actions produce consequences in different social spaces, academic or otherwise. Brummans (2006, p. 211) considers it important that researchers ask themselves:

> How am I (or are we), as a researching agent, conceptualizing, attributing, and appropriating agency, based on a set of values inhabited by

operating in this particular social space? Who am I (or we) to do so in the first place? What consequences to my (or our) actions yield? That is, do these consequences better the academic and nonacademic spaces in which I (or we) operate?

There are three significant reasons why scholars of gossip should attend to the ethical questions, principles and focus upon agency advocated by both Brummans, and a virtue ethics approach. First, virtue ethics focuses on social processes and shared values that enable meaningful interaction between agents. Second, a focus on agency and virtue ethics locates the scholarship of gossip in larger fields which push communication scholars to reflect upon their own academic and disciplinary practice/s. Third, as Cooren et al. (2006) argue, the way in which Brummans centralizes ethics 'illuminates not only the *corporate scandals* where issues of responsibility are raised, but also the interplay between *schools of thought and the politico-epistemic game* so typical of academic life' (p. 10, emphasis added). Corporate scandals abound and are unlikely to go away. They provide a rich seam of data for inter-disciplinary gossip-related research. An ethically informed CCO approach shows much promise here for future research. However, developing a theoretically and ethically sound research proposal will not necessarily guarantee access to the closed and secret spaces where gossip circulates. There are further methodological and ethical issues which need to be considered.

FURTHER METHODOLOGICAL AND ETHICAL CONSIDERATIONS

Developing a methodologically sound research ethics proposal is not necessarily easy and careful attention needs to be given to the rationale for, and limitations of, particular methods. Interviews, for example, are not the most effective, way of collecting gossip-related data. There may be problems associated with selective recall of information and confidentiality which can inhibit what, or how much, material is disclosed. Diaries are another way of collecting gossip-related data, but the privacy of absent third parties (the targets/subjects of gossip) must be assured. This can be achieved by reminding diarists not to disclose the names or inappropriate details about absent third parties. As discussed in Waddington (2012) compliance with relevant legal requirements of disclosure and data protection also needs to be taken into account with diary data. Researchers and participants also need to be aware of the law of defamation, which protects both individuals and companies, and is about reputation and the protection of reputation. Libel is concerned with the written word, and slander with the spoken word. This is of particular importance in gossip-related research, even more so perhaps in case studies and theoretical analyses of corporate scandals. In England and Wales the *Draft*

Defamation Bill (2011) is currently under consultation to introduce new measures to enable people to protect their reputation. This also applies to the protection of scholars' and researchers' *own* academic reputations and it is crucial that the threat of libel proceedings is not used to stifle robust scientific debate and academic freedom.

There is an argument to be made for studying gossip as naturally occuring talk in organizational spaces and settings. In other words, researching gossip as it happens in real time. Case study research is particularly suited to research questions which require detailed understanding of organizational processes and dynamics in context (Clegg, 2011). Case studies are defined in terms of theoretical orientation. Without a theorizing framework case studies may yield fascinating details and stories which are lacking in wider significance. Methodologically there is growing recognition of the contribution of social and business anthropology and ethnographic methods in organization studies (Connolly, 2010; Michelson & Mouly, 2002; Silverman, 2006). Case study research and organizational ethnography are useful approaches for future research into gossip and organizations. They are particularly useful with questions which explore the meanings of particular processes, practices, or concepts (Fine, Morrill, & Surianarain, 2011). Nevertheless a number of practical and procedural ethical dilemmas remain, as illustrated in the following exemplar of an ethnographic study of university corridors.

Gossip in University Corridors

Anyone who has worked in, studied in or researched universities knows that their corridors are spaces where gossip can be found. It is the same in any large municipal, public sector, or commercial organization. Corridors form part of what Gabriel (1995; 2000) refers to as the *unmanaged organization*—spaces where stories, gossip, jokes, cartoons, and graffiti can be found. Hurdley (2010a; 2010b) conducted workplace ethnography of the corridors of a university building, using a variety of methods including interviews, field notes, audio recording, and photographs. Her focus of attention was the 'material, spatialised, contingent practices that slide away unseen and unheard beneath the buzzing repetition of metaphor, icon and cliché' (Hurdley, 2010a, p. 46). This study is used as an exemplar here because the ethical issues encountered in researching corridor encounters and interactions are similar to those facing researchers of gossip. Namely, the difficulties involved in transgressing public/private boundaries and entering dangerous territory as a researcher. As Hurdley (2010b, p. 518) comments:

> The very character of corridor interactions made the corridors themselves ethically problematic as a research topic, in terms of both

observation and publication. They are both more private than the meeting room and more public. While walking the corridors as a member of the public or of the institution, I might repeat all I saw and heard; yet my sight and hearing became dangerous senses once I assumed the role of researcher.

With regard to the latter point, procedural ethical constraints resulted in the removal of gossip, rumour, backbiting, intimacy, and scheming from the subsequent writing up of the ethnography. Hurdley argues that researchers must constantly, and actively, reflect upon the confines of bureaucratic, procedural ethics, in order to develop depth and richness of insight. Ethical constraints and questions will not go away, and they do not necessarily lend themselves to easy answers. I therefore conclude the chapter by addressing some future directions for research ethics and gossip.

RESEARCH ETHICS AND GOSSIP: THE WAY FORWARD

Organizational researchers' practice is guided and regulated by professional bodies such as the *Academy of Management, British Psychological Society,* or *Social Research Association.* Universities and funding bodies such as the *European Commission* or *Australian Research Council* also have ethical standards and research governance procedures. Ethical codes of practice and standards universally specify: (i) avoidance or minimizing harm or risk of harm; (ii) the need for research participants to give informed consent; (iii) the privacy of research participants; (iv) confidentiality and anonymity of data where appropriate; and (v) minimizing the possibility of deception at all stages of the research process (Bell & Wray-Bliss, 2011). Research ethics is premised upon wider principles of respect, responsibility, competence and integrity. Yet research ethics is often practiced, and experienced, as a frustrating, form-filling, funding nightmare.

For those who have the courage and determination to research gossip, ethical issues relating to access, participation, privacy, secrecy, and confidentiality all need careful attention and scrutiny. There are particular issues relating to data collected about third parties (individuals and/or organizations) who may be unaware that they are the subject of gossip, and unaware that they are 'absent participants' in gossip-related research. Researchers will need to convince funders, ethics committees and other such monitoring and review bodies that what they are proposing is rigorous, theoretically and practically relevant and will not cause harm. The following extract from a reviewer's comments on a research proposal I submitted to a large funding body illustrates some of these issues quite aptly:

> This is an important and under-researched area. I do however have some reservations about the ethical aspects of the work. The study of gossip in organizations is surely an ethical can of worms which cannot be wrapped up in two short paragraphs that mainly focus on the research governance procedures of the applicant's institution. I'd like to see at least two pages of A4 which *talk about ethics from the perspective of a reflexive researcher*, with examples of the sorts of problems that have come up in previous work on public sector gossip, and how the team has gone about addressing these. (Extract from reviewer's comments on a gossip-related research funding proposal, emphasis added, reproduced with permission)

The idiom 'to open a can of worms' means a complex, troublesome situation which arises when a decision or action produces considerable subsequent problems. The 'can of worms' review comment above reflects the complex relationship between the procedural ethics of institutional and professional research codes and guidelines, and the microethics of real world research practice.

There is a view that gossip may be an unresearchable topic because of the ethical difficulties involved (Noon, 2001). These difficulties include covert 'eavesdropping' of conversations in public places, informed consent and right to withdraw, particularly for the absent third parties who are targets/subjects of gossip. On the other hand, ethnographers such as Marzano (2007) argue that covert non-consensual research is justified in the study of gossip. How then are researchers to practice ethically in *this* paradox? There are I would suggest at least three ways forward.

The first is to keep an open mind and not be confined by procedural ethics. There are other ways of thinking about collecting data such as 'unpeopled ethnography' (Hurdley, 2010b, p. 517), which foregrounds public places and spaces, rather than individual behaviour. The focus here is on *visual* material and situated *processes*, rather than face-to-face interactions. Pictorial representation and organizational photography are promising, but as yet under utilized methods in organizational gossip research (e.g., see Buchanan, 2001; Stiles, 2004). The second is a shift in emphasis away from a controlling orientation of ethics as formalized compliance to bureaucratic rules, toward one that is more enabling and cognizant of power dynamics, beliefs, and values. This way of thinking emphasizes the ethical *relationship* between the researcher, their topic, and those with whom they research. It invokes a virtue ethics approach because '[i]t entails a focus on how organizational researchers choose to conduct themselves, casting ethics as a matter of beliefs, thoughts, and values as well as actions' (Bell & Wray-Bliss, 2011, p. 89). The third way forward is to work *reflexively* and attend to what Guillemin & Gillam (2004, p. 276) describe as the '"ethically important moments" in research practice, in all their peculiarities.' In the final part of the chapter I talk about ethics from my perspective as a reflexive researcher and what it means to work with gossip as everyday ethics in practice.

REFLEXIVITY AND ETHICAL RESEARCH PRACTICE

Reflexivity contributes to ethical research practice as a process through which researchers can scrutinize themselves and their practices and acknowledge the dilemmas that permeate the research process. However, like gossip, reflexivity is a contested and slippery concept with a history rooted in divergent disciplinary fields, and it is difficult to capture a single definition or focus. The term is used variously to acknowledge the role, influence, subjectivity, and visibility of the researcher. But there is the risk that the role and presence of the researcher overshadows that of the 'researched.' There are also negative connotations of self-indulgent subjectivity, narcissism, and ego-ethnography (Hurdley, 2010b; Waddington, 2010). As a methodological construct, reflexivity involves examination of the broader social and political context of knowledge production and research conversations (Alvesson & Ashcraft, 2011; Cunliffe, 2003). But research conversations can occur anywhere, as demonstrated in the following reflection.

REFLECTION 4: 'I'VE JUST GIVEN YOU HALF AN HOUR OF DATA'

This comment was made following a gossipy conversation that took place on a train journey to a conference. Although it was said light-heartedly, there was also a sense of underlying indignation. I was travelling to the conference with Sam [*pseudonym*], an ex-colleague and friend. We were looking forward to catching up on the journey, having a gossip, as we hadn't seen each other for some time. When we got on the train, Sam said 'Oh look, there's professor A. N. Other over there, let's go and sit with them.' I didn't know this professor, but it quickly became evident that they and Sam also had some catching up to do. I took a book out of my bag and started to read, but was aware of the conversation going on around me. The talk moved on quickly from their respective conference papers to the relationships, research grants, publications, and promotions of people who were unknown to me. This was serious gossip.

I was in a dilemma. I felt simultaneously like an outsider, an intruder, an eavesdropper, and a voyeur. I sat quietly, trying to read my book, inwardly squirming. Eventually Sam turned to me and said 'go on, tell us about your paper,' and nodded towards their professorial colleague. 'Kathryn's interested in gossip at work you know.' 'No, I didn't know' said professor Other, rather acidly. There was a tangible silence, followed by, 'so I've just given you half an hour of data . . .' And another pause, '. . . for free.'

The 'incident' in Reflection 4 is a composite of a number of different conference experiences and ethically important moments, illustrating how data and gossip are commodities to be traded. However, I was not intentionally collecting data in those moments. It was one of the 'gossipers' who referred to their gossip as 'data.' Reflecting upon my own position I was an outsider to conversations and networks, with no 'in group' gossip to trade. But I had acquired a newfound sense of power. I had become potentially dangerous, and the indignation I sensed related to me being privy to 'inside knowledge.' There was also an assumption that I would, or could, use the conversation as data. Arguably, I have by presenting it in here, albeit in an altered form. However, the reflexive point is that because gossip is everywhere, it can be *mindfully* attended to and reflected upon. This is what I have referred to elsewhere as 'reflexive gossip' (Waddington, 2010, p. 313).

Mindfulness is a flexible state of mind involving active engagement in the present, sensitivity to new things and noticing context (Langer, 2000, cited in Weick & Putnam, 2006). Researchers and practitioners alike can mindfully attend to experiences and incidents of gossip, and critically reflect upon ethical questions such as 'Is this good gossip, bad gossip, or toxic gossip?' Context is a crucial concept here for researchers and practitioners alike. Whereas it is the individual who gossips, for virtuous or vicious motives, the organizational context and environment provide the triggers and opportunities. Mindful attention to gossip allows further exploration of communicative *contexts* and prompts further reflection upon the ethical *consequences* of future actions (or inactions).

CONCLUSION

This chapter began by asking whether gossip can be justified in an ethical and moral sense. The simple and short answer is yes, provided the potential for harm is not overlooked. Gossip is part of how we experience and come to know about the world, and as evaluative talk, gossip is the embodiment of everyday ethics in practice. Quite simply I am arguing that *the decision to participate, or not, in gossip is always an ethical one.* Gossip, people who gossip, and the consequences of gossip can all be judged as good, bad, and toxic. I have argued in this chapter that despite its miserable reputation and potential to harm, gossip can also be valuable informal talk. Closer and more mindful attention to gossip can reveal the 'messy moral heart of the organization, where its ethics are displayed in practice rather than in manuals and codes' (Clegg & van Iterson, 2009, p. 287).

The chapter also addressed the ethical issues surrounding the research task of collecting gossip-related data. Procedural, pedantic, and theoretical ethics can conspire to make this a difficult, but not impossible task. Ethical constraints can be overcome by thinking beyond the content and act of gossip to include visual, material and non-verbal representations of evaluative talk. This is a fruitful area for further exploration. I would also recommend that rather than being constrained by formalized compliance to bureaucratic rules, practitioners and researchers alike need to consider what it means to 'be ethical.' Being ethical is 'primarily a matter of being a person of good character, with virtues, emotions, values, and practical intelligence to match' (Hartman, 2008, p. 325). This chapter therefore has established ethics as a core conceptual component of the theorizing framework developed in the book. The next chapter addresses the second conceptual component of emotion.

4   Gossip and Emotion

The degree of one's emotions varies inversely with one's knowledge of the facts.

—Bertrand Russell (1872–1970)

This chapter is an examination and analysis of the role of gossip in the highly topical area of emotion at work. It draws upon a more substantial amount of empirical material than in previous chapters to illustrate how gossip is a means of expressing and managing emotion. The relationship between gossip and emotion appears to be particularly pertinent when 'knowledge of the facts' is uncertain, for example during periods of organizational change. The chapter also engages with a broader level of analysis and interpretation to ask whether gossip circulating between individuals and groups represents a form of 'spillage' of toxic organizational emotion. I argue that there is scope for further exploration of the relationship between 'gut feelings,' gossip, and intuitive knowledge which lies on the threshold of conscious perception. The overarching aim of this chapter is to illustrate how gossip as a means of expression and management of emotion is embedded in practice in nursing and healthcare organizations.

The chapter is organized as three overlapping sections. First, some broad methodological and empirical foundations are set out to foreground the primary research upon which much of this book is based. The research design adopted a mixed-methods approach and pertinent epistemological arguments relating to mixed-methods research are outlined briefly in order to: (i) give a methodological context to the empirical material presented here, and in subsequent chapters; and (ii) identify issues that researchers adopting mixed-methods approaches need to consider from the outset. Interview and diary excerpts provide key themes and primary interpretations which are then discussed in the context of contemporary theoretical perspectives and debates surrounding emotion in organizations. Finally, a reflexive and critical exploration then goes beyond what the empirical material presented in first part of the chapter was able to say. The reader is encouraged to think, and think again, about gossip and emotion.

MIXED-METHODS RESEARCH

It is all too easy to become entangled in the philosophical debates which can variously guide, plague, haunt, and stifle social and organizational inquiry.

In mixed-methods research the debate clusters around two main arguments. One argument centres on the value of retaining distinctions between qualitative, quantitative, and mixed-methods paradigms, acknowledging the value of paradigm diversity (e.g., Buchanan & Bryman, 2007; Cresswell & Plano Clark, 2011). Advocates of paradigmatic diversity argue that mixed-methods research provides a meeting point for numerous disciplines in the social and organizational sciences and promotes methodological innovation. The counter-argument advocates removing the notion of distinct paradigms altogether, adopting an approach where all methods play a role and have a key place in the research cycle 'from the generation of ideas to the rigorous testing of theories for amelioration' (e.g., Gorard, 2005, p. 162; Symonds & Gorard, 2010). Bryman (2011) comments that mixed-methods research occupies an ambiguous position in the research process because it is simultaneously both an old and a new approach. It is old because it has existed in different forms for many years. It is new because of recent and growing interest in mixed-methods research.

In Chapter 1 the metaphor of gossamer walls was introduced to think about the concept of reflexivity as a number of different relationships which occur through constantly shifting and permeable boundaries. This metaphor also invokes imagery of intellectual, political, theoretical, and epistemological 'ghosts' which appear 'sparsely, but powerfully, in social science work' (Doucet, 2008, p. 74). To avoid being haunted by the ghosts of paradigms past, which have previously negated or neglected organizational gossip, the rationale for combining methods in gossip-related research is essentially a pragmatic one. The term pragmatic is used here in a philosophical sense associated with mixed-methods research. Drawing upon ideas articulated by John Dewey, William James, and Charles Sanders Peirce, it represents an approach which is 'pluralistic and oriented towards "what works" and practice' (Cresswell & Plano Clark, 2011, p. 41). Gossip, like the contemporary organizational environments it inhabits, is volatile, uncertain, complex, and ambiguous. As a concept and an organizational phenomenon gossip is elusive, ephemeral, and highly resistant to paradigmatic summing up. Combining qualitative and quantitative approaches therefore is one way of addressing the method problems arising from such complexities.

Combining Qualitative and Quantitative Approaches

Johnson, Onwuegbuzie, and Turner (2007, p. 123) offer the following definition:

> Mixed-methods research is the type of research in which a researcher or team of researchers combines elements of qualitative and quantitative research approaches (e.g., use of qualitative and quantitative viewpoints, data collection, analysis, inference techniques) for the broad purposes of breadth and depth of understanding and corroboration.

This definition encompasses perspectives that include researchers working alone, for example doctoral students, as well as those working in inter-disciplinary teams. A contingency theory of research methodology, which recognizes the strengths and limitations of qualitative, quantitative, and mixed approaches, is a fundamental feature of this definition. All three approaches are considered to be important and relevant depending, of course, upon the research question/s, context and circumstances. Mixed-methods designs can therefore be tailored in relation to unique, ambiguous and emergent research situations. Although researchers may have a primary disciplinary 'home,' or comfort zone, it also 'makes sense for the researcher to visit other homes when his or her research can benefit from such a visit' (Johnson et al., 2007, p. 123). The benefit of visiting other disciplinary homes is the generation of greater insights than might be achieved by staying at home and adopting a unitary approach.

Critical realism has been advanced as an approach that can make a contribution to mixed-methods research (Maxwell & Mittapalli, 2010). This is a philosophical perspective which supports and validates key aspects of qualitative and quantitative approaches, seen as a 'third way' approach between naïve positivism and social constructionism (Creswell & Plano Clark, 2011; Denzin & Lincoln, 2005; Reed, 2011). 'Critical' in this context refers to a realism that rejects methodological individualism and universal claims to 'truth.' This approach to realism highlights the importance of diversity as a real phenomenon, rather than 'noise' which gets in the way of generalizability. Clearly there is no single paradigm or approach which can meaningfully justify and guide mixed-methods social and organizational inquiry (Greene, 2008), and paradigmatic pluralism is a defining feature.

Combining methods goes beyond the widely used, but not unproblematic concept of triangulation, to that of crystallization in order to reach a 'deepened, complex, and thoroughly partial understanding of the topic' (Richardson & St. Pierre, 2005, p. 963). Similarly, Denzin and Lincoln (2005) adopt the view that the model for mixed-genre research also has more than three sides, and should be seen metaphorically as a crystalline form. The imagery in the metaphor of crystallization is one of prisms which refract multiple externalities, creating within themselves different colours and patterns. The imagery is also one of flexibility rather than fixedness. Like the metaphor of gossamer walls, this imagery also chimes well with the elusive and ephemeral nature of gossip as a social and organizational phenomenon. Flexibility of thought and openness to imaginative ideas and theorizing are needed when approaching gossip-related data gathering, analysis, and interpretation.

What follows now are some illustrative examples of empirical material drawn from research into gossip and healthcare organizations (see Appendix A). Repertory grid and critical incident techniques are introduced here as methods of collecting gossip-related data. More detailed methodological consideration is given to these techniques in Chapter 5. The research was carried out in three phases, beginning with a preliminary investigation of individual and organizational factors, advancing to a more in-depth exploration of gossip and emotion as the study progressed. The themes and patterns illustrated here are based on an immersion/crystallization organizing style of analysis. This involves taking iterative and recursive 'horizontal' and 'vertical passes' through the data, looking for patterns, delving in and distancing (Borkan, 1999).

ENTERING THE FIELD

The first phase of the research used a Twenty Statements Test (TST) (Rees & Nicholson, 2004), and repertory grids (Kelly, 1955) in order to elicit the contexts and constructs of gossip. Ervin-Tripp's (1964) sociolinguistic framework, which has been used in previous empirical and theoretical analyses of gossip (Eder & Enke, 1991; Jones, D. 1980), provided an initial analytic template. There were sixty six participants in this study, working across a range of organizational roles and responsibilities ranging from newly qualified nurses to senior managers working at directorate level. First level data analysis involved examining communicative episodes of gossip with regard to (i) function, (ii) features, (iii) topic, (iv) setting, and (v) participants. Further categories were later elicited relating to emotion, interpersonal relationships, and organizational factors (see Appendix A, Figure A. 2).

The TST generated exploratory data by requiring respondents to write down their responses to the statement 'I gossip when . . .', which yielded over 400 contextual statements surrounding episodes of gossip. A third of these statements related to underlying emotions and emotional states, for example *'when I feel angry'* or *'I feel relaxed.'* Gossip also emerged as way of dealing with stress in statements such as *'I gossip when I'm stressed and I need to let off steam'* and *'as a way of coping with stressful circumstances.'* Other statements expressed concern for or about others, for example *'to support others'* or to *'help others relax and feel at ease.'*

Constructs of gossip were elicited using repertory grid technique, which has its origins in Kelly's (1955) personal construct psychology, based on the belief that individuals strive to make sense of their world through their constructs. The technique is not described in full here, but further methodological detail is given in Chapter 5 in relation to gossip and the construction of identity. In essence, repertory grids have three stages:

1. Identification of situations/entities in the area of inquiry, in this instance people who gossip, described as *elements;*
2. Comparing the elements to elicit *constructs,* expressed as contrasting dimensions of difference, for example trustworthy-untrustworthy;
3. Construction of a matrix or *grid* of elements and constructs.

Participants were asked to identify six people with whom they gossiped, or whom they would describe as someone who gossips, in order to elicit constructs. Over 500 constructs were elicited, some of which related specifically to the expression and management of anxiety. For instance:

> Are less anxious, or less likely to express their anxieties to me; vs. uses me as a sounding board for anxieties expressed in gossip.

A pattern of emotion enacted and embedded in the contexts and constructs of gossip was beginning to emerge. This took the research agenda in a different direction, and led to a re-examination and questioning of intellectual suppositions and disciplinary assumptions.

REFLECTION 5: EXPLORING UNCHARTED TERRITORY

A reminder. This was part-time doctoral research in psychology, undertaken at a time when gossip was a relatively unexplored field of organizational practice. The absence of substantive published literature which empirically examined gossip as its central topic meant that this felt, to me, like uncharted territory. The initial research aim was to examine the function of gossip at work and investigate the determinants and outcomes for the individual and the organization. So far, so safe. The study had begun from a fairly traditional psychological standpoint of individual differences and my initial research question included the terms 'antecedents' and 'consequences'. Following this exploratory phase, I had originally planned to construct a psychometric survey instrument based upon the Tendency to Gossip Questionnaire (TGQ) developed by Nevo and colleagues (1994).

At the time, I had the feeling, quite literally, of 'safety in numbers.' However, aside from my own feelings and concerns, emotion was not initially an explicit element of the research agenda. I was therefore, naïvely perhaps, surprised by the extent to which I found so much emotion in participants' responses in the first phase of the research. I began to question and critically reflect upon my intellectual assumptions and—pursuing Bergmann's metaphor of 'border-runners' introduced in Chapter 1—I followed emotion as a theme across the borders, venturing deeper into inter-disciplinary territory.

DELVING DEEPER

The ways in which emotions were enacted and embedded in gossip were explored further in qualitative interviews with ten Clinical Nurse Specialists (CNSs) (for detail see Waddington, 2005b). CNSs provide clincal expertise in particular areas of practice such as pain management, and work in a system-wide context, within and between healthcare organizations. Participants were asked to recount critical incidents of gossip, with the aim of gaining a deeper understanding of the contextual, cognitive and in particular, emotional elements (Chell, 2004). The incident summarized below illustrates how strong feelings of resentment were a catalyst for gossip:

> Let me give you an example, we had a most unfortunate member of junior medical staff who made the error of commenting upon a nurse who had A-Levels [*UK post-16 academic qualifications*] and who had given up medical training to become a nurse. 'What a waste' was the comment, in other words to waste your A-Levels on nursing, and this was taken up by the nurses, yeah, ad nauseam really and passed on through and through and through. And it was this very strong feeling of resentment about this statement that made people pass it on, it literally was passed on by everyone on the unit, and there was that feeling, that resentful feeling, maybe that occurs quite frequently. (CNS 4)

Gossip was also viewed as a cathartic process, enabling the release of emotion and as a means of gaining support and reassurance. A typical example was:

> I think a lot the gossip that goes on in the office is, um, expressing frustration. You know like 'God can you believe what that ward has done now,' and 'you'll never guess what that GP [*General Practitioner*] has done.' So it's frustration and despair you know 'aargh what have they done now.'
>
> KW: And does it help to have let off this frustration?
>
> Yeah . . . [*why?*]. Well, there are a lot of the team who have worked in a similar situation before who'll say, 'oh God yeah I worked with them before, they're really stupid, I'll tell you what I did' and then it's 'dedadedadeda . . .' So it can be a way of finding another strategy to deal with the situation, and which if you had never gone and said 'aargh' it might never have occurred to you. (CNS 2)

Gossip can also be cruel and hurtful:

> Well, it's a shared understanding that the weakest person in the chain is probably 'her,'[*said with emphasis*] because 'she has lots of problems,' and again that's probably through gossip that we know that. So, it could be then that that person becomes a kind of scapegoat, via the gossip channels. And I think also that gossip feeds gossip, so somebody's already down there in the kind of misfortune, they've fallen off the tracks, and the gossip gets juicier and juicier. It's where the pack instinct comes in. So I think gossip, yeah, can be fairly cruel. (CNS 7)

To summarize thus far, the patterns of emotion enacted and embedded in the contexts and constructs of gossip were also emerging as a strategy to manage negative emotions about colleagues. For *individuals* this was means of gaining support, reassurance and a 'sympathetic ear' from others. On the other hand, strong emotions which were *shared by a group* could also act as a catalyst or trigger for gossip about others.

RETURNING TO THE SURFACE

In the final phase of the research structured diary records of incidents of gossip, recorded over a two-week period were used with a sample of twenty participants (for details see Waddington, 2005c; 2012). The record sheets included (amongst other things) the emotions associated with each incident of gossip (see Appendix A, Table A.1), as well as a more detailed description of one critical incident. These critical incidents were followed up during a telephone interview carried out after participants had completed their diary records.

Overall, gossiping was perceived and quantitatively rated as being a more pleasant than unpleasant activity. Contrarily however, qualitative analysis of the emotions associated with incidents of gossip suggested more a negative dimension, expressed in terms such as '*annoyed*,' '*hurt*,' '*angry*,' '*embarrassed*,' '*guilty*,' or '*uncomfortable*.' A theme to emerge from the diary records was that of 'mixed emotions,' illustrated in the following diary extracts:

> I felt frustrated, but it was also good to talk to someone about it, you know then the other person feels the same way;

> Annoyed, here we go again, devalued, it doesn't surprise me, some resignation, apathy, yet also a feeling of solidarity and mutual support;

> Fine about the gossip, not fine about some of the people being gossiped about.

Follow-up telephone interviews explored the emotions and organizational relationships associated with the critical incidents of gossip in more depth. The intention with these interviews was to position the feeling, thinking, and actions represented in particular episodes of communication within an organizational context. This is illustrated in the following interview extract with a senior operational manager.

> *KW:* What were the key factors which contributed to the occurrence of this particular incident?

> Number one, a breakdown in the professional relationship between the person being gossiped about and the person I was gossiping with who

was their immediate line manager. Number two, a feeling of being left behind by organizational change.

K W: In your diary records you also wrote about people feeling left behind by organizational change, can you say more about this?

Change creates instability and feelings of insecurity and lack of self-confidence and belief in the organization. People build on the lack of understanding by creating their own mythical bubble. It makes as much sense as the organization, but at least for the moment they have real control.

K W: So people gossip to create their own realities and security?

Yes [*pause*] to get some degree of control over their life at work . . . I mean that in a large organization because of lack of knowledge of what is occurring elsewhere people create the facts for themselves with an inevitable spin. My experience is that despite IT [*information technology*], or perhaps because of it, we have lost the ability to communicate on an understandable level. Things seem to be more rather than less complicated with more opportunity for misunderstanding.

The crucial issue—as another manager in a different organization commented—is quite simply, '*people speculate and gossip when they do not know.*' Not knowing makes people feel anxious, apprehensive, or excluded and, as the quote from Bertrand Russell which introduced this chapter suggests, the less we know, the more intensely we feel.

THEMES AND INSIGHTS

The empirical material selected for this chapter should not be seen as definitive data illustrating the relationship between gossip and emotion. It was gathered and is positioned in a professional/organizational context of nursing and healthcare in the UK, and a disciplinary home of psychology. The constructs and consequences of gossip to emerge are bound to reflect this. One interpretation is that the material is illustrative of professional resentments that have become embedded in the discourse and culture of nursing. Taking this view, gossip does little more than reinforce what can become, quite literally, a vicious circle. Another interpretation is that the emotions expressed were simply a reflection of the stressful nature of healthcare practice. Healthcare organizations in particular have long been seen as 'emotional zones' (Bolton, 2005, p. 56); misunderstandings, professional rivalries, competing priorities, and strong feelings are to be expected here.

On the other hand, as Alvesson and Sköldberg (2009, p. 304) argue, '[e]mpirical material should be seen as an argument in efforts to make a *case for a particular way of understanding social reality, in the context of a never ending debate'* (original emphasis). My argument here is that (re) examination of the patterns and themes of emotion found in gossip can yield fresh insights into existing multi-level understandings and dimensions of emotion in organizations. Furthermore, I also contend that this (re)examination also draws attention to previously neglected dimensions such as intuition.

UNDERSTANDING ORGANIZATIONAL GOSSIP AND EMOTION

This section begins with an indicative rather than definitive review of debates and issues in the field of organizational emotional. As Fineman, (2005, p. 10) points out, gossip is but one of many forms of organizational emotion which are 'framed, rehearsed and politicised in organising processes.'

Conceptually, emotion can be understood from a range of disciplinary perspectives including sociology, neuroscience, psychology anthropology, and more recently economics (Becker et al., 2011; Lewis, Haviland-Jones, & Barrett, 2008; von Scheve & von Leude, 2005). The term 'affect' is an all-encompassing expression for any emotionalized activity, with important differences to be drawn between three associated constructs of feeling, emotion, and mood. *Feelings* are subjective, self-referential, and privately experienced emotional states and in the psychodynamic literature relating to organizations, feelings of anxiety and fear dominate. *Mood* on the other hand is a more general term that lacks the object directedness of emotion, and its cause or trigger may be obscure; moods are feelings that linger in the background. *Emotions* are the external displays of feelings, usually directed towards something or someone in the external world or towards the self, and which are short term and transient (Briner & Kiefer, 2005; Elfenbein, 2007; Grandey, 2008). Debate continues regarding precisely what an emotion is; however, there is consensus that it involves a wide-ranging number of elements including cognitive and physiological components, motivational, and communicative aspects and wider social factors.

The growth of interest and research into emotion and organizations over the last thirty years or so has been attributed to the rising service sector and work that is increasingly customer facing. Of particular note is the relationship between commercial value and competitive advantage (Bolton, 2005; Fineman, 2000; 2003; 2005; Noon & Blyton, 2007). Such relationships are constructed in terms of customer care, consumers, clients, compliments, and complaints; terms that have now become a yardstick of 'service user' and employee satisfaction. Changes in technological and economic aspects of society have also impacted on the understanding of professional and client relationships (Weir & Waddington, 2008). The term 'client' is used here to refer to any person who interacts with an employee, such as patients, customers, passengers, and the like. Organizational emotion thus encompasses 'service-with-a-smile' industries (e.g., the hotel business and fast food outlets), and work where employees are in direct, and indirect, interpersonal contact with the public (e.g., lawyers, nurses, police officers, and call centre workers). Emotion is a valuable resource, available for management and development, something to be harnessed in pursuit of customer satisfaction (Bolton, 2005). However the pursuit of customer satisfaction is often characterized by strong emotion, leading Stein (2007) to adopt the imagery and metaphor of 'toxicity' in his examination of the employee-customer interface and emotion.

Emotion at work has grown to become one of the most popular, and popularized, areas of organizational scholarship (see Ashkanasy & Cooper, 2008; Elfenbein, 2007; Sieben & Wettergren, 2010). Prior to this popularization, emotional aspects of organizations were ignored, dismissed, or written out—a situation not dissimilar to gossip and organizations at the moment. There appears to have been a view that emotion at work and organizational goals and management were both contradictory and mutually exclusive issues. Fineman's (1993) *Emotion in Organizations* challenged this view, and brought emotion issues more explicitly onto organizational research agendas in a range of disciplines. Fineman draws upon the sociological perspective of Hochschild (1979; 1983) whose writings on the 'managed heart' have inspired much research into emotion at work. Indeed as Bolton (2005) observes little is written about emotion and organizations that does not take Hochschild's (1983) *The Managed Heart: Commercialization of Human Feeling* as a reference point. Hochschild's study of flight attendants showed that a substantial part of the job entailed dealing with passengers' emotions, and an associated need for employees to regulate their own emotions.

Briner and Kiefer (2005) note that at the time of Hochschild's early work the emotional experience of employees was described and understood in terms of job satisfaction and stress. More recently, empirical, and conceptual work has centred on a number of key themes, which include discrete and contested topics such as emotional intelligence, emotion work, emotional labour, and affective well-being (e.g., Briner & Kiefer, 2009; Conte, 2005; Côté & Hideg, 2011; Mayer, Roberts, & Barsade, 2008; Skakon, Nielsen, Borg, & Guzman, 2010). Emotional intelligence (EI) refers to the ability to perceive, to process, to understand, and to manage emotions in self and others (Mayer & Salovey, 1997). EI has burgeoned into a veritable emotion industry of publications and testing, educational, and organizational consultancy. However, the size of this industry is not matched by what is regarded as relevant research in the field. Critics argue that EI is an invalid concept because it is defined in too many ways (Locke 2005, cited in Mayer et al., 2008). This has cast a shadow over the concept, and concerns about is value and meaning as an over-idealized commodity packaged in sales gloss.

The concept of emotion work, like EI, also refers to management of emotion in self and others. Emotion work refers to the effort individuals put in to presenting and re-presenting their feelings in order to best 'fit' external expectations (Hochschild, 1983). Emotion work also relates to the effort that is expended in 'displaying' or presenting such feelings, based on Goffman's (1959) dramaturgical model of role performance. This happens, for example, when private, subjective emotions and opinions are suppressed so as not to hurt the feelings of others. There is debate over the extent to which emotion work and the associated term emotional labour can and should be used interchangeably, and this can be confusing as there are overlapping as well as differentiating features. It is beyond the remit of this chapter to address these issues in detail (but see Weir & Waddington, 2008; Zapf & Holz, 2006). In essence, emotional labour is commodified, paid emotion work, which involves having to present an appropriate—in other words managerially, professionally or organizationally prescribed—emotional appearance and response to others (Hochschild, 1983). However, what is less clear is an understanding of the interpersonal processes and means by which individuals and groups learn *how to*, and in practice *do*, emotional labour/emotion work.

The mass popularization of emotion has resulted in exaggerated claims about the importance of emotion and emotional intelligence in the workplace. It has also resulted in research which is driven by commercial need rather than practical or human value. Furthermore, the literature is dominated by Eurocentric and North American perspectives. Research findings and the issues they raise are therefore located in a predominantly Westernized context. Unsurprisingly then, there is dissent regarding the extent to which the concepts of organizational emotion and emotion work can be assumed to be universal phenomena (Chong, 2009; Mirchandani, 2003; Rowe, 2005). Yet emotion permeates all aspects of our lives and cultures. We are human beings who experience many emotions such as joy, anger, surprise, grief, despair, and pride. Psychoanalysis has always been immersed in the study and understanding of emotion, exploring the origin, meaning and grip that it has in, and on, our lives (Gabriel, 1999). Therefore as understandings about the role of emotion in organizations have grown, so too have the opportunities for psychoanalytic and psychodynamic understandings.

WORKING BELOW THE SURFACE

Working below the surface is a phrase used to characterize a distinctive psychoanalytically informed approach which:

> focuses primarily on the human side of enterprise; both what is known and consciously attended to and also what is *unknown,* unattended,

or unconscious in the individual and/or in the group. The working hypothesis that informs it is that bringing this undertow of experience and behaviour into view (to the surface) *can shed new light* on the challenges and dilemmas that an organization and its members are facing. (Armstrong & Huffington, 2004, p.3, emphasis added)

Paying attention to gossip is a way of bringing the emotional undertow of organizations into view. Emotion and gossip then become features of the 'organization-in-context' (Armstrong, 2004, p.11), rather than simply being features of the individual, their relationships and/or the group. This is important, as we need to move beyond commercially driven research evaluating the emotional 'savvy' of individuals to that which has practical value for improving organizational emotional experiences more generally. This then allows for a deeper understanding of emotion, based on underpinning psychoanalytic assumptions that:

- Behaviour is often influenced by conscious and unconscious mental processes, which also need to be taken into account in the study of organizing processes;
- Individuals create a subjective emotional reality of the organization, social interaction and the attribution of meaning link human experience and organizational reality;
- There is a dynamic interaction between organizational structures and individual and group behaviour and experience;
- Social defences emerge when individuals and groups unconsciously attempt to deal with anxiety and threats to self-esteem; such defences are often dysfunctional and detrimental to task performance.

The notion of working below the surface can also be associated with the metaphorical 'dark side' of interpersonal relationships and communication (Cupach & Spitzberg, 2011; Spitzberg & Cupach, 2007). A dark side perspective draws attention to that which is ambivalent, surprising, paradoxical, and difficult; to that which is unknown, unattended, or outside of our conscious awareness. Spitzberg & Cupach, (2007) suggest that the conceptual coherence of the dark side metaphor requires ongoing examination. For example, there is a risk that the metaphor runs the risk of appearing like everything and nothing However, as Stein (2007, p. 1223) comments, metaphors which have unconscious framings are also valuable ways of drawing attention to a 'deep reservoir' of human experience by using tangible images to symbolize intangible emotions and processes. Stein's metaphorical use of the term toxocity is linked to notions of poison, dirt, and Mary Douglas's (1966) claim that when boundaries are permeated or become confused, the fear of pollution or contagion is heightened. 'Dishing the dirt' is a term which means the spread of unpleasant or shocking personal information about someone through the medium of gossip

(Clegg & van Iterson, 2009; Wilkes, 2002). As discussed in the previous chapter, gossip can be variously differentiated as good, bad and toxic. The metaphor and imagery of toxicity are therefore also highly pertinent to new understandings of gossip and emotion.

In summary, emotion in organizations has been studied from a variety of disciplinary perspectives with some associated paradigm tensions. As Fineman (2005) points out, for many social scientists, to know emotion is to measure it and this can be problematic. The act of measurement can result in studies that may not fully capture the richness and authenticity of emotional experiences. In comparison, interpretivist approaches can provide fine-grained analyses and inductive insights that may *appear* meaningful, but lack a sense or feeling of day-to-day reality. As we have seen from empirical material presented thus far, the day-to-day realities and demands of working in and 'managing' the public and private worlds of emotion in organizations provide core environmental conditions for gossip to flourish. Yet the burgeoning literature surrounding emotion in organizations has paid scant attention to gossip, and it is time to think again about gossip and emotion.

THINKING AGAIN ABOUT GOSSIP AND EMOTION

Rather than using the empirical material presented earlier to support various views on 'how emotion is' or 'how gossip is,' the intention now is to use it think about new ideas and areas of inquiry. The material was gathered in healthcare organizations where gossip and emotion abound due to the nature of the work carried out there. Healthcare organizations are sites of intense emotion, both for the people who need their services and care, and the practitioners who provide services and care (Kahn, 2005). They hold rich seams and undercurrents of material for real world research because they are quite simply hotbeds of gossip and rumour (e.g., Bordia et al., 2004; 2006; Department of Health, 2005; Thomas & Rozell, 2007).

The emotion themes discerned in healthcare organizational gossip can be summarized thus: (i) emotion triggers gossip; (ii) gossip is a way of communicating and expressing emotion in general and anxiety in particular; (iii) gossip is associated with emotional dissonance; and (iv) gossiping results in emotional outcomes for individuals and groups that may be positive, negative, or mixed. The paradoxical pleasure associated with gossip represents an element of *schadenfreude* or malicious enjoyment of other people's misfortunes, and is indicative of the dark side of gossip. For example, participants said they felt better after gossiping, and terms such as '*cathartic*' and '*therapeutic*' were used fairly frequently. There is a risk however that the 'quick fix' which makes people feel better in the short term may not address underlying longer-term organizational issues and problems.

Looked at another way however, gossiping may also have a protective function for employees and organizations, preventing the build up of feelings that it is inappropriate to express or display in public. It has been suggested that the healthiest emotional labourers are those who are allowed to, or are taught to express their true feelings (Kruml & Geddes, 2000). Therefore, gossip also acts as a way of *doing* emotion work by reducing the emotional dissonance characterised by feeling one thing, and having to express something different. Much of the literature surrounding emotion work/emotional labour seems to focus primarily upon the expression or suppression of emotion in relation to the client or customer, although there are some studies that include colleagues and peers in their analyses (e.g., Tschan, Rochat, & Zapf, 2005; Zerbe, 2000). Gossiping about colleagues and co-workers privately, behind closed doors, is a way of 'keeping up appearances' in public and managing emotion in the workplace.

In summary, gossip plays a role in doing emotion work and dealing with the emotional dissonance of conflicting public, professional, and organizational expectations and emotional display rules. The psychodynamic processes and defensive practices which arise in the face of strong emotions in healthcare organizations are well understood, and are not rehearsed here (e.g., see Hinshelwood & Skogsdad, 2000; Menzies, 1989; Obholzer & Roberts 1994a). For example, Obholzer (2005) refers to '"emotional toxins" arising from the underlying psychic raw material that the staff is dealing with' (p. 298). Gossiping in this sense can be seen as a form of 'organizational detox.'

GOSSIP, SENSEMAKING, AND KNOWING

It is evident that emotional spillage of resentment, anger, and frustration precipitate gossip. However, as Mark (2005, citing Weick, 1995) argues, emotional spillage is a component part of an organization's sensemaking apparatus and a potentially important indicator of organizational health. Sensemaking is about developing ideas, putting things into frameworks, constructing meaning and mutual understanding, redressing surprise, and patterning (Weick, 1995a). This is encapsulated in CNS 2's comment '*so it* [gossip] *can be a way of finding another strategy to deal with the situation, and which if you had never gone and said 'aargh' it might never have occurred to you.*' In other words, emotions of frustration and irritation trigger gossip, an outcome of which is sensemaking and problem solving. The essence of sensemaking is language, talk and communication, and gossip also plays an important role here in the telling of anecdotes and stories.

Gossip provides the means through which stories of individual, managerial, or organizational triumph and failure circulate and re-circulate through talk in emotionalized backstage zones. Gossiping is a process through which tales of the unexpected, of individual and organizational misfortunes, and of incompetence are told. This is a micro level of analysis that seeks to demonstrate how an understanding of a seemingly trivial and transient organizational phenomenon can lead to deeper level understandings of macro level organizational processes and ways of knowing. Emotions are a means by which we make sense of, and relate to, our physical, social, and organizational worlds (Holland, 2007). Consequently, according to Game (1997, cited in Holland) emotion is a way of knowing the world. Therefore it can be argued that gossip as a means of expressing and communicating emotion has epistemological significance as a form of narrative and intuitive knowledge.

Gossiping and storytelling are social practices in organizations which can play a crucial role in developing organizational knowledge. For example, Sims (2004) argues that stories are the means by which knowledge is held, stored, and transferred from one person to another. Notably 'this transfer is an encouragingly critical process, because people are better able to hear stories critically than less narrative forms of communication' (p.165). Gossip is also a critical process because it is evaluative talk between at least two people that may be spoken, written, or visual. Gossip also contains elements of constructing meaning and shared understandings about people and work, exploring hunches and dealing with surprise and unexpected events. The practice of gossiping is also a way of developing ideas and getting informal feedback and opinion. This line of thinking can be extended to suggest that there is potential relationship between gossip, curiosity, and human inquiry. In other words, gossiping is a way of formulating real world working hypotheses which can be tested in everyday contexts (Michelson & Mouly, 2000; Spacks, 1985).

Ayim (1994) takes this a little further, using the term 'investigative gossip' to reference the role of gossip in *eliciting* information (rather than imparting or applying information). She goes on to argue that the enormous appeal, importance, and veracity of gossip are such that:

> we are obliged not just to condone gossip but to encourage it; for gossip is virtually ubiquitous, providing avenues of access to inquiry in terrains too steep, too marshy, too eroded, and far too dangerous for science to operate. (Ayim, 1994, p. 99)

Viewed this way, gossip can be seen an emergent organizational process and informal method of inquiry. As Prins (2006) observes, the psychodynamic perspective provides 'additional insight in the study of what *actually happens* in an emergent organizational process' (p.351, emphasis added). Gossip also potentially yields powerful insights into the 'dark side' of organizational processes and practices. It reveals an aspect of work that is collusive, dysfunctional, and detrimental to healthy and effective interpersonal and organizational relationships. A psychodynamic understanding of gossip provides a means of judging levels of organizational anxiety and emotion that accommodates both individual *and* organizational perspectives. This is significant, because when gossip is seen as a purely personal attribute there is a risk that it may simply be understood as an individual's negative or unprofessional behaviour. Although this may indeed be the case, as Mark (2005) points out, patterns of gossip may also be symptomatic of more general issues of emotional and organizational concern and should not be ignored.

The empirical themes and insights addressed here are not without their limitations. Cultural understandings and concepts of gossip and emotion were not specifically addressed, and these are significant areas for future research. My research focused upon a particular organizational context, and what is presented and discussed in this chapter may simply be a representation of the culture and practices of healthcare organizations and professions. The research sites and participants were chosen as information-rich sources of data because of the centrality of communication in their practices. There is therefore a 'sense,' or 'scent' (see below), of large, historically hierarchical, bureaucratic, and predominantly public sector organizations which permeates the empirical material. The following reflection illustrates this more fully. The rationale for its inclusion here is to try and show *how* sensemaking and immersion/crystallization was enacted in my reflexive research practice. These issues are also discussed more fully in Waddington (2010).

REFLECTION 6: SMELLS LIKE GOSSIP

I was enjoying the uninterrupted quiet time on a train travelling on my own to a conference, thinking about my presentation which was about using metaphor in the research process. I was trying to anticipate and plan for questions that might arise—such as what if someone asks me 'What is your metaphor for gossip?' As I was thinking that question (not thinking about the answer, that came later), an image came to mind of a stagnant pond with visible vapour coming off it. Working and thinking reflexively over a period of time, I have learned to trust images such as this which appear without conscious thought, and the valuable insights they can yield. But it hasn't always been easy to work with, or to explain to other people and I also feel a little bit apprehensive about including it in this chapter. So, I thought to myself on the train, gossip is like a bad, toxic smell, coming off something that is stagnant. Oh dear. But smells are also nice, like fresh coffee or flowers. And smells, nice or nasty, are pervasive. People often used the terms like 'filters through the organization' when talking about gossip. So metaphorically then gossip is like a smell?

And then I thought more deeply and quite literally about 'sense'-making and the other four senses. Hearing—'Have you heard . . . ?' is a frequent precursor to gossip, but you don't always have to hear gossip to know it's happening. Sight—you can see it in the huddles in corners or by the photocopier, in the raised eyebrows and little aside nods in meetings. Taste—this is the 'juicy,' 'tasty gossip,' but also the bad taste in the mouth which can linger after excessive, negative, or malicious gossip. Touch – people may be touched lightly or heavily by gossip either as an expression of care and concern, and also as that which causes harm. I also speculated about a 'sixth sense' of intuition—is this where gossip and 'aha' sensemaking moments connect? Is gossip a bridge between day-to-day experience and unconscious insights and intuition?

GOSSIP AND INTUITION

Thinking about gossip as in terms of a smell is, for me anyway, yet another interesting and intuitively appealing organizing metaphor. It accounts for the way gossip cuts across boundaries, and filters through organizations. How people can be exposed to it, contaminated by it, protected from it, and not least of all, how difficult it is to define a smell. Smells can also be uplifting and invigorating or can make you feel sick. Working with the metaphor of gossip as smell also enabled the concept of sensemaking to be applied and developed in an imaginative way. Thinking about gossip as a bridge to insights and intuition is also interesting and timely and there are areas where gossip and intuition share some noteworthy similarities.

The concept of intuition, historically consigned to the fringes of psychology, is, like gossip, emerging as a legitimate area of inquiry. Intuiting involves:

> a complex set of inter-related cognitive, *affective* and somatic processes, in which there is no apparent intrusion of deliberate, rational thought. Moreover, *the outcome of this process (an intuition) can be difficult to articulate.* The outcomes of intuition can be experienced as an holistic 'hunch' or 'gut feel', a sense of calling or overpowering certainty, and *an awareness of a knowledge that is on the threshold* of conscious perception. (Hodgkinson, Langan-Fox, & Sadler-Smith, 2008, p. 4, emphasis added)

There is an as yet understudied link between intuitive knowing, emotion, and gossip. The challenge for researchers, and practitioners, is to think beyond the negative emotions and stereotypes associated with gossip, and think again about what might lie beneath the surface. In other words gossip, which may be triggered by negative or distressing emotions such as anger, resentment or anxiety, is a 'surface manifestation' of underlying individual, group and organizational emotion. The *emotional* outcome of gossiping may be experienced as pleasant or positive, for example feeling supported, or as a strengthening of interpersonal relationships. However, for individuals and organizations what lies beneath the emotional triggers for gossip are intuitive perceptions and holistic information processing and sensemaking which are occurring beyond a conscious level of awareness. Recent theorizing of intuition which draws upon inter-disciplinary and multi-level models of social and organizational neuroscience, sensemaking ethics, and emotion offer promising avenues for future research (e.g., Becker et al., 2011; Dane & Pratt, 2007; Sinclair & Ashkanasy, 2005; Sonenshein, 2007).

It is evident that the inter-disciplinary scholarship of gossip is an emergent field of inquiry with potentially much to contribute to the field of emotion in organizations. There is also much to learn from emotion in organizations regarding challenges, opportunities, and ideas for future research and theory development.

ORGANIZATIONAL GOSSIP: AN EMERGENT FIELD OF INQUIRY

Gossip and emotion are, respectively, emergent and emerged fields of inquiry in work and organizational settings. The escalating literature and subsequent reviews of emotion in organizations and organizing over the last thirty years suggests that this is a fairly well-established field. It is also a field that has been heavily popularized, and areas such as emotional intelligence have grown prolifically, but as Elfenbein (2007) notes:

> Popularization has led to many sweeping—yet often poorly substantiated (e.g., Goleman, 1995)—claims about the power of emotion to be harnessed for the bottom line. The academic literature has been extensive, but often only a loosely connected body of work with disparate themes all included under the banner of emotion . . . At some extremes, arguments claim that nearly everything is emotion and that it now encompasses every phenomenon heretofore studied across management and organization. One question, then, is *how to articulate boundaries* because, for emotion to mean anything, it cannot mean everything. (p. 316, emphasis added)

In Chapter 2, organizational communication and knowledge were advanced as boundary conditions within which to better understand and theorize gossip. Without clearly articulated boundaries organizational gossip risks becoming a meaningless fad or fashion that may only briefly capture the imagination of organizational scholars. We need to ask therefore what can be learned from the more established field of emotion, and what current indicators of growth in the scholarship of gossip look like.

The first lesson is to guard against diluting the scholarship of gossip with the clichéd 'everything except the kitchen sink' approaches which have characterized some aspects of emotion in organizations. The second is to keep a look out for conceptual cowboys and free-riders seeking to profit from sales of spurious organizational tools and remedies. Scholarly writing and research needs to differentiate itself from 'airport organizational theory' and have a sound evidence base. But we also need to steer clear of research that produces one-dimensional accounts, dull pictures and dead descriptions that bear little resemblance to the realities of gossip. There are small but significant indicators of healthy growth evident in empirical work and case studies contributing to conceptual and methodological developments in the field (e.g., Beersma & van Kleef, 2011; Grosser et al., 2010; Hallett et al., 2009; Kniffin & Wilson, 2010; Michelson et al., 2010; Mills 2010; van Iterson & Clegg, 2008; van Iterson et al., 2011). This book will also, I hope, be an important landmark.

The wider challenge for current and future researchers is how to represent and 'preserve' the transient, equivocal, ephemeral, and shifting nature of gossip as we know it. Gossip must not be empirically or epistemologically cleansed of all of its negative attributes and assumptions and transformed into an acceptable organizational resource, discourse, or artefact. Gossip can be simultaneously healthy and harmful, trivial and toxic; it can make you happy and it can also hurt. Researchers should not uncouple or ignore the dark side of gossip. A particular methodological challenge therefore is that of how to accurately, and ethically, capture the nuances and dynamics of 'gossip-in-situ.' Inter-disciplinary approaches and methods from the field of emotion relating to employee happiness, which capture fleeting and fluctuating experiences at work across a range of levels may prove valuable here (see Ashkanasy, 2011; Bakker & Daniels, 2012; Fisher, 2010). These include diaries, the day reconstruction method, event and experience sampling research approaches, which study experiences as they happen or very close to the time that they happen.

CONCLUSION

It is evident that gossip is an important aspect of social and organizational practices of emotion at work. Gossip is also a potentially useful avenue of inquiry in organizational neuroscience, positive emotion, and happiness at work. There may be particular resonance in the so-called meso-level paradigm, where relationships that link phenomena across different levels of analysis are studied (Ashkanasy, 2011; Von Scheve & Von Leude, 2005). It has been suggested that multi-level approaches to organizational emotion incorporating a neurological basis for affect can help to extend existing theoretical perspectives and understandings (Ashkanasy, 2003). A pragmatic, multiparadigm approach is essential to navigate the terrain between and beyond reductionist 'neuroessentialism' and the popularized neuroscience of emotion (Becker et al., 2011, p. 951; Elfenbein, 2007).

The crucial point is that future scholars of organizational gossip develop and engage with research agendas which are unfettered by attachment to narrow specialist methods and/or defensive disciplinary perspectives. As Becker et al. (2011, p. 951) comment, '[b]rain science has much to contribute, but it also could learn much from other perspectives and levels of explanation.' Arguably there is potential here for collaborative inter-disciplinary research between neuroscientists, and organizational theorists who adopt a communicative contstitution of organization (CCO) perspective. The latter encapsulates notions of going from the small to the big, and 'scaling up from interactions to organization' (Cooren & Fairhurst, 2009, p. 141) and is addressed more fully in the next (and subsequent) chapter/s.

5 Gossip and Identity

Considering how much we are all given to discuss the characters of others, and discuss them often not in the strictest spirit of charity, it is singular how little we are inclined to think that others can speak ill-naturedly of us, and how angry and hurt we are when proof reaches us that they have done so.

—Anthony Trollope, *Barchester Towers*, 1857

Identity is dynamic, socially constructed and therefore susceptible to change, and this chapter explores how the nature of identity as constructed via gossip emerges. It includes consideration of how leaving and joining organizations act as trigger points for gossip, and how leaders' identities are narrated as stories circulated as, and through, gossip. This leads to consideration of the role and identity of followers, as the messengers and dealers of gossip. I take a reflexive stance from a personal identity position as a practice-based academic (which I how I currently describe myself). Empirically, the chapter introduces material from a recent study into human resource management strategies and academic engagement in UK universities[1] (Waddington & Lister, 2010). The problematic field of communicative technologies of organizational knowledge (Canary & McPhee, 2011b) is addressed in the context of electronic, or 'e-gossip.' I also draw upon empirical material from the mixed-methods study of gossip in healthcare organizations described more fully in the previous chapter. Methodologically, further attention is given to the use of repertory grids and critical incidents as techniques for transforming gossip into data.

First, recent theoretical work on organizational identity, including its metaphorical construction and the contribution of communicative constitution of organization scholarship are briefly reviewed. Then I develop the principles of reflexive inquiry introduced in Chapter 1, using empirical material to illustrate the how nature of identity as constructed via gossip emerges. Finally, McPhee and Zaug's (2000; 2009) four flows model is used to examine gossip-related data and academic identities.

ORGANIZATIONAL IDENTITY

Organizational identity represents the ways that organizational members define themselves as a social group in relation to their social environment, and understand themselves to be different from their competitors. The concept of identity integrates individual, collective, and organizational levels of

---

1. This was a Small Development Project funded by the UK Leadership Foundation for Higher Education (LFHE).

analysis around a sense of who and how *we are*, and who and how *I am*. Organizational identity is a theoretically diverse and contested field of scholarship. For example, du Gay (2007), writing from a sociological-anthropological approach wonders whether '"Identity", "Identification" and their conceptual fellow-travellers . . . [have] run out of steam' (p. 1). Conversely, social identity remains an area of contemporary inquiry in organizational identity studies (e.g., Huy, 2011; Jones, C. & Volpe, 2011). More broadly, social identity also draws together a number of phenomena such as leadership, motivation, power, and decision making (e.g., Haslam, S. A., 2004; Haslam S. A., & Ellemers 2005; Haslam, S. A., Reicher, & Platow 2011; Pfeffer & Fong 2005; van Dick, Ullrich, & Tissington, 2006). Identity is a theoretically diverse field and Cornelissen (2006b; 2007) argues that appreciation of the concept of organizational identity as a metaphor—because organizations cannot *literally* possess an identity—is a means of better understanding such theoretical and disciplinary diversity.

Metaphors have been interwoven throughout the book to provide imagery and concepts which lead to the articulation of a framework for theorizing organizational gossip. Identity is one of five core concepts within this framework (the others being ethics, emotion, power, and sensemaking). Cornelissen's (2006b; 2007) analysis of the different image-schemata (abstract imaginative structures) of 'identity' and 'organization' reveals six distinct research traditions in play in the field of organizational identity, (i) organizational behaviour, (ii) cognitive framing, (iii) institutional theory (iv) discursive psychology, (v) social identity, and (vi) organizational communication. This chapter focuses on the latter two research traditions in particular for two reasons. First, social identity provides a theoretical construct with which to understand the empirical and reflexive material presented in the chapter. Second, as Cooren et al. (2011) argue, communicative constitution of organization scholarship provides a valuable complementary perspective to social identity and social psychological theories. Social identity is therefore a core element of CCO thinking and theorizing.

Cornelissen (2006b) contends that the image-schematic view of metaphor is 'a pervasive and cognitively fundamental way of structuring human understanding where meaning is created through the creative juxtaposition of concepts that are not normally interrelated' (p. 687). An image-schema is an abstract imaginative structure that is triggered by the target concept (in this instance 'organization') and source concept (in this instance 'identity') which are correlated in a metaphor. Content analysis of dimensions of 'organizational identity' metaphors in the literature revealed the following views of social identity and organizational communication research traditions.

- *Social identity:* here the image-schema of 'organization' is the *collective product* of group cognitions, sensemaking and behaviour. The image-schema of 'identity' is established through categorizing individuals in *groups* and making *social comparisons* between them. The emergent meaning is that organizational identity resides in shared group cognition or 'oneness' with the organization;

- *Organizational communication:* here the image-schema of 'organization' is one which is *constituted* in and through language. The image-schema of 'identity' is as something which *exists* in and through language. The emergent meaning is of organizational identity as 'the imposition of the actor ("corporate rhetor") in and through corporate language' (Cornelissen, 2007, p. 47).

GOSSIP AND SOCIAL IDENTITY

T. Watson (2007) differentiates three forms of social identity: (i) *category identities*, such as gender, nationality, class, ethnicity; (ii) *formal role identities*, such as occupation, job title, citizenship, and so on; and (iii) *local-personal identities*, where individuals are characterized in terms of how they are described by others in the context of specific situations of events. The latter is particularly pertinent to the analysis of gossip, as it implies an evaluative component, for example 'the scary nurse,' 'the compassionate leader,' or 'the strategic martyr.' These analytical categories can also be understood in terms of identity work as presentation of self (Goffman, 1959). As a writer, I am presenting aspects of myself as a 'scholar,' 'psychologist,' 'nurse,' and as someone who has something different to say about the topic of gossip.

Notably Bergmann (1993, p. 78), comments that anyone who wishes to avoid being labelled a 'notorious gossip' should try and contextualize their 'affinity for gossip' so that it appears unintended, accidental, and excusable. Arguably an affinity for gossip is to some extent legitimized in the guise of academic scholarship, research, and peer review. For example, Carmel's (2011) examination of the role of gossip in gaining and retaining 'social access' in a work place ethnography led him to ask the question 'are ethnographers gossips?' (p. 551). Developing the reflexive inquiry position introduced in Chapter 1, I now critically reflect on my affinity for gossip from a social identity perspective.

Who Am I, and Why Am I Interested in Gossip?

As discussed in Chapter 1, a reflexive inquiry position is constituted in terms of relationships within which researchers construct knowledge (Cunliffe, 2003; Doucet, 2008). Following T. Watson (2007), this section illustrates the value of attending to the interplay between 'self' and 'social category' aspects of identity work. I therefore now reflect upon the ways that my own identity as a practice-based academic has evolved. The personal identity work that we all do addresses questions of who we are and where we come from. However, such questions often remain in the background of our taken-for-grantedness for much of the time. I now move briefly into autobiographical mode to connect who I am as an academic who is interested in the scholarship of gossip with where I come from.

REFLECTION 7: DOING AND BEING

I grew up in North East England in the 1960s and 1970s, in an area characterized by heavy industries of shipbuilding, steelworks, and chemical plants. I have lived, studied, and worked in the working-class neighbourhoods of 'women's talk.' I illustrated this by including pictures of Edwin and Daisy, my grandparents, in Chapter 2. Gossip is in the background of things I have taken for granted. I left the North East to 'do nursing' in London, and later whilst working in clinical practice as a nurse teacher I studied for a part-time psychology degree. On graduating I recall being asked this question by my dissertation supervisor, 'So Kathryn, what now. Are you going to be an academic nurse, or a nurse academic?' The question troubled me a little at first. My professional identity at the time was predominantly that of clinical nurse teacher. But I was moving into the transitional space between 'doing' nursing and 'being' an academic. I have since worked in universities in a variety of academic, management and leadership roles. I am a hybrid of both academic and nurse which has undoubtedly influenced some of the metaphors I use and the things I see—and don't see—as a reflexive researcher and reflective practitioner.

As T. Watson (2007, p. 149) puts it:

> We all need to be epistemologically reflexive and conscious of how our own life experiences and our own identity work can both inspire and constrain our research creativity . . . personal circumstances and experiences can only ever be understood within the public, historical, and structural contexts of which they are a part.

Having done a bit of personal identity work by revealing aspects of my personal, professional, and academic identity, the next section looks more closely at how social identities are created and recreated through gossip.

CREATING AND RECREATING IDENTITY THROUGH GOSSIP

A core argument of *Gossip and Organizations* is that gossip is constitutive of organizational realities. In other words that gossip as communication is embedded in processes, patterns, and products which constitute organizing and organization. Here I argue that gossip can also be used as a means of seeing and making sense of individual and group identities in different ways. Identities are the lenses through which people make sense of their experience (Weick, 1995a), although relatively little has been said about *how* individuals and groups access and use identity related information to construct, maintain, revise, or repair these identities. Notably, Myers and colleagues examined the socialization of municipal firefighters, including how new members learn organizational and group based norms. Probationary firefighters reported that they learned most through interaction with others 'in the trenches' (Myers, 2011, p. 296). Informal socialization, listening to stories, and narratives facilitates newcomer learning and distribution of organizational knowledge. Pratt, Rockmann, and Kaufmann's (2006) longitudinal study into the construction of professional identity in medical residents also shows how informal feedback and the grapevine are powerful sources of professional identity validation.

Gossip and identity are also closely related to the dynamics of inclusion and exclusion (Elias & Scotson, 1965; Soeters & van Iterson, 2002; Stacey, 2010). At a group level, individuals are included or excluded in a dynamic which expresses a pattern of power relations and underlying ideology such as 'good' and 'bad.' Gossip sustains this ideology. People direct praise gossip to their 'own' group, and blame gossip to the 'other' stigmatized group. The splitting of 'good' from 'bad' and consequent inclusion-exclusion dynamics can also be explained in psychodynamic terms of splitting and projection (Gabriel, 1999; Obholzer & Roberts, 1994b). This is a defence by which institutional difficulties are often attributed to the personalities, and therefore identity, of others. Particular individuals or groups become identified as 'troublesome.' There is often much blaming, and gossiping, between employees, between employees and managers, or between organizations and their external environments. The underlying assumption is that 'all would be well if only the evil ones, the trouble-makers, could be got rid of' (Obholzer & Roberts, 1994b, p. 129). The dynamics of inclusion-exclusion can also be understood in relation to organizational identity and socialization and the processes through which individuals adapt from being 'outsider' to 'insider.' This includes changes in and learning of new skills, knowledge, values, attitudes, and relationships, and the development of appropriate sensemaking frameworks (Cooper-Thomas & Anderson, 2006). Socialization is also a feature of membership negotiation, one of the communication flows discussed later in the chapter.

Social identity is also closely linked to personal reputation in organizations. That is 'the extent to which individuals are perceived by others, over time, as performing their jobs competently, and being helpful to others in the workplace' (Zinko et al., 2012, p. 157). Personal reputation is shared and transmitted by word of mouth, in other words gossip. Similarly, the reputation of teams, professions, organizational departments and sections are also shared and transmitted through gossip. What follows now are incidents of gossip which illustrate some of the issues relating to social identity and reputation in more depth and detail. This empirical material is drawn from qualitative interviews with Clinical Nurse Specialists (CNSs), using critical incident technique to capture participants' thought processes and feelings about incidents of gossip. The methodological principles underlying the technique are that it is:

a qualitative interview procedure, which facilitates the investigation of significant occurrences (events, incidents, processes or issues), identified by the respondent, the way they are managed, and the outcomes in terms of perceived effects. The objective is to gain an understanding of the incident from the perspective of the individual, taking into account cognitive, affective and behavioural elements. (Chell, 2004, p. 48)

Bradley (1992, p. 98) asserts that critical incident technique is a useful method of 'turning anecdotes into data', and the technique has value for researchers and practitioners alike. Close and careful analysis of incidents of gossip is a means of picking up and honouring what might be seen as discarded trivia and trifles, and turning them into something useful. Critical incident technique is a way of turning gossip into practice-based knowledge and theorizing, in this instance about identity, as demonstrated in the following incidents.

'I Had a Picture in My Head . . .'

The first incident below illustrates the way that untrue gossip can create a distorted picture of individual identity.

INCIDENT 1: I HAD A PICTURE IN MY HEAD—WAS IT CORRECT?

It's quite fascinating, it happens all of the time, I think people love to gossip, but with nurses, Chinese whispers goes on all the time. I was at an update session with a colleague and she told me this gossip about another member of staff, and really it was just hearsay. And there had been some confusion, and she was being quite indiscreet. Until we got it all sorted out *I had a picture in my head* of this other person, and *I could have got it all wrong and made a terrible mistake.* (CNS 8, emphasis added)

This incident highlights the dangers of gossip and the way that inaccurate perceptions can influence the pictures we hold of people with resultant harm. But how do people access internalized knowledge held by others?

Knowing the Picture

The following example demonstrates two things. The first is how people joining the organization act as a trigger for gossip. The second is awareness on the part of the research participant of how their team and the service they delivered was perceived by others in the organization.

INCIDENT 2: KNOWING THE PICTURE—WHAT'S GOING ON HERE?

My recent example of that is that we've just appointed someone to work in the team and gossip works in a couple of ways doesn't it? There were a couple of internal applicants and the person appointed was an external applicant, so already there's a kind of mythology about the person that's coming into post, they are going to be compared to the existing post holder, or the previous one if they are a replacement . . . and that can create some very negative things to start with. Now [CNS] jobs are high profile, you work across the directorate, *you know, you can turn up, show off, make a mess and leave again, and I think that's how we are seen across the board.* If I know there is an area where our service is viewed negatively, I can send Louise [the newcomer/pseudonym] in and just by listening to what people say she can also get a flavour of what's going on (CNS 6, emphasis added).

This incident highlights the role that gossip plays in giving a flavour or impression of what is going on but again illustrates the need for caution in taking gossip at face value. The participant's use of the term 'flavour' links back to the metaphorical and literal use of 'sense'-making to better understand gossip used in Reflection 6 in the previous chapter. The incident also illustrates ways that gossip about newcomers circulates, and offers insight into how this participant understood perceptions of their role and service. These perceptions were not necessarily positive—but did this matter? This incident can be used to highlight a dimension of social reflexivity in teams, which according to West (2000), includes reflection upon the overall social climate of the team. The overall social climate of a team may well be influenced by the way that they are perceived, either positively or negatively, and gossip as evaluative talk may reinforce perceptions of groups and individuals. However, gossip can also be used to change perceptions and pictures in people's heads.

Changing the Picture

The next incident, again provided by CNS 6, relates to the use of anecdotes as a means of debriefing and supporting staff. Incident 3 relates to quite specific clinical issues surrounding healthcare professionals' attitudes, perceptions, and emotions following a cardiac arrest situation. However, it can also be interpreted in a wider organizational (rather than clinical) perspective, to demonstrate how an anecdote about one person—the doctor who had 'freaked out'—circulating as gossip, was used help people feel better after a distressing event. Thus, a positive outcome for some individuals was achieved at the expense of another's reputation. An incident became a personalized anecdote, retold, and no doubt embellished, through gossip. However gossip is also evaluative talk

---

INCIDENT 3: CHANGING THE PICTURE USING ANECDOTES

Um, right, every now and again [pause] if you want to bolster people, if you want to support people who feel they have been involved in some disastrous clinical event, then you can pick on bits of information you know are common knowledge, are still hot gossip about disastrous events in other hospitals, terrible events in our own hospitals, things that compare to things that a group of people have just been through. And with that comparison that group of people must feel better about what they have just been through. Um . . . I can give you an example of that from this time last week. A patient on a ward had a cardiac arrest [and] the ward staff were having a hard time coming to terms with it. The anecdote there was about another patient who had collapsed over a year ago, and the doctor who was standing there when that patient collapsed freaked out so much, all commonsense went out of the window. *So immediately everyone felt better because I'd shared with them what had become a piece of gossip.* (CNS 6, emphasis added)

---

about other people's private and personal lives, as well as about particular events and incidents and this too influences reputation and identity.

Gossip as Strategy

Adopting a wider organizational perspective, this incident illustrates how the judicious choice of the 'messenger' of gossip was used proactively to set the scene for planned future change.

INCIDENT 4: GOSSIP AS STRATEGY—SETTING THE SCENE

Um, I can think of an occasion in my last job with my boss, there were things about that person which were happening in their private life which initially were kept fairly quiet, but then they *chose to let people know about their change in circumstances* by using the gossip channel. So they told one person, and said, 'I don't mind if other people know.' So it was a kind of acknowledged channel of communication, but rather than tell everybody that their life had changed in some sort of way, it just filtered down in a fairly productive way. They would choose carefully the people they would tell a certain amount of detail to, and would keep back detail from other people. But it *struck me as a fairly, kind of, strategic use of gossip,* because it was a fairly small organization.

KW: And did the strategy work?

It did, yes, the outcome was that everyone then knew the situation of that person, and *the ground was laid for, um, other changes* which became gossip in themselves, which was about an intimate relationship at work with a colleague, and it was all, it seemed to me that the gossip prepared the ground for that to happen, and then when that event happened it was less of a shock. (CNS 7, emphasis added)

In this instance, the change was in an individual's personal circumstances, but gossip can also be used strategically to set the scene and gauge reactions for future organizational change. Incident 4 also highlights awareness and understanding that gossip about other people's private lives and relationships is not uncommon. The above incidents show how formal role identities (e.g., occupation, role, and local-personal identity, where individuals are characterized in terms of how they are described by others) are shaped by, and through, the medium of gossip. The way in which gossip constructs, destructs, and reconstructs identity is also influenced by factors such as gender, position in the organization and personality. These issues are considered next.

WOMEN GOSSIP, MEN TALK?

It is a myth that women gossip more than men. The intention in the book is to dispel, once and for all, the myth that women gossip and men have conversations. The real difference between men and women with regard to gossip is much more to do with (a) the way that gossip is perceived and used as a term in everyday conversations, and (b) different relational practices (see also Fletcher, J., 1999). Women seem to feel more comfortable with using the term 'gossip' in both a positive and negative sense, whereas men may tend to only see the negative stereotype/s and perceptions of gossip. Women may be more likely to say 'What's the gossip?' whereas men may feel more comfortable saying 'What's been going on?' In Chapter 3, I reflected upon how, during my doctoral research, men often began interviews with comments such as 'Well of course, I'm not one to gossip, but,' or 'I'm not sure how much use I'll be for your research but I'll try . . .' They would then go on to talk about gossip for quite some time. This was certainly the case in the interview study that yielded the incidents of gossip used above, where the men's interviews and transcripts were on average 50% longer than the women's. That study did not seek to specifically examine differences in men and women's gossip (as the focus was on sensemaking, socialization, and emotion). However, an earlier interview study using repertory grid technique demonstrated some differences between the way that men and women conceptualize and use gossip, and these differences are discussed next.

Using Repertory Grid Technique to Identify Constructs of Gossip

Repertory grid technique is a useful method for eliciting constructs of gossip because of its capacity to illuminate subjective meanings of particular phenomenon. The theoretical background to the technique is George Kelly's personal construct psychology (PCP), which originated in a therapeutic context in clinical psychology (Kelly, 1955). It is a well-recognized technique within psychological research and has been utilized in clinical, educational, and organizational contexts (Cassell & Walsh, 2004). Personal constructs are the often unarticulated or implicit frameworks within which individuals view the world, and repertory grids provide the means to make these constructs explicit. A key notion within PCP is that it is about sensemaking, and repertory grid technique offers a form of 'conversational technology providing the stimulus through which the researcher and the researched can discuss often complex issues' (Cassell & Walsh, 2004, p. 70). Repertory grids are therefore a potentially very valuable method in gossip research. Their value lies in the way they can provide significant cues and clues about the characteristics and constructs of gossip and people who gossip.

The technique itself is quite complex, which is one of its limitations, as research participants may struggle to grasp what the technique is about. Repertory grids were created by asking participants to identify six individuals with whom they gossiped, or whom they regarded as gossips. To preserve confidentiality of these absent third parties they were not referred to by name, but identified by a letter A to F. Thus individuals, identified by participants as 'people who gossip' were the elements of the grid. This part of the technique was not difficult, reflected in comments like 'Oh, that's easy!' and 'The problem is who to leave out!' The elements were then presented in up to twenty varying triad combinations, for example: 'Individuals A, D, and E,' and participants were asked to characterize how two were similar in some respect, but also different from the third. Where possible, constructs were explored in behavioural, rather than propositional (e.g., young/old, male/female) terms. When propositional constructs were generated, participants were asked to explore similarities and differences with regard to the nature of the gossip. This process elicited over 500 constructs of gossip, and people who gossip, expressed as contrasting dimensions of difference. For example:

> Have a closer interpersonal relationship with me; vs. is not so close, doesn't know me that well.

Repertory grid constructs were collected from a sample of thirty six participants, which contained an equal number of men and women. Because I was interested in how position in the organization influences who gossips to whom about what, the sample in this study ranged from newly qualified nurses to senior managers holding directorate level positions. The constructs were analyzed qualitatively to identify broad categories of gossip, summarized in Table 5.1, which were then used to draw comparisons between men and women, managers and non-managers using quasi-statistical analysis (King, 1994).

Table 5.1   Categories and Constructs of Gossip

Categories	Examples of Constructs
Interpersonal relationship context: described the nature of the relationship	Knows me well/doesn't know me well Social relationship/work relationship
Organizational context: described role and position in the organization	My boss/subordinate Works with me/ doesn't work with me
The nature of the gossip: described the topic/content of the gossip	Personal/work related Malicious/innocent
Personality factors: described aspects of an individual's personality	Extrovert/introvert Good sense of humour/no sense of humour
Social behaviour: described behaviours not directly attributable to personality	Smoker/non smoker Socializes after work/doesn't socialize
Propositional factors: described observable attributes	Male/female Young/old

Initial descriptive statistical analysis identified some gender differences. 26% of women's constructs related to an interpersonal relationship context as compared to 11% of the men's constructs. In brief, the interpersonal relationship context referred to constructs describing the nature of the relationship, for example:

Are colleagues, I'd be less inclined to talk about other work colleagues, they wouldn't act as a 'sounding board';
vs.
Is not a nurse, acts as a 'sounding board' e.g., when my boss is being a pain in the neck. (Female manager)

The differences observed between men and women related to the *frequency* of occurrence of interpersonal relationships constructs, rather than *how* to interpersonal relationships are construed.

20% of the men's constructs related to the organizational context, as compared to 11% of the women's constructs. Organizational context referred to constructs relating to position in the organization, for example:

Are in management positions, have to be careful, are selective in their use of gossip, use gossip to diffuse difficult situations;
vs.
Is not in a management position, still 'in the ranks' is less discriminating in who they gossip with. (Male non-manager)

As with gender differences in the interpersonal relationship context, women's constructs relating to the organizational context were *similar* to those of the men, but appeared *less frequently*. Additionally when managers' and non-managers' constructs were compared there was also an observed difference relating to the number of constructs relating to the organizational context. Organizational context accounted for 24% of managers' constructs and for only 9% of non-managers' constructs. This suggests, unsurprisingly, that position in the organization was more a salient issue for managers. The purpose of quasi-statistical analysis in this study was to turn textual data into quantitative data to enable a broad comparison of the distribution of constructs across groups (King, 1994). It also helped to guide subsequent qualitative analyses around key themes.

It is pertinent to consider the gender differences observed in gossip and interpersonal relationships in the workplace in the context of J. Fletcher's (1999) research. She showed how women's relational practice—described in terms of task accomplishment, enabling others, self-achievement and teamwork—is often invisible and overlooked:

> Why is it that though there is an espoused organizational belief in collaboration and supportive teamwork, people who exhibit such behavior seem to get *disappeared* from the organizational screen? (J. Fletcher, 1999, pp. 2–3, original emphasis)

The constructs illustrated, unsurprisingly, that one of the frames of reference with which women view the world is a relational one. It is also therefore no surprise that gossip constructed in this way is also likely to 'get disappeared'. Men's constructs on the other hand reflected a different frame of reference relating to organizational role and position. These findings could be understood in terms of differences in psychological distance between men and women with regard to interpersonal relationships (Levin & Arluke, 1985), with men's constructs relating to position in the organization being a feature of maintaining psychological distance. The above differences between men and women, managers and non-managers relate to expressive and instrumental work relationships, practices, purposes and outcomes.

Two exemplars are now given of individuals who 'stood out' as extreme examples, described in repertory grid constructs as 'out and out' and 'destructive' gossips.

The 'Out and Out' and 'Destructive' Gossip

Constructs relating to some of the individuals used as elements in the repertory grids (i.e., one of the six people identified by participants as people they gossiped with, or who they regarded as gossips) were described in disapproving terms such as an 'out and out' and 'destructive' gossip. The constructs used to describe the characteristics of such individuals (altered slightly for reasons of confidentiality) are summarized in Table 5.2.

Table 5.2   Characteristics of the 'Out and Out' and 'Destructive' Gossip

The 'Out and Out' Gossip	The 'Destructive' Gossip
Is an out and out gossip, they go out of their way to gossip	They use gossip to lull people into a false sense of security
Is more disorganised/chaotic in their approach to life	Has a senior job, the amount they gossip is inappropriate to their role
Won't check out it out, the story gets bigger every time they tell it	Uses information to destroy people and their careers
Will gossip and ferret out information, seems to know who to go to	Has spread gossip about others to higher echelons of the organization
Is indiscreet, they gossip indiscriminately	Can be friendly, but uses gossip to harm people's reputations
Has no power in themselves and no sense of separate identity	

The composite characteristics presented in Table 5.2 represent a combination of individual, formal, and informal organizational factors. They may appear to be extreme and unrecognizable, or they may be uncomfortably familiar. As discussed in Chapter 3, gossip is an example of everyday ethics in practice, and its potential to harm should not be overlooked. The 'out and out' gossip had reasons (i.e., they sold home-made products) to cross multiple organizational boundaries and hierarchies—rather like smokers who huddle outside of the physical boundaries of organizations and workplaces. They combined their need for gossip with the creation of opportunities to gossip, but any harm done was mainly to their own reputation.

The 'destructive' gossip, on the other hand, had seniority and position power, and caused wider reaching harm to others, which is a characteristic of toxic leadership (see Kellerman, 2004; Lipman-Blumen, 2005). The profile of the 'destructive' gossip is also in many ways similar to Van Fleet and Van Fleet's (2006, p.767) profile of 'the internal terrorist':

> Internal terrorists (also sometimes termed 'organizational terrorists,' see for example McCurley and Vineyard, 1998) or psycho-terrorists are members, former members, or other constituents of an organization who use gossip, political tactics, harassment, intimidation and threats to create a climate of fear that will enable them to further their own objectives within an organization (Kinney, 1995, p. 96). More colloquially they are referred to as cancers within organizations, although they frequently present such a positive face to many that they have many supporters.

These are strong words, with the potential to provoke emotive and upsetting images and responses, and there are three important points to note. First, vivid words draw attention to new possibilities, images, and vocabularies for understanding gossip and organizations. Second, further research is necessary in order to identify those aspects of organizations and professions that foster or attract the behaviours associated with malicious, destructive 'toxic gossip'. Third, as Van Fleet and Van Fleet (2006) note, leaders within organizations may contribute towards the creation of internal environments and climates that diminish, contain or further inflame the spread of malicious gossip. Some of the wider issues relating to leaders and followers as messengers and dealers of gossip are now addressed.

You Need to Know Your Dealer

At the end of the repertory grid interviews participants were asked to reflect upon their recent experiences of gossip. George (pseudonym) had recently had been promoted to a more senior leadership position in mental health services, and noticed a difference in the 'quality' of gossip post-promotion. This was described in terms of its 'purity,' and the following observation was made:

> Gossip is addictive, and like with illicit drugs, you need to know your dealer. Gossip from a dealer above me is pure, but less useful in terms of how I can use it. It's so 'pure,' in other words true, but because it has come from higher up I can only use it at certain levels, if at all, and certainly not lower down. It's so pure it can be dangerous. Gossip from a dealer lower down is 'raw,' and may have a lot of impurities in it, in other words it may not be so 'true' or accurate. This can be equally dangerous, like using drugs from a street dealer that are cut with lots of other stuff.

This is an insightful observation and metaphor for gossip that highlights the purity and danger of gossip as something that is addictive and toxic (see also Douglas, 1966; Clegg and van Iterson, 2009). Use of the term 'use' is also significant here. George, unlike the 'destructive' gossip described in Table 5.2, was mindful of the dangers of misusing gossip and showed an awareness of its potential to harm. This example also provides insights into the dynamics and qualities of leader-follower relationships and identities that have not necessarily been examined in depth or fully tested in previous research.

As discussed above, notions of 'bad,' 'toxic,' or 'dysfunctional' leadership are now beginning to feature in the psychodynamic, organizational, and leadership and management literature. Recent business scandals such as Enron and WorldCom in the United States and Parmalat in Europe (and there are obviously many more) have turned researchers' attention to the ethical consequences of irresponsible leadership (e.g., Boddy, 2011; Pless, 2007). Arguably, closer analysis of the role that gossip plays in irresponsible and toxic leadership is warranted, as is the role of gossip in leader-follower identities and relationships. The question of when, where, and how gossip constitutes an early warning signal of failure is an important area for future research. As is the question of when, why, and how gossip contributes to organizational silence and the creation of a climate of fear (see also van Iterson et al., 2011). These questions are addressed more fully in Chapter 7. Next in this chapter however is an exploration of gossip and academic identities from a comminicative constitution of organization (CCO) perspective.

EXPLORING ACADEMIC IDENTITIES
WITH THE FOUR FLOWS MODEL

In this section the theoretical emphasis shifts to CCO thinking and McPhee and Zaug's (2000; 2009) four flows model, which were addressed more thoroughly in Chapter 2. The flows (membership negotiation, organizational self-structuring, activity co-ordination, institutional positioning) are analytically distinct and conceptually separate, they can drift into each other's spaces. Following Browning et al. (2009), here I revisit empirical material from a recent research example and examine the emergent complexity among the flows as a guide for analysis. The example used in this instance is a study of human resource management (HRM) strategies and academic engagement. The aim of this study was to explore the degree of engagement of academic staff with universities' HRM strategies and associated HR-driven initiatives, and to ascertain reasons for the levels of engagement reported. It was a small scale study carried out in six English universities in 2010 (for details see Appendix B; Waddington & Lister, 2010).

Most scholars seem to agree that engagement includes strong identification with one's work and an element of energy or vigour (Leiter & Bakker, 2010). In universities, engagement, energy, and identification are clustered around multiple individual, collective/disciplinary, and organizational *identities* and *reputations*. Like heathcare organizations, universities also provide rich pickings for gossip-related research, not least because of the importance of reputation and institutional positioning in the sector:

> The concept of institutional reputation [in universities] represents the point where internal self-image meets various relatively uncontrollable aspects of external evaluation . . . Story-telling also validates the concept of the "reputational reservoir" [which] has an odd relationship with the practice of *praise* and *blame*. (D. Watson. 2009, p. 113, original emphasis)

As discussed in Chapters 1 and 2, gossip is associated with story telling and has many different forms, variously described in terms which include good, bad, critical, uncritical, healing, blame and praise. Thinking about gossip in terms of the communication flow of *membership negotiation* includes aspects of identification, self-positioning and socialization. *Organizational self-structuring* as a communication flow includes 'official' documents such as organization charts, policies, procedures, and strategies. Pairing these two flows is thus highly pertinent to an examination of academic engagement with HR strategies and initiatives. The focus here is on how the flows overlap, with the intention of providing a very partial and essentially emergent exemplar of gossip and CCO thinking. Empirical material has been 'lightly edited' to preserve respondents' confidentiality and disguise institutional identity.

Membership Negotiation and Organizational Self-Structuring

The University of Arbitrary County (a pseudonym—obviously) is now used as a short case example of disengagement, disconnection, and dissonant communication processes. The data extracts below were gathered during interviews with members of the senior management team (e.g., HR Director, Pro-Vice Chancellor, Deans), and a focus group interview with academic staff.

> The VC [*Vice Chancellor*] announced a new strategy which they had discussed with the senior management team [*SMT*] that was brilliantly espoused in a series of presentations. And in my time in the sector we have never been able to focus upon one thing which is so conceptual and so easily graspable. Yet the staff survey showed a lack of engagement with staff and almost an impermeable membrane. There was a feeling [*in the SMT*] that the message was not getting down. (HR Director)

Compare the above with a focus group comment from an academic who described the poor communication practices of management '*oh, there were cries going up and down the corridors.*' The underlying meaning was that the cries went unheard, yet the SMT also recognized '*sometimes the ideas that are coming up from the shopfloor are brilliant and we need to absorb them.*' The university engaged management consultants to address the lack of engagement revealed by the staff survey. Some academic staff did not engage with this idea:

> The very worst thing you can do is bring in a team of management consultants, because you get them in at enormous expense to tell senior management what they really know already, but they really can't face. The consultants say: 'You know it already, but I'm telling you because nobody else will.' So what you need is to get someone inside the organization who is bold enough and protected enough to say to senior management 'by the way, you're doing this wrong.' And they [*SMT*]

will say 'you've shot yourself in the foot there.' (Composite data extract from a focus group with academic staff)

The argument being developed here is that gossip *may* drift in and out of communication flows through metaphorical 'gossamer walls,' which were introduced earlier in Chapter 1. However, in the University of Arbitrary County, the walls between the flows were impermeable and academic staff were disengaged. This is not unusual in the higher education sector. It has been said (anecdotally) that universities are places where academics are joined together by central heating and/or air conditioning systems. Arguably universities are not unique in this respect. Put another way, organizational members experience little coherence in the *internal interactions* of the organizational world which they inhabit. Another senior academic at Arbitrary County commented:

> In the health service you have 'the Gods' who think because they are doing brain surgery they can't be treated the same as everybody else and it can be the same with the professoriat—they're all employed for their/our intellectual property. So it is about their 'uniqueness'—that's why we employ them—therefore they think that they are 'Gods' that they are 'untouchable' that they don't have to obey the rules. However . . . there is total transparency and decisions are made very openly and wrong decisions are openly admitted, 'sorry, I got it wrong.' (A Dean)

There was however some dissonance between this view of transparency and the perceptions and experience of respondents in the focus group:

> People were disengaged because you're working all these hours, but we're not allowed to say anything. When I asked for the rationale behind a management decision—I wasn't being difficult, I was quite polite—I got the sense that my question wasn't welcome. It was like opening a can of worms; they [SMT] didn't want that. So, on the one hand they are proclaiming wonderful openness, and on the other hand it's all empty verbiage. (Composite data extract)

Loyalty to, and identification with, the institution was limited:

> If you ask an academic where his or her loyalties lie, that first loyalty is not necessarily to the University and its mission and objectives, that loyalty is to their subject/discipline and an academic will have more in common with a professor in X [another university] than with the professor next door. Indeed they probably hate the professor next door because what the professor next door espouses is probably heresy and he/she alone and the prof in X are the one true faith. (HR Director)

The University of Arbitrary County was not an unusual or extreme case. It illustrates how, in universities, academic discipline takes precedent over institutional affiliation in the identity stakes, and how *external interactions* have greater significance. In this particular instance there was minimal overlap between the flows; the organization as constituted in this pairing of membership negotiation and organizational self-structuring was disconnected.

External interactions are also significant in communication flows about individual and institutional academic identities and reputations which spread *beyond* the organization as constituted through the multiple media of gossip (spoken, written, and visual). The communication flow of *institutional positioning* asks the question 'What external forces provide legitimacy, and what kinds of communication are necessary to please them?' (Browning et al., 2009, p. 92). Collaborative inter- and intra-disciplinary networks, the marketization of higher education and widespread use of communicative technologies have a role to play in understanding the role of gossip, academic identities, and institutional positioning. These are considered next through the medium of '*e-gossip*,' which illustrates aspects of the problem field of 'communicative technologies of organizational knowledge' (see Canary & McPhee, 2011b, p. 8). The problem in this instance being that knowledge circulating electronically as gossip leaves a permanent trace, is largely unregulated and open to abuse, harmful, and in some instances, hateful speech (Levmore & Nussbaum, 2011).

Institutional Positioning and e-gossip

Students, as consumers, can access a range of formal (e.g., league tables, university guides) and informal (e.g., social networking sites, websites, and blogs) metrics and sources of information about universities. Bradshaw and Saha (2011), for example, discuss the challenges universities and administrators face from social-networking websites such as JuicyCampus, a website in the United States which solicited anonymous gossip, and operated from 2007 to 2009. The site became a place where offensive postings and cyber bullying caused distress and harm to individuals and institutions, and was subject of two investigations by Attorneys General (Ivester, 2011).

> JuicyCampus was, at its core, an anonymous (no login required) message board organized by college campus. Students could select their school, and then post a message on their campus's page, whether it be about a class they were taking, a professor they liked or disliked, or some juicy bit of gossip about a fellow classmate. (Ivester, 2011, p. xvi)

This is 'e-gossip.' That is, informal evaluative talk about organizational (in this instance university/academic) issues occurring in information and communication technology (ICT) supported networks. Not all e-gossip is informative; some can be very nasty, offensive, defamatory, and verbally abusive. E-gossip abounds on the 'Readers' comments' section of the *Times Higher Education* journal's website (http://www.timeshighereducation. co.uk). An example can be seen in the following short extract of posts commenting on an original article written by a professor of English and comparative literature:

alex: Why is it that people who study literature—the one subject which any literate person can have a go at with a few bob in their pocket and access to Amazon—feel able to pontificate on the 'true' purpose of 'the University'?

@alex: The fallacy in your post is called 'ad hominem'. It was already identified by the academic profession in the Middle Ages, or earlier. The post also contains (which is something different) *gratuitous verbal abuse* (for example the groundless suggestion that the author as well as others "with access to Amazon" etc. have "no purpose"). (http://www. timeshighereducation.co.uk/story.asp?storycode=418076, accessed 11 November 2011, emphasis added, names have been changed)

The above is an example of one of the shorter, less inflammatory exchanges which can be found on websites such as this. Even though this exchange might be dismissed as background 'noise in the system' and 'academic points scoring', e-gossip is potentially harmful to individual and institutional identities and reputations.

E-gossip is also an overlooked, but potentially problematic, aspect of organizational knowledge. On the one hand, e-gossip circulating via email, blogs, tweets and such like can facilitate sharing information and knowledge. Furthermore, fragments of e-gossip can be used, with other sources of data/evidence to build up a composite picture of what is 'really going on' or to identify trends and themes which can be cross-referenced to ascertain their accuracy, or otherwise. The work of scholars who adopt a naturalistic sensemaking paradigm is pertinent here, particularly with regard to the creation of sensemaking databases (see Snowden, 2010). Such a database can contain anecdotes, gossip, drawings, pictures, sound files; anything that allows people to make sense of complexity. However Kurtz and Snowden (2007) also caution that a sensemaking database is not an expert system, nor a knowledge base, although it may work in close collaboration with such systems.

While the naturalistic sensemaking paradigm—which adopts an epistemology which draws upon natural science—shares some similarities with that of Weick (1995a) there are some important differences. Naturalizing sensemaking challenges notions of retrospective coherence in order to create models for future action. There is thus a greater emphasis on understanding the present, and such an approach has potentially much to offer for understanding 'gossip-in-situ'. In other words gossip as it happens in real time. The indelibility of e-gossip may leave a potentially damaging legacy for individuals and institutions touched by harmful gossip—a permanent digital trace and audit trail for others, employers, or researchers for example, to access. Conversely, digital permanence may push organizational gossip further underground, away from the eyes and ears of researchers and other interested parties.

CONCLUSION: GOSSIP, IDENTITY AND CCO THEORY BUILDING

This chapter has demonstrated the utility of critical incident and repertory grid techniques in understanding how social identity and reputation, as constructed, destructed and reconstructed via gossp, emerges and changes. It also addressed related issues of organizational identity and reputation from a 'gossip-as-CCO' perspective. The important point that this chapter has illustrated is how the communicative flows of membership negotiation, organizational self-structuring and institutional positioning intermingle together through the medium of gossip. E-gossip flows, or indeed surges, through the internet, which has dramatically altered the speed with which reputations can be made and altered (Levmore & Nussbaum, 2010). Gossip, as informal evaluative talk, also flows through metaphorical gossamer walls in organizations at a speed far greater than formal communication flows. Gossip coalesces at various points within and between the flows, and individual, collective and institutional identities emerge and evolve. This chapter has provided a fresh perspective upon organizational identity, bringing together micro-level constructs and incidents of gossip and macro-level perspectives of organizational communication.

This brief exploration of gossip, identity and the communication flows offers some tangible insights to substantiate claims that organizations are constituted through communication. Such claims are arguably meaningless unless we can articulate and analyze the processes that operate in constituting organizations and organizing. Such claims are also of limited value unless they impact upon management thinking and practice. As Leclercq-Vandelannoitte (2011) points out, the CCO argument has made a significant contribution to organizational communication studies, 'but it has had limited impact on management, because communicative explanations emphasize symbolic over material aspects' (p. 1249). Organizations exist in their tangible architecture, artefacts, and technologies, *as well as* being invoked in communication.

A building, for example, constitutes an organization and its identity, through what it looks like, the values, norms, and ideologies communicated and the impact it has upon visitors and employees. Materiality, which is experienced through the artefacts and technologies with which we interact, is pertinent to the arguments about gossip and identity developed in this chapter for at least two reasons. First, material objects such as websites, logos, strategy documents, and other manifestations of corporate communication can become the subject matter of gossip. Repositioning gossip as an example of CCO thinking highlights connections between corporate and organizational communication. This is important, and as Christensen and Cornelissen (2011) argue, there is potential for greater cross-fertilization between these two areas of communication to enhance links between micro and macro level analyses. Second, buildings contain unmanaged spaces and technologies where face-to-face *and* e-gossip circulates. Gossip is constitutive of *cross-currents* between flows, moving through metaphorical gossamer walls. There is clearly scope for inclusion of gossip in future CCO theory building to better understand how organizing and organizations emerge from blended *and* disconnected flows.

In conclusion, Weick (1995a) famously recounts the sensemaking story of the little girl who, being told to be sure of her meaning before she spoke, asked the question '[h]ow can I know what I think till I see what I say?' (p. 12). Gossip is informal evaluative talk that may be spoken (most common), written (less common) or visual. Paraphrasing Weick, arguably the important gossip and identity question is this: *How do we really know who we are until we see and hear how others talk about us?*

6 The Politics of Gossip

It's not what you know, and it's not who you know—it's what you know about who you know that's important in this place.

—(Anon)

The above 'advice' about organizational politics was given to a friend of mine shortly after they had joined the organization. It was then told to me, much later, in what might be described as a gossip-about-gossip conversation. That is, evaluative talk between two friends who were exchanging views, opinions and information about what was going on in their lives. Unsurprisingly, I was talking about writing this book. We talked about gossip as the 'how' you get to know, how the 'where' you get to know is determined by access to often 'unmanaged' social and organizational spaces, and that there is an often an ethical dimension to 'what' you know. This brief anecdote sets the scene for consideration of the politics of gossip.

The politics of gossip should not be confused with the 'gossip of politics.' The lines between politicians and celebrities are blurred, but this book is about organizational rather than celebrity or political gossip. Historically however there is anecdotal evidence that early politicians sought feedback from the public to determine what the people considered important. Politicians sent their assistants to local taverns and bars to drink ale and listen to people's conversations and political concerns.'You go sip here, you go sip there.' The two words 'go sip' were eventually combined when referring to the local opinion and, thus we have the term 'gossip.' Etymologically this is not proven, but it makes intuitive sense. While this book is not about the gossip of politics, its arguments, analyses, and frameworks do also *apply* to 'politics with a big P.' The work of politicians has been an under-researched area in organization studies and organizational psychology (Silvester, 2008), and the work of politicians is a promising area for future gossip-related research. For instance, as I have discussed elsewhere, commentators and politicians from Samuel Pepys's (1633–1703) time onwards have written political diaries and memoirs for posterity through archives, and profit through publication (Waddington, 2012). Politicians' and political commentators' diaries and blogs are potentially rich sources of gossip-related data in the public domain, available for secondary analysis.

This chapter builds upon some of the broader themes identified in previous chapters. That is, it conceptualizes gossip and politics as organizing processes within and between individuals, groups and organizations that include both formal and informal activities. In this chapter I argue that power, knowledge, and ethics are loosely connected concepts which contribute towards a framework for theorizing and understanding gossip and organizations. Organizational communication and knowledge were introduced in Chapter 2 as boundary conditions for theorizing gossip. Following on from Chapter 3, the concept of gossip as everyday ethics in practice and the theoretical perspective of virtue ethics are developed further. Continuing with the approach adopted in Chapter 5, Mc Phee and Zaug's four flows model is used to further illustrate how gossip is communication constitutive of organization (CCO). In the latter part of this chapter the communication flows of 'organizational self-structuring' and 'activity coordination' are used as an organizing framework to re-describe, re-present, interrogate and vary data. This invokes Alvesson and Sköldberg's (2009, p. 313) notion of R-reflexivity, and the intention here is to open up new lines of interpretation to produce 'better' research politically, ethically, and theoretically.

Organizational politics and power are key terms used in this chapter; their meanings are contested, changing, and complex, and first I summarize the ways in which they are understood and adopted here.

ORGANIZATIONAL POLITICS

Looking at gossip and organizations through a political lens involves consideration of organizations as political systems. That is, as webs of interdependent members who use power, influence, and political manoeuvring in pursuit of goal satisfaction (Sussman, Adams, Kuzmits, & Raho, 2002). But like gossip, politics is a dirty word. There is ostensibly a double helping of dirt in this chapter. Organizational politics often involves activities which are unsanctioned by the organization, leading to dissent. Political behaviour has been described as 'neither formally authorized, widely accepted, nor officially certified . . . [it] is typically divisive and conflictive, often pitting individuals and groups against formal authority, accepted ideology and/or certified expertise or against each other' (Mintzberg, 1985, cited in Silvester, 2008, p. 110). Ferris et al. (2005, p. 127) define political skill, or savvy as 'the ability to effectively understand others at work, and to use such knowledge to influence others to act in ways that enhance one's personal and/or organizational objectives.' A meta-analysis of the outcomes of perceptions of organizational politics concluded:

> From a research perspective, models of job satisfaction, job stress, turnover, and organizational commitment should all consider politics perceptions' adverse effects. Researchers performing empirical tests of each of these critically important worker-related factors should consider the impact of organizational politics perceptions as a predictor

or, at least, as a control variable. (Miller, Rutherford, & Kolodinsky, 2008, p. 216)

The above definitions and perceptions reflect a view of politics as a variable that can be measured and manipulated within an organizational container. As discussed in Chapter 2 the 'communicative constitution of organization' (CCO) approach sees the root metaphor of organization as container as 'superficially simple' (Ashcraft et al., 2009; Putnam et al., 2009, p.2). Mumby (2001) offers a definition of oganizational politics that aligns more closely with the CCO approach, and is the one adopted for the purposes of this chapter.

> *Politics:* The articulation of various individual and group interests through the everyday enactment of communicative processes that produce, reproduce, resist, and transform collective (intersubjective) structures of meaning. Politics is power enacted and resisted. (Mumby, 2001, p. 587)

There is a prevailing assumption that organizational politics are indicative of the 'dark side' of organizational practices (Gotsis & Kortezi, 2010, p. 497). The 'dark side' of politics is characterized by destructive self-serving opportunism and dysfunctional game playing. However, comparatively few researchers have critically evaluated the assumption that politics is inherently harmful and divisive. Essentially then there are two views of organizational politics. The first sees organizational politics as self-serving unsanctioned negative behaviour. The second, broader perspective sees politics as a manifestation of social influence processes which can yield beneficial organizational outcomes. There is growing interest in a more positive side of organizational politics and political behaviour. Researchers are beginning to explore how political skill can be nurtured and developed in order to enhance individual and organizational performance (Silvester, 2008).

Organizational politics encompasses multiple perspectives and its perception as either positive or negative clearly depends upon the views and interests of the observer. There is a need to develop a more critical understanding of how organizational practitioners, managers and leaders experience politics in the workplace. For example, UK surveys of managers in public, private, and voluntary sectors have identified the need for a shared understanding of political skills (Buchanan, 2008; Hartley et al., 2007). Politics can be understood in terms of alliance building to achieve organizational objectives, and something which is necessary, and ethical. Buchanan's (2008) study found a willingness to engage in politics, but also an implicit 'you stab my back, I'll stab yours' attitude, and the study was inconclusive with regard to gender differences. Conversely in Hartley et al.'s (2007) study, fewer respondents viewed politics solely in terms of people 'protecting their turf,' and there was a significant gender bias. Women were more inclined to view politics as alliance building and reconciling conflict, whereas men were more inclined to view politics as the pursuit of self-interest.

Hartley et al.'s (2007) findings are similar to the gender differences in expressive and instrumental work relationships, practices, purposes and outcomes of gossip discussed in the previous chapter. To recap, analysis of repertory grid constructs revealed that women were more likely to describe gossip in terms of interpersonal relationships, while men were more likely to describe it in terms of role and position in the organization. Women's gossip is relational and expressive, men's gossip is instrumental and political. Similarly, Davey (2008, p. 650) argues:

> Organizational political processes are seen as fundamental to gender in organizations, first, because political activity is seen as gendered and masculine and contrary to female identity; secondly, because politics is part of the informal system which constructs organization from which outsiders are excluded; and finally, because political activity is linked to the performance, achievement and maintenance of power.

Gossip, Power and Politics

The role of gossip, power and politics is illustrated, albeit implicitly, in S. Taylor, Bell, Grugulis, Storey, and Taylor's (2010) analysis of the short-lived UK National Health Service (NHS) University (NHSU). The NHSU was a public sector organizational training and learning initiative, based on the private sector model of corporate universities as a means of developing learning organizations. It was located within, and caught between, two highly politicized contexts; the NHS (a publicly funded healthcare system) and the higher education sector. The NHSU's positioning within such a complex web of institutions, power relations and interest groups make it a noteworthy case for analysis. The pertinent issue for this chapter relate to the negative impact of being outside of formal and informal power structures and spaces. As one respondent commented 'I think the decision [to abolish the NHSU] came primarily from within the Department [of Health] . . . we weren't part of the structure there, *we weren't walking round the corridors*, we weren't friendly with the key people there' (Taylor, S. et al., 2010, p. 96, emphasis added). 'Walking round the corridors' is a means of accessing the 'power of corridors' and gossip. Chance meetings and corridor conversations, are 'keys to the hidden kingdoms of power beyond the visible territories of the institution' (Hurdley, 2010a, p. 518).

It is evident from this brief and selective overview that organizational gossip and politics are inter-connected, and in some respects they share a number of similarities. Both have had miserable reputations in the past but are now being recognized as important aspects of management and organizational practice. Organizational politics has been associated with negative assumptions, emotive descriptions and connotations of disreputable self-interested individual behaviour. Like gossip, little attention has been paid to the potential for any positive organizational consequences. However there is also new academic and scholarly interest in both fields that goes beyond the level of individual behaviour to a yield a deeper understanding of the organizational dynamics, relationships and processes of power.

POWER AND KNOWLEDGE

Here the focus is upon the key aspects of power that are theoretically relevant and useful to the understanding of the politics of gossip-as-knowledge. The introductory comment at the start of this chapter suggests that, from an organizational member's viewpoint, gossip, power and politics are closely connected with knowledge. As discussed above, politics is power enacted and resisted. Lyon and Chesebro (2011) argue that the political aspects of organizational knowledge and its management have consequences for the relative health of organizations. Knowledge is constructed in epistemic communities and dominant groups tend to defend their knowledge territory in ways that reproduce and distort dominant-subordinate relationships. This is particularly evident in 'expert' communities and professional groups, where complex language or highly technical terminology serves to exclude 'non-experts.' As Gluckman (1963) observed, the more exclusive the group, the greater the amount of gossip within it. The more highly organized the profession, the more effective is the role of gossip:

> the professional group, like lawyers or anthropologists, whose gossip is built into technical discussion so tightly that the outsider cannot always detect the slight personal knockdown which is concealed in a technical recital, or the technical sneer which is contained in a personal gibe. This is, therefore, the most irritating kind of group to crash into, because one has no clue to the undercurrents, no apparatus for taking soundings. (Gluckman, 1963, p. 309)

Jargon and gratuitously complex language found in exclusive groups and professions, and overly academic/managerialist writing may also become the subject of gossip and jokes by those who feel irritated and excluded. Sturdy, Clark, Fincham, and Handley's (2008) case study of humour discourses around management consultancy provides some examples:

> her colleague teasingly asked the consultant: 'Can we use any of the terminology about methodology that was in your . . . paper? Or is that just bollocks?' And, in another case study project meeting, the client CEO commented, with a broad smile, that he had initially been sent the consultants' report but had not understood it—'now I've got the English version!' (p. 144)

More generally, knowledge is closely related to power. A power/knowledge connection reflects the Foucauldian assumption that it is impossible to separate power from knowledge, that they are not neutral and that all knowledge is dangerous. Foucault asserts:

> we should admit rather that power produces knowledge . . . that power and knowledge directly imply one another; that there is no power relation without the correlative constitution of a field of knowledge, nor any knowledge that does not presuppose and constitute at the same time power relations. These "power-knowledge relations" are to be analysed, therefore, not on the basis of a subject of knowledge who is or is not free in relation to the power system, but, on the contrary, the subject who knows, the objects to be known and the modalities of knowledge must be regarded as so many effects of these fundamental implications of power-knowledge and their historical transformations. (1979, pp. 27–28)

Foucault's discussion of power is extensive, complex and can be challenging to read and comprehend, not least because the raw materials for his analysis of power are scattered through a fragmented body of work (Clegg, 1989, citing Wickham, 1983). Foucault did not define power, nor did he construct a clear theory of power (Alvesson & Sköldberg, 2009). The most important feature of Foucault's thinking about power centres on the premise that power is not a '"thing" or a "capacity" which can be owned either by State, social class or particular individuals' (O'Farrell, 2005, p. 99). Put differently, power can come from anywhere. Power produces knowledge and power and knowledge directly imply one another. Readers seeking more detailed exposition of Foucault's work than is given here are directed to Danaher, Schirato, and Webb (2000), Dreyfus and Rabinow (1983), and O'Farrell (2005).

Foucault's discussion of power/knowledge embraces a number of issues that hold particular relevance for scholars of gossip. These are the conceptualization of power as: (i) a network of relations that are localized, dispersed, diffused, and typically disguised through a social system; (ii) productive of particular types of knowledge and social order; and (iii) operating at the most micro levels of social relations. A Foucauldian approach to power and power relationships allows for the development of new lines of thought through the inversion of perspectives, offering new approaches and re-exploration of issues. Although Foucault's notions of power are buried in the roots of CCO theorizing, critics have argued that power is poorly conceptualized in CCO scholarship. There are a number of gaps, ambiguities, and challenges. For example:

> The conditions in which organizations are created through communication are not clear. What does it mean that an organization is constituted through human communication? In which conditions does communication create organization and through which focal processes

does power get manifested and shape organizational reality? How can we understand the interplay between agency and structure? How do these processes relate to the symbolic and material elements that form an organization? Despite abundant and multidisciplinary research, the claim that communication constitutes organizations has not been satisfactorily explained. (Leclercq-Vandelannoitte, 2011, p. 1249)

In addition, Reed (2010) contends that the process or practice-based conception of organizational power and control in CCO theorizing fails to access the wider structures of relational power within which ongoing political processes and practices are embedded:

There is a recurring failure to recognize and elucidate the dynamics of domination within and between complex organizations because this would require a conception of institutionalized hierarchical power/control relationships which is ontologically and analytically inadmissible within the CCO position. (Reed, 2010, p. 154)

In order to address the above challenges and clarify the nature of these various relationships, Leclercq-Vandelannoitte (2011) proposes an approach to CCO thinking and theorizing based much more *explicitly* upon Foucault's work. A Foucauldian lens brings the relationships among communication technology, power, knowledge, discourse, discipline, and subjects into a sharper focus. Dynamic political processes that combine material and symbolic elements into the constitution of organizations then become much more overt. Methodologically, Leclercq-Vandelannoitte provides a comprehensive example of a qualitative case study of a large building company in France which had implemented new mobile technologies used by foremen. This implementation was officially presented as empowering foremen by promoting their autonomy and self-discipline, although it created new forms of surveillance and control of their activities. This created discrepancies between official and unofficial discourses, disruption and resistance by some of the foremen. These findings are not dissimilar to my own research.

I re-interpreted as gossip being 'unofficial' nursing discourse, used as a means of expressing resistance to dominant discourses such as health service reform and managerialism. Power is also manifest in the informal and unofficial discourse of gossip and the interpersonal relationships and networks it sustains. (Waddington 2010, p. 320)

Case study research can provide the fine-grained contextual detail with which to theorize power and politics in organizations (Clegg, 2011). Leclercq-Vandelannoitte's (2011) case study is therefore highly pertinent to the ideas and arguments presented in this chapter. It shows how communication processes act as loci of resistance and domination, through which knowledge, power, and ethics are relationally constructed, deconstructed, and reconstructed. In particular, it supports the argument that power, knowledge, and ethics are loosely connected concepts which contribute towards a framework for theorizing and understanding gossip and organizations. This leads us now to consider extant theoretical frameworks of power, politics and gossip, and their relevance and applicability to the future scholarship of organizational gossip.

FRAMEWORKS OF POWER AND GOSSIP

Two frameworks are advanced here which articulate dynamics and concepts of power and gossip. This is followed by consideration of ethical principles for managing negative organizational politics and promoting positive political practices in the workplace. The intention is to provide an overview of conceptual aspects of power underpinning the new theorizing framework articulated in Chapter 8.

Circuits of Power Framework

Clegg's (1989) circuits of power framework has played an important and enduring role in the development of social and organizational theory and research into phenomena aligned to gossip such as bullying and organizational politics (e.g., Hutchinson, Vickers, Jackson, & Wilkes, 2010; McPhee, 2004; Mumby, 2004, van Iterson & Clegg, 2008). Clegg draws upon Foucauldian notions of power, knowledge, and resistance, viewing power as a constitutive force which flows in three distinct but interacting circuits which are episodic, dispositional, and facilitative.

1. *Episodic agency power:* this is the most visible circuit of power, operating at the day-to-day level of social interaction, such as meetings or other arenas of struggle in which agencies use 'means in order to control resources which have consequential outcomes for the scope of action of these agents' (Clegg, 1989, p. 215). However, a later application of the circuits of power framework found the 1989 model too *static*, suggesting there is no fixed starting point for episodic power. Rather it 'can start wholly *outside* the formally established relations between organizations, and episodic circuits tend to *intersect*' (van Iterson & Clegg 2008, p. 1133, original emphasis). Even if it is assumed that this circuit of power has stabilized, it is always capable of being influenced and reconfigured by other the other two circuits, and gossip plays a key role in these relations.

2. *Dispositional power:* here the power of social integration focuses on group membership, relationships of meaning, and rules of practice.

This circuit is concerned with 'fixing or refixing relations of meaning and of membership' (Clegg, 1989, p. 224).

3. *Facilitative power:* is concerned with 'the empowerment and disempowerment of agencies' capacities, as these become more or less strategic as transformations occur which are incumbent upon changes in techniques of production and discipline' (Clegg, 1989, p. 224). This circuit is related to the previous one, and together they can be seen as 'integrative' as well as 'disintegrative' through the notion of 'obligatory points of passage' (p. 224).

The enduring strengths of the circuits of power framework centre on the following: (i) recognition of a plurality of processes involving power; (ii) the idea of obligatory passage points, which act as conduits between the three circuits; (iii) its potential to provide fresh insights into the power dynamics of many organizational phenomena; and (iv) recognition that the exercise of power through socially constituted 'rules of practice' has the potential to both negate or constrain, and also to create and enable more productive aspects of power (Hutchinson et al., 2010; McPhee, 2004). Applying the circuits of power framework specifically to gossip, it is evident that there are two diverse and disconnected rationalities at play. For gossipers, there is a situational and contextual rationality in play, moving through the circuit of dispositional power. Gossip also has the potential to change the relations of meaning between organization members. In this context, it is both a community-building device and something that 'gnaws away at the grounds of propriety, legitimacy and respect, dividing organizations' (Clegg & van Iterson, 2009, p. 286). There are links here with the short case study of the University of Arbitrary County, discussed in the previous chapter, where disengagement and disconnection of communication flows was evident.

Clegg's framework is therefore both relevant and applicable to future theorizing of organizational gossip for two compelling reasons. First, because of the way the framework draws upon Foucauldian notions of power, knowledge, and resistance. This supports Leclercq-Vandelannoitte's (2011) argument for an approach to CCO thinking and theorizing based more explicitly upon Foucault's work. Second, the framework draws attention to the analysis of the *everyday* constitution of power, underpinned by a concern for the moral and ethical questions of power and responsibility. This recalls and reinforces the notion of gossip as the enactment of everyday ethics in practice, as illustrated in the following extract from an interview with a Clinical Nurse Specialist (CNS 6):

I knew that X [*a board member*] was going to resign but it was kept a secret from the organization. Now I don't necessarily think that is right, I don't agree with it, however, I can understand the rationale behind it. Having been inadvertently exposed to it I chose to maintain the corporate silence. And then a month later I met Y [*a senior nurse*] and I revealed to her what I knew and she got flustered and said 'you shouldn't know' and 'you must keep it quiet' and I was a bit offended that I wasn't seen to have the maturity in the organization. But equally, suddenly, you know, you are involved in other peoples' agendas and there was a political thing going on between the union and X at the time. So then I was involved in some gossip, and to be honest, I wish I wasn't a part of it, it leaves me with dilemmas that I didn't want to be privy to.

This extract shows how gossip impacts upon ethical aspects organizational communication and knowledge practices, and also illustrates a number of themes addressed in previous chapters. It touches on emotion and identity in the way that the participant felt *'offended'* by their perceived lack of organizational maturity. The ethical and 'toxic' element is reflected in the notion of having been *'inadvertently exposed to gossip'* and consequential ethical *'dilemmas I didn't want to be privy to'* relating to confidentiality and secrecy. However, as I discuss next, there has been little explicit reference to ethical concepts in earlier work addressing gossip and power.

Gossip and Power in the Workplace

Kurland and Pelled (2000) have adopted a rather different approach to gossip and power in the work place than the arguments advanced here. They cite Pfeffer's (1992) description of power as the potential ability to influence behaviour, overcome resistance, and get people to do things they would not otherwise do. Their model of gossip and power identifies specific predictions relating to the linkages between positive and negative gossip and the gossiper's coercive, reward, expert, and referent power over gossip recipients. Influenced by French and Raven's construction of power, the model also predicts that the effects of gossip on different types of power will be moderated by gossip credibility, quality of interpersonal relationship and organizational culture. The model reflects a precise, yet questionably narrow conceptual framework that fails to take into account or acknowledge a Foucauldian power/knowledge connection. Gossip and power are treated as variables in the workplace, with power as the dependent variable. For example:

> *Proposition 9*: The effects of gossip on coercive, reward, expert, and referent power will be moderated by organizational culture. Any tendency for gossip to enhance coercive, reward, and expert power will be weaker when the culture discourages informal communication. Any tendency for gossip to reduce referent power will be stronger when the culture discourages informal communication. (Kurland & Pelled, 2000, p. 435, original emphasis)

Kurland and Pelled's model is noteworthy as one of the first theoreticals model of workplace gossip and its consequences, and is widely cited (e.g., Bordia et al., 2006; Farley, 2011; Fox, 2001; Kniffin & Wilson, 2005; Michelson & Mouly, 2002; 2004). There are also *conceptual elements* in the model which are worth considering further with regard to the politics of gossip, but not necessarily in the way originally envisioned. For example, the model includes contextual factors of *relationship quality* and *organizational culture* which have a bearing upon the the connections and relationships between knowers (see also Lyon & Chesebro, 2011; van Iterson et al., 2011). There is little empirical evidence that the gossip and power in the workplace model was subject to further testing or development. This may be a reflection of the shift towards CCO thinking which has taken place since McPhee and Zaug's (2000) initial influential paper. It may also simply be a reflection of the ethical challenges facing researchers, which have resulted in gossip remaining a relatively untouched area of organizational experience (Hurdley, 2010a; 2010b; Noon, 2001).

However, this also begs the question of why have ethical concepts been so conspicuously absent in previous models of organizational gossip? The power of language is an important ethical consideration, particularly given the argument that language evolved to enable people to gossip (Dunbar, 1996). The power of language to harm is evident in relation to malicious gossip and bullying (Hutchinson et al., 2010; Tehrani, 2004), underscoring the argument advanced in Chapter 3 that the decision to participate, or not, in gossip is always an ethical one. Therefore, the discussion now turns to ethical principles and organizational politics.

ETHICAL PRINCIPLES AND ORGANIZATIONAL POLITICS

In this section I undertake a further analysis of gossip and organizational politics from an ethical perspective, and bring in a little more empirical material as argument. As we have seen, organizational politics can broadly be viewed in two ways. Either as self-serving unsanctioned negative behaviour, or as a process of social influence with beneficial organizational outcomes. Politics and power are two sides of the same coin. The circuits of power framework, discussed above, recognizes that the exercise of power through socially constituted 'rules of practice' has the potential to negate or constrain. It also has the positive potential to create and enable the more productive aspects of power. There is now growing interest in a more positive side of organizational politics and political behaviour, and a reframing of the role of politics and political skills in organizational life (Hartley et al., 2007; Silvester, 2008). Thinking differently about politics in the workplace calls for a re-evaluation its normative ethical foundations. Gotsis & Kortezi (2010) suggest that a deontological approach is important for the management of negative political behaviour, whereas a virtue ethics approach can be adopted to foster positive political behaviour in the workplace.

Kantian deontology (which derives from the Greek *deon* or duty and *logos* or study) is primarily an ethics of duties towards others, based upon respect for others' humanity by treating them as we would wish to be treated (Michelson et al., 2010). Deontology guides decisions and actions on the basis of that which is morally forbidden, allowed, or required, rather than the consequences of such decisions or actions. Kantian deontology effectively constrains negative political behaviour because it 'encourages individual autonomy, ensures meaningful work, and fosters leadership styles that facilitate workers' participation and enhance perceived fairness in the workplace' (Gotsis & Kortezi, 2010, p. 503). Equally important, and particularly pertinent to gossip, are ethical principles based on theories of justice, where obligations such as fairness and equity facilitate the just allocation of resources and corporate cooperation (Prasad, 2008). Distributive justice states that 'rules should be applied consistently, and those in similar circumstances should be treated equally, and individuals should not be held responsible for matters beyond their control' (Buchanan & Badham, 2008, p. 85).

Unsurprisingly, management decisions and actions which are evaluated as 'unfair' by employees are organizational triggers for gossip. In the previous chapter, critical incidents were used to illustrate aspects of gossip and identity which were drawn from qualitative interviews. The incidents used in this chapter were collected using paper-and-pencil diary methods and follow up telephone interviews (see Appendix A, Figure A.1; Waddington, 2005c; 2012).

INCIDENT 5: ETHICS AND EMOTIONS

Q1. Why did you choose this particular incident?

Because I felt very strongly about it. A decision had been taken by the management group about a colleague which I felt was morally wrong.

Q2: How did you feel at the time?

Extremely angry

Q3: Where, when and who was involved?

Two other colleagues and myself—we discussed the management decision prior to a staff meeting when the decision was about to be made public.

Q4: Briefly describe the nature of the gossip.*

It was instigated by myself because I felt that the management group had made a decision to reallocate part of the budget to an area of the service that I thought was inappropriate and disadvantageous to a particular client group.

---

*Note that in order to protect the confidentiality of absent third parties, the structured diary records had explicit instructions for participants to record salient points only, and not to refer to individuals by name.

This incident reveals a strong emotion of anger associated with the ethical evaluation that the management decision was perceived by this participant as both *'morally wrong'* and *'disadvantageous'* to a particular group. For this participant there were ethical principles of deontology and justice being played out in this incident of gossip. However, ethical principles are variously applied in practice and across cultures (Robertson, Crittenden, Brady, & Hoffman, 2002). Judgements of consistency, similarity, and responsibility, for example, are subjective and likely to vary from one context to another. National cultures vary with regard to what is considered to be morally significant and how inequalities and power distance in the workplace are addressed (Ho, 2010; Hofstede et al., 2010). Furthermore, perceptions of organizational politics differ substantially across sectors, proving higher in the public sector than in the private sector. The reason for this Gotsis and Kortezi (2010) suggest, is that public sector employees are more likely to view their work environment as political in nature, and thus unfair and unjust.

There may be some dissonance between the need to lead and manage with political awareness and an individual's personal or professional standards of ethics and practice. This is the problem, or question, of 'dirty hands' (Provis, 2005, p. 283), which occurs when ethical and political obligations collide. In other words, is what is *ethically* the 'right thing to do' that which is *politically* the 'right thing to do?' The answer is not always yes, and it is more often a case of being 'damned if you do and damned if you don't.' Political awareness and skill involves, amongst many things, establishing and building relationships, and gossip plays an important role here. The following aggregate (created in order to protect confidentiality) from interviews with Clinical Nurse Specialists illustrates the dissonance between the ethics and politics:

> I'm not a good gossiper, I don't like it, but I do it [*why?*]. It helped with teamwork, I work in a multidisciplinary team and gossip helps to build social relationships and teamwork. I suppose it can be useful for trade-offs, I can tell you something if you can tell me something. So then on an individual basis you can use it as a power base as well. But I still don't like it [*say a bit more?*]. When I started in this role it was quite a distressing element, I take my job very seriously, and other people's gossip was detrimental and hurtful. It's to do with my Christian beliefs that it's wrong to talk about people behind their back. But it can also give you status in the hierarchy if you've got gossip attached to you, but it depends on what the gossip is about, obviously. (Composite data extract from interviews with CNSs)

These participants understood the dynamics of professional power and organizational politics, and saw gossip as a 'necessary evil' which promoted effective collaborative interprofessional relationships and team work.

Because gossip is evaluative talk, value judgments may be made about the content or practice of gossip during the process of establishing and building relationships. This is not to suggest that the content is unimportant, but rather that the topics of gossip are not the primary objective of the talk between the gossiper and listener/respondent (Michelson et al., 2010).

It is not just perceptions of organizational politics which differ across sectors. Perceptions about the role and importance of ethics in the workplace also differ across public and private sector organizations, although this is an under-researched area (Svensson, Wood, & Callaghan, 2010). A recent survey of British employees indicated that public sector workers were notably more aware of misconduct in their organizations than private sector workers (Webley & Werner, 2009). In the UK, a higher proportion of public sector organizations had ethics programmes in place than in the private sector. Conversely, in Sweden, although codes of ethics are developing in across private *and* public sector organizations, and being recognized and acted on at an organizational level, this was found to a lesser extent in the public sector (Svensson et al., 2010).

Problematically, the existence of an ethical code of practice does not necessarily ensure ethical behaviour by employees, nor does it guarantee an ethical corporate culture. Having an ethical code does not necessarily equate to the enactment of everyday ethics in practice. In order to address this problem and promote a more positive side of politics in the workplace, some commentators argue for adoption of a virtue ethics approach (Arjoon, 2008; Gotsis & Kortezi, 2010; Hartman, 2008; Robertson et al., 2002). This also calls for what Buchanan and Badham (2008, p. 102) refer to as 'a situational ethics, in which rules and principles inform our decisions and actions, but where our judgement also takes other factors into consideration, including context, warrants, accounts, and reputations.'

Virtue Ethics

Virtue ethics, which is based on an Aristotelian approach which favours virtue and character over principles, consists of ethical positions which emphasize the cultivation of virtuous individual character traits (Hartman, 2008). The notion of character includes virtues, vices, values, emotions, and actions. Aristotle also distinguishes between intellectual (acquired through education) and moral (developed through practice) virtues. The former include *sophia* (theoretical wisdom), *episteme* (science), *nous* (intuitive understanding), *phronesis* (practical wisdom or judgement), and craft expertise. The latter—moral virtues—include justice, temperance and fortitude, representing primary modes by which individuals approach a 'human good as discerned by practical wisdom' (Arjoon, 2008, p. 226).

Critics of virtue ethics have argued that the notion of stable or enduring character traits has been disputed by social psychologists, who point to situational determinants of behaviour. There have also been historical challenges which revealed a 'string of theoretical failures' (Walker & Ivanhoe, 2009, p. 7). Nevertheless, virtue ethics is re-emerging in the field of contemporary ethics and organization studies as a form of practical ethics. Arjoon (2008), for example, argues that both situational/organizational and inner characteristics/virtues are powerful influences upon moral and ethical behaviour. Virtue ethics provides a resource for moral thinking, and some commentators regard it as superior to rule theories for the practice of ethics in business and other settings (Audi, 2012). Virtue ethics is an agent- (rather than action-)based approach. As such it may be regarded as 'transcending the dichotomy between utilitarianism and deontology because it acknowledges that in the real world, agents are concerned with both consequences and duties, but subject to social relations and context' (Gotsis & Kortezi, 2010, p. 506, citing Van Staveren, 2007).

Virtue ethics also has a place in the growing field of 'positive organizational scholarship' (POS) which emphasizes the need for more focused theory building, research, and effective application of positive traits, states, and behaviours of employees in organizations (e.g., Bakker & Schaufeli, 2008; Caza & Caza, 2008). Gotsis and Kurtezi (2010) have also argued that positive political behaviour can be grounded in a virtue ethics framework based on shared power, inclusivity, connectedness, participation, excellence, and an encompassing value system. However, before we get carried away by a wave of virtuous positivity, we need to remind ourselves that virtue ethics is still a normative ethical approach. The long line of increasingly significant business scandals and institutional failures over the past four decades has led Brenkert (2010) to conclude that normative business ethics arguments lack power, persuasiveness, and effectiveness:

> [Because] we lack an account of business organizations as they develop and change both individually and systemically within these conditions. We need to focus new efforts (as some have been doing) on understanding businesses, not simply as economic organizations, but also as social and political organizations themselves that change over time. (p. 708)

The following extract from a telephone interview (following up on data gathered using diary methods) illustrates the role of gossip in change:

KW: In your experience, how does organizational uncertainty and change impact upon gossip?

Most certainly yes—most gossip where I work is as a result of high levels of uncertainly and change, which causes people to behave in a particular way which then triggers gossip [*meaning?*] That the people who respond in a particularly irrational way get gossiped about, while others gossip because they want to find out more about how the change will affect them personally. The way change is communicated like email or letters act as a trigger. Letters, emails or the information in them prompt people to pick up the phone and say 'my God, now look what they've done/ said/ want us to do.' (Jo [pseudonym], Community Mental Health Practitioner)

I have argued elsewhere (Waddington & Michelson, 2007) that paying closer attention to gossip in and about organizations through research and reflective practice yields fresh understandings of organizations as they undergo change. Analysis of gossip provides insight into power relationships, political actions, reactions to change and communication flows. The final part of the chapter now attempts to draw these elements together using McPhee and Zaug's (2000; 2009) communication flows of 'organizational self-structuring' and 'activity coordination.'

ORGANIZATIONAL SELF-STRUCTURING AND ACTIVITY COORDINATION

As in Chapter 5, the flows are synthesized, and used as an organizing framework to re-describe, re-present, interrogate and vary empirical material within the overall theme of this chapter. Empirical material from participants working in different organizations provides indicative examples of potential relationships and interactions between gossip and communication flows, which could inform future case study research. *Organizational self-structuring* asks the question 'What rules do we operate by?' It refers to 'official' documents such as organization charts, policy and strategy documents, processes of employee evaluation and feedback and 'the more casual announcements that often substitute for them' (McPhee & Zaug, 2009, p. 36). As we have seen in the data extract from Jo which concluded the last section, such documents can become 'triggers for gossip.' For example, Jo went on to say:

Oh the wording—if it's aggressive or dismissive—it provokes verbal comments about the management which can be inflammatory. And then we were given three volumes of rules and regulations about child protection and you just think 'please! Can't I just get on with my work?'

Another participant referred to the dissonance between what was espoused as organizational values, and what was experienced in practice in a diary incident of gossip.

INCIDENT 6: HUMAN RESOURCES HYPOCRISY

Q1. Why did you choose this particular incident?

My work situation is proving very stressful to my team members and myself. My manager has empathy and supports me and shared some of my frustration about a post being re-graded [to a more senior grade]. Trust policy is supposed to encourage retention of staff, but I can't retain people once their post has changed. It seems hypocritical to preach and encourage personal and service development, and not feel supported to retain staff.

Q2: How did you feel at the time?

Irritated, cross, frustrated that HR didn't seem to understand the complexity of the post and that it was a crucial part of the team. I am aware my service is often held up as a model for personal/service development/skill mix, and I felt let down.

Q3: Where, when, and who was involved?

Staff room of Trust Headquarters after a business meeting. My line manager (who shares my philosophy of learning and developing, investing in staff and trying to practice the Trust's 'learning organization' philosophy and culture).

Q4: Briefly describe the nature of the gossip*

About the HR department and having to rewrite the job description twice.

*Note that in order to protect the confidentiality of absent third parties, the structured diary records had explicit instructions for participants to record salient points only, and not to refer to individuals by name.

Other participants' diary records contained incidents of gossip that were triggered by emotional responses to formal communication or requests for information, for example:

> When I was first asked for this information I felt quite overwhelmed at having to collect what was required in such a short time span, as well as carrying on with routine work. The feeling of being overwhelmed turned to frustration and anger at having to rearrange my schedule in order to collect the information required, which ultimately meant more work had to be undertaken during the evening to redress the balance. The information requested was data for a workload analysis. (Nancy [pseudonym], Lecturer)

These data extracts illustrate the murmurs of discontent which characterize reaction and resistance to formal rules, roles and organizational policies and procedures. They also provide examples of the 'background talk' occurring in 'unmanaged spaces' through which resistance to formal organization is organized. These examples illustrate how organizational structuring and control activities act as breeding grounds for gossip.

Activity coordination asks the question 'What work are we doing together?' At one level, gossip can simply serve to help people to get to know each other in order to work better together:

> Well, I've been working with X for the last year and a half, and it's been hard to get to know them because they just don't gossip. And then they did. And it was a relief, and it made me feel I know them better, from just, it wasn't malicious, just a couple of odd lines, but I was relieved, I know them better and our working relationship is better. (CNS 10)

Beyond the level of interpersonal working relationships, the communication flow of 'activity coordination' is very pertinent to power and politics because 'members can coordinate on how *not to do work*, or coordination may be in abeyance as members seek *power over one another* or external advantage for themselves from the system' (McPhee & Zaug, 2009, p. 39, emphasis added). The power of gossip lies in its potentially destructive and damaging impact on people's reputations and self esteem. For example:

> Um, if I'm jealous of an individual, or what's happened to them personally, or to their department, if I'm jealous then I can portray that jealousy in quite a positive light, you know 'Have you heard?' You know 'Who did they have to get involved with to have that happen to them?' But [*pause*] if I was particularly angry with someone then it's easy to make up malicious gossip that's completely false, or take one very insignificant action or reaction of theirs and turn it into a big deal just in the way that I present it. (CNS 6)

The above interview extract illustrates a subtle manipulation of gossip which had a potentially powerful, adverse impact upon the target of gossip. This research participant was a Clinical Nurse Specialist who held a relatively powerful position in the professional and hospital hierarchy. People with relatively little position power, for example students, administrative and unqualified staff, were perceived to gossip more, and in a less subtle way, than managers. For instance:

> Gossip increases with the amount of change—people discuss change and speculate about change, but I think it's more the people who are most vulnerable to change who will gossip more. Nurses and doctors will always be able to find jobs and are often in a more powerful position than receptionists say. Receptionists will also often tell you salacious gossip, but they are usually last in a long line of power. (Margaret [pseudonym], Community Nurse Practitioner)

For groups who are relatively powerless, gossip can be used as an expression of power, expressed as '"hidden transcripts" of counter power' (Clegg & van Iterson, 2008, p. 280; Jones, D., 1980). Exercise of this type of power through gossip can also be interpreted as a form of sabotage, the hindering or slowing down of work, and also as an expression of resistance to change (Gabriel, 2000). Gossip represents 'unofficial' discourse, used as a means of expressing resistance to the dominant or 'official' discourses such as health service reform and organizational change. This exercise of power through socially constituted 'rules of practice' can both constrain activity coordination and also create collaborative working relationships. This was evident in the composite interview extract discussed earlier in this chapter, which illustrated dissonance between ethics and politics and gossip as a 'necessary evil.'

Gossip can be re-interpreted in relation to Foucauldian notions of the 'micropolitics' of everyday talk. The following interview extract illustrates some of the issues:

> I guess it's about everyone recognising there is a problem, about everybody feeling hard done by in some way, but nobody is prepared to take the bull by the horns, in a lot of cases. Yes we could all sit down and talk about it, but why is it that no one is speaking directly to that person, or going to their manager and saying we've identified a problem [*why?*] I guess no one wants to make trouble for anyone else . . . because in some respects it's just easier to get on with it . . . It's almost like if you know this person is like that, you build up a strategy around them, and it's easier if someone goes along with that strategy than be challenging them or being confrontational about it. (CNS 2)

'Micropolitics' relates to the choices people make in accepting, challenging or colluding with practices which maintain, rather than challenge the status quote. In the above data extract, gossip circulates around a perceived 'problematic' colleague as a collusive, dysfunctional strategy. The key point is that gossip is a potentially powerful influence in organizations, but the argument is complicated and paradoxical. As long as gossip exists in informal and unmanaged spaces, it serves to maintain the status quo. Yet in order to preserve (rather than conceptually cleanse) the nature of gossip, it must also remain in informal and unmanaged spaces. The four flows model and a CCO approach based more explicitly upon Foucault's work are useful resources for understanding the 'micropolitics' of gossip. Such approaches honour the elusive, ephemeral nature of gossip. Delineating more explicit links with power/knowledge also draws gossip away from functional analyses and narrow disciplinary domains. Additionally, the 'circuits of power' framework provides a demonstrably useful approach to understanding communication dynamics, and offers another resource for theorizing gossip (Clegg, 1989; Clegg & van Iterson, 2009; Hutchinson et al., 2010; van Iterson & Clegg, 2008).

In conclusion, this chapter has drawn together aspects of organizational politics, power, knowledge and ethics which contribute towards a framework for theorizing and understanding gossip and organizations. It has focused upon the dynamics of gossip and politics as power which is enacted and resisted, and which have both positive and negative aspects.

CONCLUDING REFLECTION

The chapter began with an anecdote, and ends with critical reflection upon toxic gossip, which is a manifestation of of the dark side of organizational politics and the power of gossip to harm.

REFLECTION 8: TOXIC GOSSIP—A SILENT KILLER?

Here I reflect upon CNS 6's experience (outlined earlier in the chapter) of being 'inadvertently *exposed* to gossip'. This evokes imagery of harmful toxic matter such as ionizing radiation or carbon monoxide. These environmental toxins are largely invisible—they are 'silent killers' which require specialized detectors. Metaphorically, gossip can be seen as 'toxic gas'—pun intended—as 'to gas' means to talk or chat (http://www.websters-online-dictionary.org). A gas is also a state of matter, consisting of a collection of particles without a definite shape or volume, which also reflects the elusive and ephemeral nature of organizational gossip and the problems of quantifying and measuring it. Taking the metaphor a bit further, carbon monoxide poisoning is caused by gas appliances and flues that have not been properly installed, maintained or that are poorly ventilated. Levels that do not kill can cause serious harm to health if breathed in over a long period. Organizations need carbon monoxide detectors to pick up early warning signs of danger ahead.

The following chapter takes these metaphorical reflections into the real world, where, amongst other things, case analyses of public inquiries illustrate the consequences of failing to detect the silent, or silenced, signals expressed as gossip.

7   The Management of Gossip

Where is the wisdom we have lost in the knowledge?
—T. S Eliot, *The Rock*, 1934

Much of the debate on gossip from a management and organizational perspective has been based on assumptions that gossip is detrimental to work productivity and employee morale. There is an associated assumption that managers must do something about 'the problem' of gossip. This chapter challenges these assumptions, and explores further the individual and organizational consequences of gossip, and the managerial interventions advanced to remedy 'the problem.' The chapter asks the question, 'What is *really* the problem?' Is it the activity, content and consequences of gossip, as some of the business and management literature would have us believe (e.g., Chapman with Sharkey, 2009). Such literature reflects a view of gossip as shallow, inconsequential or damaging organizational talk, which undoubtedly is the case in some instances. Therefore, any consideration of the meaning and management of gossip needs also to address gossip as communication which is constitutive of organizational violence and bullying.

However I also contend that gossip may also be constitutive of deeper, more far-reaching and disturbing organizational issues. In other words gossip represents the 'problem-behind-the-problem' (Henriksen & Dayton, 2006, p. 1550). Gossip may foreshadow a disaster, yet its importance and value as an early warning system often only becomes apparent in retrospective investigations into organizational disasters and failures of management and leadership. The Kerr / Haslam Inquiry (Department of Health [DH], 2005) into the handling of allegations about psychiatrists' performance and conduct in the UK is therefore used as a substantive case study in this chapter. Shorter case analyses of other inquiries and disasters are also included to illustrate theoretical relevance of this type of case material.

Theoretically, this chapter further considers sensemaking as a concept in the evolving theorizing framework for organizational gossip (Snowden, 2010; Weick, 1995a). Sensemaking is the final conceptual piece in the framework. In particular this chapter examines how sensemaking contributes to understanding the role of gossip in organizational disasters and failure. Finally, the chapter also considers the role of gossip *as* management, and how it might be used effectively as a form of organizational knowledge and thus promote team reflexivity. As in previous chapters, empirical material is included, not as unequivocal clear-cut data, but rather to support the arguments and theoretical claims being made. There are fewer data extracts in this chapter because the focus here is upon novel ways of thinking about using organizational sensemaking in the management of gossip. Chia's (2005) description of managing provides a useful starting point from which to expand the arguments advanced in the chapter:

> Managing is firstly and fundamentally the task of *becoming aware*, attending to, sorting out, and prioritising an inherently messy, fluxing chaotic world of competing demands that are placed on a manager's attention. It is creating order out of chaos. *It is an art, not a science.* Active perceptual organization and the *astute allocation of attention* is a central feature of the managerial task. (p. 1092, emphasis added)

The overarching intention in this chapter is to suggest a hypothetical new line to T. S. Eliot's poem *The Rock* (1934), and ask '*Where is the knowledge we have lost in the gossip?*'

MANAGING THE CONSEQUENCES OF GOSSIP

Gossip has been viewed as a form of 'social cement' holding individuals and organizations together, with noteworthy and contradictory consequences. For example, gossip allows employees to understand and predict their bosses' behaviour, yet can also be used to ruin the reputation of others, whereas the informal context encourages the development of social networks and relationships (Doyle, 2000; Emler, 1994). Gossip often (but not always) involves sharing negative stories and attitudes about others, and this can have positive consequences in that it promotes closeness and friendship (Bosson et al., 2006). Gossip provides a cathartic means of releasing anger and frustration for individuals and groups, which may be restorative and beneficial (Foster, 2004; Medini & Rosenberg, 1976; Waddington, 2005b). Gossip establishes in-group/out-group boundaries, boosts self-esteem, and is a source of information, influence and entertainment (Elias & Scotson, 1965; Gluckman, 1963; Fine & Rosnow, 1978; Soeters & van Iterson, 2002).

Michelson et al. (2010) provide a fuller analysis of the consequences of gossip than that considered here. Their analysis demonstrates important individual, social and organizational consequences. Individual and organizational outcomes may be simultaneously positive and negative, intended and unintended, inconsequential and significant. The management implications are complex, and raise a number of ethical questions. For example, what are the implications and consequences of not managing gossip? How should the positive consequences and benefits of gossip be managed and maintained? Is it possible to transform gossip into useful and actionable organizational knowledge and management information? This chapter attempts to answer these questions in order to advance some guiding principles and enable us to begin to differentiate sense from nonsense, and non-trivia from trivia.

As discussed above, and also in Chapters 2 and 3, managerially and historically there has been a tendency to cast gossip in a negative light. This concurs with the popular view of gossip as a typically destructive or mischievous social phenomenon and form of indirect aggression. When the consequences of organizational gossip are harmful, for example psychological injury and distress to citizens, damage to an individual's self-esteem or destruction of an organization's reputation, then clearly managerial action must be taken. In these circumstances, gossip may also be accompanied by unsubstantiated rumours, and on the one hand can be considered and managed as a form of workplace bullying and violence. On the other hand, and paradoxically, gossip and rumour may constitute prescient aspects of organizations that need to be surfaced and managed.

Gossip and Workplace Bullying

Workplace bullying has been defined differently by different stakeholders, and there are debates surrounding interpersonal and organizational levels, intentionality and subjective versus objective bullying (Einarsen, Hoel, Zapf, & Cooper, 2003). Bullying at work includes harassing, offending, and socially excluding someone; it is a gradual, often hidden, and intensely harming experience. Gossip and rumour represent just a small part of a wide spectrum of unacceptable behaviours related to the personal degradation of others, which are associated with physical and psychological ill health in their targets (Beswick, Gore, & Palferman, 2006). Empirically, this is illustrated in the following interview composite (presented in this way to protect participant confidentiality):

> I left my last job because I was the victim of gossip. There were big emotions there when I found out what people were saying about me, which was completely untrue. It was unnerving and upsetting. I really think that when someone tells you something about another person you should look at their [*the gossiper's*] origins, intentions and purpose and ask yourself why are they telling me this? (Composite data extract)

Hutchinson et al. (2010) employed a multidimensional model of bullying which importantly—given the discussion of gossip and power in the previous chapter—draws upon Clegg's (1989) 'circuits of power' framework. Their analysis of bullying in nursing in Australia revealed complex flows of power where networked relationships and informal alliances played a crucial role. Actors in the alliances were able to control obligatory passage points because of their knowledge and control over circuits of power. In

Hutchinson et al.'s study, this enabled individuals to influence meaning and day-to-day interactions and control work and resources, giving them *power over*. Empirically this was exemplified in my own research in the 'disclaimer' that one participant included at the beginning of their diary records.

> I don't generally approve of gossip as in my experience it is generally negative, and can, if not balanced by external sources, get out of control—i.e., one person's slightly different working practices or habits can be so reinforced in peoples' minds after successive gossip sessions amongst a small number of mostly senior staff that it can lead to victimization—trial without independent jury. (Sam [pseudonym], Clinical Lead)

The examples given thus far relate to bullying, gossip, and victimization in public sector healthcare organizations and nursing in Australia and the UK. The ethics and values of care and justice are central to this context, but they are frequently absent from day-to-day practice and experience. Psychological and sociological analyses of caring relationships reveal a darker side of uncaring and abuse (Roberts, 1994; Traynor, 1999). Practitioners are exposed as 'manipulative and/or oppressive characters, quick to make judgemental and moral evaluations of their patients, or as agents of a deterministic social or political system' (Fox, 1993, cited in Traynor, 1999, p. 154). Historically, nursing has a legacy of verbal abuse by colleagues; the problem is deep seated and has existed for many years. For example, one Clinical Nurse Specialist recalled stories and gossip from their student days:

> It could be quite terrifying really, hearing the stories 'she doesn't like it done that way' and I remember things like that when I was training, things were so terribly different then, I think there was more kind of negative gossip then, because it was to do with the relationships between the students and the senior nurses, nursing officers then, the harridans, and some of the stories that I heard were quite terrifying. (CNS 5)

They went on to reflect that professional relationships nursing have now changed with the advent of *'a new kind of modern breed of nurse, who you can call by their first name and have a much more positive relationship with.'* Yet I was asked the following question fairly recently by an American nurse in the UK on an educational visit. *'Do nurses in the UK eat their young like we do in the States?'* It was said lightheartedly; part of the small talk of breaking the ice and finding common ground. Nevertheless the question is illustrative of underlying passive-aggressive professional behaviours. For example Rowe and Sherlock (2005, p. 242) have asked 'do burned out nurses eat their young?' They argue that nurses who experience burnout are more likely to verbally abuse other nurses. Although these are quite professionally specific examples of verbal abuse and bullying in nursing and the public sector, there is no doubt that workplace bullying is a widespread global phenomenon (Bartlett & Bartlett, 2011). There are similarities and differences across cultures. For example, Escartín, Zapf, Arrieta, and Rodríguez-Carballeira's (2011) cross-cultural study found that employees in Central America placed greater emphasis on the physical components than their Southern European counterparts. However both Southern European and Central American employees defined workplace bullying as a hierarchical phenomenon, and Hutchinson et al. (2010) contend that *all institutions* are both a source and solution to workplace bullying.

As discussed in the previous chapter, the exercise of power through socially constituted rules and circuits has the potential to both negate and constrain, but also create and enable, more productive aspects of power (Clegg, 1989). Importantly however, drawing attention to power and ethics offers an insight into potential solutions to the problem of bullying. For example, managers might reconsider how resistance may be usefully employed 'as a legitimate strategy to uphold the ethics of care and justice in the workplace' (Hutchinson et al., 2010, p. 39, citing Thomas & Davies, 2005). The challenge is to find new ways of thinking about productive aspects of power in everyday organizational experience. This means finding new ways of thinking about gossip as a representation of wider issues of organizational concern which should be surfaced. This also means breaking the 'organizational silence'.

GOSSIP AND ORGANIZATIONAL SILENCE

Organizational silence refers to a 'collective-level phenomenon of saying or doing very little in response to significant problems that face an organization' (Henriksen & Dayton, 2006, p. 1539). Some of the thinking about organizational silence can be traced back to Hans Christian Anderson's story of *The Emperor's New Clothes* published in 1837. This is the well-known story about a vain Emperor who cares only about his appearance. He hires two weavers to produce a new suit of clothes from a fabric which they claim is invisible to anyone who is either unfit for their position or just plain stupid. Neither the Emperor nor his ministers can see the fabric, but they pretend they can. The weavers make a lot of money, given to them for materials they did not buy. When the suit is 'finished' the Emperor goes in procession before his subjects who also play along with the pretence. Suddenly a child cries out 'but he has nothing on,' and the cry is taken up by the crowd. The Emperor suspects that the child and the crowd are right but thinks 'I must go through with the procession.' So he holds his head higher and carries on (http://www.bartleby.com/17/3/3.html). The message, or moral, of this story is also found in the idiomatic expression 'the elephant in the room' which applies to an obvious truth, problem, or risk which is being ignored.

Janis's (1972) theory of 'groupthink' and Harvey's (1974) 'Abilene paradox' have classical theoretical relevance for understanding organizational silence. Briefly, groupthink refers to faulty decision making in highly cohesive groups which are under pressure to make a quality decision. Janis's theory of groupthink has been applied to decisions involving the Bay of Pigs invasion of Cuba and the space shuttle *Challenger* accident (Esser & Lindoerfer, 1989). The Abilene paradox on the other hand is explained as a story about a family who make a trip to Abilene in Texas, which none of them want to make, but none would admit to when the trip is suggested and planned.

In organizations the Abilene paradox refers to the dysfunction which occurs when individuals fail to communicate their true thoughts and knowledge. Time and resources are wasted on projects that 'everybody knows' are destined to fail. An example of the Abilene paradox is given by a respondent in Taylor S. et al.'s (2010) study of the political processes surrounding the development and demise of the NHS University (NHSU) (which was also discussed in the previous chapter). 'There'd been this big announcement, "they're going to have a university for the NHS" and policy advisors had not actually sat ministers down and said this doesn't fly' (Taylor, S. et al, 2010, p. 94). Leonard Cohen's lyrics also ring true here (*Everybody Knows*, Leonard Cohen/Sharon Robinson, 1988):

> Everybody knows that the boat is leaking
> Everybody knows that the captain lied

Rubin and Dierdorff (2011) have also used the Abilene paradox to explain curricular misalignment of MBA programmes:

> In this sense, MBA programs have adopted a form of *pluralistic ignorance* in which stakeholders seem to *privately agree* what competencies ought to be emphasized, but *fail to manage such agreement in practice*, inevitably maintaining the curricular misalignment that remains so persistent. (p.154, emphasis added)

The Abilene paradox therefore does not stem from the inability to manage conflict or disagreement, but rather from the inability to manage agreement. That which is unsaid and silent, or silenced, is therefore as, if not more, important to that which is communicated formally. Organizational silence spans a range of issues. 'Undiscussable' topics include concerns about management practices, conflicts and concerns with co-worker performance, bad news, and personal issues such as balancing work-family relationships and care responsibilities (McGowan, 2009; Milliken, Morrison, & Hewlin,

2003). Unsurprisingly, such topics re-emerge in other narrative forms such as stories which are 'ignored, silenced or missed by the hegemonic managerialist narrative' (Vickers, 2008, p. 560). Organizationally silent or silenced topics also appear in gossip, for example about colleagues who 'don't pull their weight,' poor practice, and managers who are perceived to be doing nothing about these issues (Waddington & Fletcher, 2005).

For individuals, reasons for remaining silent include the fear of being viewed or labelled negatively as a 'troublemaker' and damage to valued relationships (Milliken et al., 2003, p. 1463). For organizations, groupthink, organizational cultures that fail to understand the interdependencies of complex systems and 'microclimates of distrust' all contribute to the maintenance of organizational silence (Henriksen & Dayton, 2006, p. 1545). Morrison and Milliken's (2000) theoretically grounded model of organizational silence suggests three types of factors that can bring about a climate of silence. These are, organizational structures/policies, managerial practices, and the degree of demographic dissimilarity between employees and top managers. The key point to be made here, is that gossip may be a surface manifestation of underlying organizational problems. When viewed uncritically through a managerialist lens of gossip as problematic discourse and behaviour (which of course it sometimes is), concerns expressed as gossip will be unheard. That which is often widely known as and through gossip is often either silently accepted, or silenced, and yet gossip can provide important insights into what is really going on in organizations.

The next section draws upon material from a UK healthcare public inquiry to illustrate the complex aspects of gossip and organizational silence. It could be argued that there are issues relating to power and control, hierarchy, history, emotion, professional relationships and discourses which are irrelevant to other business or organizational contexts. To some extent, it is up to the reader to judge and decide whether or not this is the case. However I contend that there are also insights that can be elicited from this case analysis of organizational silence in healthcare settings that transcend organizational and professional boundaries and limits. For example, as noted in the Kerr / Haslam Inquiry into how the UK National Health Service (NHS) handled allegations about doctors' performance and conduct:

> Gossip and rumour can provide the background against which subsequent action or inaction can be considered and tested . . .The approach of an institution to such 'soft' information as gossip, rumour, innuendo, informal soundings, expressions of concern etc, may also be relevant to how the institution sees its responsibilities within society. (Department of Health [DH], 2005, p. 671)

The *Kerr / Haslam Inquiry Report* (DH, 2005) and other inquiry reports are under-utilized resources in the wider scholarship of organizational gossip. As we have seen, organization and management studies are themselves also relatively silent when it comes to the scholarship of organizational gossip. Inquiry reports into organizational failure and tragedy, sadly, provide a legitimizing point of reference with which to break the organizational silence around gossip in both practice and theory.

THE KERR / HASLAM INQUIRY

The Kerr / Haslam Inquiry is used here as an illustrative case of gossip, rumour, organizational and professional silence. The material used is taken from information available in the public domain at the UK Government's Department of Health (DH) website (http://www.dh.gov.uk). There are clearly many other complex factors at play in this particular case, such as whistle-blowing, tolerance of poor practice and sexualized behaviour, patient confidentiality, gendered professional/patient relationships, boundaries, and power in psychiatry. These are acknowledged, but not discussed in detail here, as the focus of this chapter is sensemaking the management of gossip. Rather, the intention is to draw out the *failures in the management of gossip* highlighted by the inquiry report for further discussion.

The Kerr / Haslam Inquiry is just one of a number of inquiries in the UK healthcare sector that have revealed that knowledge of poor and dangerous practice exists as informal professional talk. The rationale for choosing this inquiry over others, for example the *Kennedy Report* into the deaths of children at the Bristol Royal Infirmary (Kennedy, 2001), is that the latter has already been subject to academic scrutiny and analysis (e.g., Alaszewski, 2002; Weick, Sutcliffe, & Obstfeld, 2005). Whereas the Kerr / Haslam Inquiry has received professional scrutiny and analysis (e.g., Subotsky, 2010), this is the first substantive scholarly analysis. Notably, the lengthy inquiry report contains a chapter explicitly entitled 'Dealing with rumour: hearing the warning bells' (DH, 2005, pp. 668–683). In particular, this chapter in the inquiry report considered management of information which may be unreliable, exaggerated or simply wrong, but which may also be an indicator of concerns.

The report provides a disturbing, and some might say extreme, example of gossip and rumour that occurred in mental health services in the UK during the 1970s and 1980s. There are nevertheless some issues in the inquiry which have wider application to organization and management studies and practice. First, however, the key issues in the inquiry are identified to provide context.

Key Issues in the Kerr / Haslam Inquiry

The inquiry panel examined the response to complaints and concerns about two male consultant psychiatrists and the sexual abuse of female patients that took place over more than two decades. It was one of three inquiries initiated in 2001 by the UK Secretary of State for Health into how the NHS handled allegations about doctors' conduct. By the time the police investigations and this inquiry were completed, sixty-seven patients had declared themselves as victims of William Kerr and at least ten of Michael Haslam. Both psychiatrists worked in the same hospital in York, North Yorkshire, during the 1970s and 1980s. Kerr was deemed unfit to stand trial, and following a Trial of the Facts conducted in his absence in 2000, was convicted on one count of indecent assault. In 2003 Haslam was convicted of four counts of indecent assault on patients, and given a three-year prison sentence. A conviction of rape was later quashed on appeal, and Haslam has consistently denied any form of wrongdoing in relation to his patients (DH, 2005; Haslam, M., 2006). The inquiry, which began in September 2002, and reported in July 2005, at a cost of £3.2 million, addressed the following central questions:

- How could it be that the voices of the patients and former patients of William Kerr and Michael Haslam were not heard?
- Why were so many opportunities to respond and investigate missed?
- How could it happen that the abuse of patients, evidenced by the convictions of William Kerr and Michael Haslam, went undetected for so long?

The report reveals that within the local general practitioner (GP) communities there was widespread belief, circulating as gossip and rumour, that something was seriously wrong with the practices of the two consultants. Box 7.1 illustrates a typical example of rumour and gossip evidence received by the inquiry.

Box 7.1   Rumour and gossip evidence in the Kerr / Haslam Inquiry
(DH, 2005, p. 668)

A GP hears from a colleague that a consultant to whom the GP refers has a reputation for having sexual relations with his patients—a rumour, just gossip. The GP. does nothing with that information—why should he/she do anything? A patient of the GP then discloses to the GP that she is having a sexual relationship with that consultant, or he has propositioned her, or the consultant has behaved improperly towards her, or he has even sexually assaulted her. What was merely gossip and rumour for the GP is now apparently supported by the account of the patient. The GP, otherwise reluctant to take the patient's disclosure seriously (for whatever reason) may then react completely differently, and proceed on the basis that that patient may be, even probably is, telling the truth.

GPs reported that their expressions of concern and complaints were met with silence, and a culture that such matters should not be raised:

> It was other meetings where I raised the issue . . ., always preserving confidentiality, but asking if other people had picked up any whispers or ideas. It just felt like there was a brick wall . . . It was very much silence from the other end of the phone when I was trying to go through what I felt I must act on. (DH, 2005, p. 334)

The inquiry report notes that organizational gossip and rumour exists, and that in social or professional organizations it 'may have some value' (p. 668), but must always be treated with caution. It is clearly dangerous and unfair to base decisions and actions upon such a fragile and unsupported basis. Gossip and rumour may be inaccurate, untrue and may have originated from a malicious or jealous source. However the inquiry report also notes contradictorily—but such is the paradox of gossip—that it would also be naïve to proceed on the basis that gossip and rumour are irrelevant. The panel therefore undertook extensive consideration of the importance of rumour and gossip, and local NHS organizations were keen to receive guidance as to when gossip and rumour should be acted upon. The conclusion was that this very much depends upon the subject matter of the gossip, the prevalence, and source of the gossip.

The panel also concluded that where there are issues concerning patient safety, or where the rumour and gossip is of sufficient intensity that comes to the attention of managers there must always be some response and investigation. If there is no truth in the gossip or rumour, then the investigation will be inconsequential, but better to be safe than sorry. On the other hand if the gossip and rumour reveals an underlying problem and further investigation may produce more information. This is an example of gossip as 'soft' information being used as an indicator for further inquiry and development of professional/organizational knowledge. A total of thirty-four root causes of the comprehensive failure to attend to patient concerns were identified. Table 7.1 is a partial summary of factors which contributed to the failure to heed warning signs of failure and impeded appropriate investigation and action.

As a result of this, and other NHS inquiries such as *The Mid Staffordshire NHS Foundation Trust Inquiry* (2010), there have been significant changes to complaints systems, governance techniques and reporting mechanisms in the NHS. Working practices are now very different, but gossip and rumour remain, and more work needs to be done:

> In answer to the question—when should rumour etcetera, be acted upon, and in what form should that action be taken—*we can only invite further research* into the fine tuning of the content of the of the positive obligation to inform NHS management of areas of concern. (DH, 2005, p. 683, emphasis added)

Table 7.1   Factors Contributing to Failure to Heed Warning Signs of Failure
(adapted from DH, 2005, pp. 14-16)

Organizational

Power and influence of defensive legal advice

Several changes of NHS hospital and management structures

Cultural

Consultants had undue power and unclear accountability

No attempt to investigate/explore recurring rumours

Structural

Consensus management, which militated against leadership and pro-activity

A management hierarchy for each function within the NHS with no overview of the whole

Professional Practice

Absence of multi-disciplinary working

A belief that doctors could not harm patients—and a reluctance to discuss what was and what was not unacceptable behaviours

Individual Failings

Hospital doctors and GPs who did not act on concerns

Nursing staff who failed to report patient concerns and ignored patient concerns

NHS managers who neglected to take action, took a line of least resistance and failed to investigate expressed concerns

This particular inquiry may have extraordinarily vivid features regarding sexual abuse of vulnerable women at a particular time in the history of psychiatry in the UK. However it is also a real-world case of management failure, communication failure, and organizational silence. It highlights a significant gap between formal management knowledge and informal professional knowledge circulating as gossip and rumour. It is a case that highlights the value and importance to organizations of listening, and responding *appropriately* to, gossip and rumour, rather than adopting a blanket 'do not gossip' management approach. There are clearly times when such gossip and rumour will be unreliable, exaggerated, or just plain wrong. However gossip and rumour are also alarm bells and indicators of important underlying concerns that managers and their organizations need to attend to and address.

THEORETICAL INSIGHTS FROM OTHER INQUIRIES

When gossip and rumour are seen from individual and group levels of analysis, wider dynamics and processes, such as organizational power may be obscured or ignored. For example, DiFonzo and Bordia (2007)

contend that rumours help people make sense of the world at the level of individual cognition and through interacting with others. Their theoretical position is set within the context of social psychological processes of explanation, attribution, illusory associations and relationships. van Iterson and Clegg (2008) extended these perspectives by focussing on *inter-organizational* gossip which spreads fact-based rumour, in terms of their shifting role in circuits of power. They use the Cole Inquiry into the conduct of the Australian Wheat Board and UN Resolution 661 as a case study of dissonance between officially formulated accounts, and rumoured gossip. Key aspects of the Cole Inquiry case are summarized in Box 7.2.

Theoretically, van Iterson and Clegg (2008, p. 1118) differentiate between 'formulation' and 'gloss' (citing Garfinkel, 1967). 'Formulations' are statements officially released as organizationally legitimate messages, whereas 'glosses,' such as gossip and rumour, are not officially formulated and not organizationally legitimated. In the case of the Cole Inquiry, rumoured gossip, circulating in faxes and e-mails which were never *formally* acknowledged, was assembled and seen as a non-issue. However, once gossip was reassembled into legal circuits of power outside the arena of governmental administrative power, its status as an issue or non-issue came into sharper focus. As van Iterson and Clegg (2008, p. 1121) comment more generally:

> Whether 'true' or 'false,' rumoured gossip can enhance organizations' value markedly (Pixley, 2004) or make them bankrupt—witness the recent UK case of the run on the Northern Rock bank, which only stopped when the bank's debts were effectively assumed by the government. Once scaled up to the organizational level—especially when its rumours have bottomline implications—gossip becomes an acute currency in the politics of organizations.

Case studies of public inquiries provide a rich seam of empirical material in the public domain, providing immeasurable detail with which to develop further theorizing of organizational gossip. They expose gaps between formal and informal knowledge, demonstrate the role of gossip and rumour as warning signals, and identify systemic factors which collude in the maintenance of organizational silence. The Cole Inquiry highlighted the politics of gossip and the spread of fact based rumours as one of inter-organizational power relations flowing through circuits of formulation and gloss. The issues raised in this inquiry have wider application and relevance concerning power, responsibility, choices and actions. The next section extends the theme of organizational failure and disaster, drawing attention to sensemaking and psychoanalytic thinking as practical and theoretical resources for better understanding organizational gossip.

Box 7.2   Key aspects of the Cole Inquiry (van Iterson & Clegg, 2008)

In particular, we looked at the sanctions imposed on Saddam Hussein's Iraq that were authorized under the United Nations Security Council Resolution 661 passed on 6 August 1990. The sanctions were designed to save the lives of many children and other vulnerable Iraqi citizens by using a UN escrow account for the purpose of providing food and medicines (p. 1119).

A Royal Commission of Inquiry, known as the Cole Inquiry (after the name of the Commissioner, Mr Terence Cole), was established into allegations about the role of certain Australian companies into what became known as the Oil-for-Food case. The Royal Commission's public hearings began in mid-January 2006 and continued through to the end of September that year. Transcripts of the entire proceedings, from December 2005 to September 2006, are posted on an official government website [http://www.offi.gov.au/agd/WWW/unoilfor-foodinquiry.nsf/Page/Transcripts]. The authors followed the case day by day, reading and listening to the media reports and cross-checking the transcripts as they were posted (p. 1122).

SENSEMAKING AND THEORIZING GOSSIP

Sensemaking is an important theorizing concept for understanding gossip as communication which is constitutive of organization (CCO). A CCO approach to sensemaking views organizations as emerging in, and constituted by, local episodes of communication (Cooren et al., 2011). To some extent gossip and sensemaking go hand in hand, and one of my intentions is to take sensemaking into new and novel contexts (see Sutcliffe, Brown, & Putnam, 2006). Another intention is to use sensemaking as a device for thinking about gossip in novel ways, as a means of realizing different forms of organizational knowledge and management information. This involves thinking about gossip as information with potential for transformation into useful and actionable organizational knowledge, rather than clinging on to stereotypes of gossip as trivial pejorative talk. This is not to say however, that gossip as pejorative talk does not exist and does not need to be managed, as illustrated in the earlier discussion in this chapter regarding bullying and victimization. The challenge lies in finding ethical and responsible ways to detect, discern and differentiate good, bad and toxic gossip. Organizational sensemaking provides one way of responding to this challenge.

The concept of sensemaking is most usually associated with Weick (1995a), and classically defined as 'placement of items into frameworks, comprehending, redressing surprise, constructing meaning, interacting in pursuit of mutual understanding, and patterning' (p. 6). In Chapter 5, I introduced Snowden's (2010; Kurtz & Snowden, 2007) naturalistic sensemaking paradigm and epistemology, which draws upon the natural sciences. In a naturalistic paradigm, 'the term *sensemaking* is used to emphasize that we are talking about a diverse and constantly evolving collection of processes that synthesize human and machine capabilities' (Snowden, 2010, p. 224, original emphasis). The processual aspects of sensemaking and its constituent components provide useful theoretical grounds for gossip-related research and theorizing (Michelson et al., 2010; Mills, 2010; Waddington, 2005a). It is pertinent to note, especially with regard to the case studies of public inquiries discussed above, that a core component of sensemaking for both Snowden and Weick is a preoccupation with failure rather than success (see also Snowden & Boone, 2007). When things appear to be running smoothly, leaders may become complacent, and if the context changes they may miss what is going on 'under their noses'. Success may be such an emotional and fulfilling experience that it can lead to hubris, which if left unchecked can in itself lead to failure (Weick & Sutcliffe, 2007).

Stein's (2003) analysis of the near collapse of the hedge fund Long Term Capital Management (LTCM) in 1998 focuses on the way in which LTCM developed a highly exaggerated, idealized view of itself. Drawing upon the psychoanalytic concept of organizational narcissism, Stein notes that the media (e.g., *The Economist* and the *Financial Times*) and the President of the Federal Reserve Bank both used the term 'hubris' to describe LTCM. Hubris, alongside omnipotence, omniscience, dismissiveness, and triumphant contempt are aspects of narcissistic organizations. Stein (2003) contends that the presence of organizational narcissism within LTCM allowed, and indeed facilitated, the incubation of the impending disaster facing the hedge fund.

The incubation period of disasters refers to the often lengthy time, lasting from months to decades, during which problems are known about but not acted upon (Borodzicz, 2005; Stein, 2003, 2004). The incubation period of disasters is also a time when gossip circulates and may be a valuable early warning indicator of 'storms ahead.' But this is not always the case, and individual and organizational denial is such that the signals are often ignored. The blind eye and the deaf ear prevail (Gabriel, 1999; Obholzer, 2005). Gabriel and Schwartz's (1999) psychoanalytically informed analysis of the NASA *Challenger* accident in 1986 describes how NASA officials failed to recognize numerous warning signs. The officials appeared blind to the failures, and blind to the fact that the agency was preventing and, thus silencing, staff from expressing legitimate concerns. Gabriel and Schwartz's analysis concludes that NASA officials kept themselves from knowing; they deceived themselves because it was too painful to acknowledge that the organization they loved and cared for was fallible.

Preoccupation with failure in sensemaking entails watching for early warning signals, looking for small signs of larger problems, and involves collecting, synthesizing and using information from a range of sources. Our interest now lies in a closer examination of the process/es involved in transforming gossip from its status and position of raw, unreliable information, to usable knowledge. However, unless it is noticed and heard, such gossip-as-knowledge remains locked in unmanaged spaces, part of the comfort trap of organizational and managerial ignorance and silence. Problems and concerns, talked about as gossip, can go unnoticed and unreported for a long time. This is maybe because if practitioners and managers know too much, they will have to take action. Action involves confronting discomforting knowledge, taking responsibility and dealing with the difficult issues that lie beneath and behind the problem of gossip.

Chapter 2 marked the conceptual repositioning of gossip as constitutive of organizational communication and knowledge. It is through the processes of *telling and attending to* gossip that we can begin to address the practical question of how organizational knowledges and ways of knowing emerge in practice. Tsoukas's (2005) position on this is quoted at length, as it is central to my thesis:

> However, in a social context, the crucial feature of tacit knowledge is that it provides the *unarticulated background*—a set of evaluative distinctions—of what is taken for granted, which is a necessary prerequisite for action. Such an unarticulated background is learned through actors' participation into a social practice, a form of life, and that is why the locus of an actor's tacit knowledge is not in his/her head but in the practice he/she is a member of. At both the individual and collective levels of analysis, tacit knowledge is the process of instrumentalizing experiences—the lapse into unawareness of the manner in which tools, be they physical and/or intellectual are used (Polanyi, 1962, 59–65). *There is no conversion of tacit knowledge to explicit, but of a shift of attention from focal awareness to subsidiary awareness.* (p. 615, emphasis added)

A shift of attention from focal awareness to subsidiary awareness links back to the figure-ground visual metaphor introduced in Chapter 2. Here, I am arguing for a metaphorical reversal of figure-ground, in other words attending to the 'background noise' of gossip. This involves the process of noticing, which is the means by which cues for sensemaking are extracted, and includes the activities of filtering, classifying and comparing (Starbuck & Milliken, 1988, cited in Weick, 1995a). And as Weick (1995a) additionally notes 'we need also need to pay attention to ways people notice, extract cues, and *embellish* that which they extract' (p. 49, emphasis added). The relationship between Weick's position and gossip is aptly illustrated by the following interview extract:

> I think you get triangulation of gossip to check accuracy [*KW:* meaning?] It's the verification of tittle-tattle, versus the embellishment of story. If I hear the same piece of information from different sources, I think it is more likely to be accurate. (A Director of Nursing)

This is precisely what happened in the Kerr / Haslam Inquiry; professional gossip was verified when women raised and concerns with their GPs. What is crucial to a sensemaking perspective and gossip is the *action* that follows the noticing. Thus, the advantage of embedding a sensemaking perspective lies in its practical commitment to *noticing, thinking,* and *action.* It enables us to think about gossip as a communicative process of realizing practice-based knowledge, rather than simply as a problem to be managed.

Notably, Mills's (2010) examination of gossip and sensemaking as part of in a wider context of change-related communication yielded insights which suggest that gossip is experienced as coupled to, or embedded in, other forms of change communication. Findings from Mills's study support the arguments advanced in this chapter:

> For the manager, the findings suggest gossip should not be condemned, controlled, or eliminated but appreciated as a social process that needs to be understood and strategized in the same way as other legitimate organizational processes. The challenge is to find ways to be aware of the gossip that is occurring so that its nature and consequences can be assessed. (Mills, 2010, p. 235)

Mills's work marks an important landmark in the scholarship of gossip and a transition point for future research and theorizing. It contributes to a shift in attention away from thinking of gossip as a 'problem' to be managed, ignored or silenced. It underscores the relevance of sensemaking and importance of understanding gossip related data as situated in the context in which they are created. Gossip does not occur in isolation, and the boundaries between formal and informal communication, gossip and rumour are blurred. Collective sensemaking takes place in interactive talk and gossip can be re-presented as 'moments of sensemaking.' The task for organizational scholars is to 'stretch those moments, scrutinize them, and name them in the belief that they affect how action gets routinized, flux gets tamed, objects get enacted, and precedents get set' (Weick et al., 2005, p. 419).

MANAGING WITH GOSSIP

Finally, the role of gossip *as* management is addressed, alongside consideration of how it might be used to promote team reflexivity. Some managers use gossip proactively in the way they manage their departments/services and organizational change. For example:

> Gossip can be a good early warning system, especially if you're looking at implementing change. You're not going to please everyone with change—some will be very vocal, but maybe not to you, and then you'll find out about it through a certain number of people and you'll know what to expect. (A Clinical Services Manager)

Returning to Chia's definition of managing introduced at the beginning of this chapter, this clinical services manager demonstrates *awareness* of the value of gossip as a change management strategy and early warning system. They also appear to actively use gossip as a form of management information, acknowledging the need to use a third party as the collector and 'messenger of gossip.' Use of a third party demonstrates astuteness in their judgement and awareness of the responsibilities of their role and position in the organization. The above data extract points to the need for the *'triangulation of gossip'* identified earlier by the participant who made the distinction between *'verification of tittle-tattle, versus the embellishment of story.'* This can be achieved by cross checking information (seen/heard as gossip) with other sources in order to enhance accuracy and potentially transform 'raw' gossip into useable, contextual and actionable working knowledge.

The above selective case analyses of organizational failures and public inquiries show that managers and organizations facing potential disasters tend to adopt three dysfunctional responses:

1. Disregarding warning signs of danger because they are expressed as gossip and rumour;
2. Dismissing the gossip as defeatist or cynical talk; or
3. Constructing defensive, dysfunctional systems and structures to keep the potential disaster (and gossip) at bay.

These are dangerous and risky strategies. As Tourish and Robson (2006) warn, the consequence is that when managers fail to notice, ignore, suppress or scorn warning signals from their internal or external environments, they end up effectively driving through a red light. On the other hand, organizations may develop and implement policies and procedures to try and reduce or eliminate damaging, negative gossip. These are necessary to deal with bullying, protect individuals, and are to some extent examples of good ethical practice. Organizations may also develop good communication strategies, and effective formal communication methods, potentially reducing the need for gossip *about* the organization. However this does not necessarily stop gossip; it merely tends to shift the topic from organizational issues to individual issues or drives the gossip further underground into deeper unmanaged spaces (Waddington, 2005b; Waddington & Fletcher, 2005).

However, as dicussed in the previous chapter, possession of ethical or communication codes of practice and strategies does not guarantee that they will be enacted. The case example of the University of Arbitrary County in Chapter 5 also illustrated disengagement of employees with organizational strategies. Furthermore, communication strategies, policies and action plans in particular tend to be 'iatrogenic' in nature

(Tourish & Robson, 2006, p. 723). In other words, managers are likely to deal with organizational problems arising from previous management interventions which were optimistically intended to have a beneficial effect. The real issue is to understand how the amount, content and consequences of gossip are indicators of the health of an organization (Nicholson, 2001). This could be achieved by using the concept of reflexive gossip (introduced in Chapter 3) as a tool for developing team reflexivity.

Reflexive Gossip

I define reflexive gossip as mindful attention to evaluative talk in and about organizations that is spoken, written or visual. Weick and Putnam (2006, p. 280) cite Langer's (2000) description of mindfulness as 'a flexible state of mind in which we are actively engaged in the present, noticing new things and sensitive to context.' Being mindful involves having a greater sensitivity to one's environment and openness to new information; it is also about creating new categories for structuring perception, and an enhanced awareness of multiple perspectives in problem solving.

Mindfulness is important for the management of gossip for two reasons. First, it draws attention to the crucial elements of awareness, judgement, choice, and action. Second, because its opposite, 'mindlessness,' implies rigidity of thinking and lack of awareness which can create the conditions where warning signs of failure and disaster go unheard. In advancing the concepts of mindful attention and reflexive gossip the ubiquitous question 'What's the gossip?' can be stretched to '*What's the gossip, what is it saying about the organization and now what should we do?*' This brings meaning and sensemaking into play, and even if the answer is that nothing needs to be done, the decision to do nothing becomes an informed and ethical one.

The concept of reflexive gossip can also be used to enhance team reflexivity, which is the extent to which teams reflect upon, and communicate about, their objectives, strategies and processes, and adapt them to current or anticipated circumstances (West, 2000).Teams could focus on such questions as:

- How much gossip has come to our attention recently?
- What are the underlying issues, gaps and themes?
- What is the mix of good, bad and toxic gossip?
- Do we need to take any action?

Questions such as these call for a shift in attention, away from silencing to noticing and listening. I have noticed that even just mentioning in passing conversation that I am researching or writing about gossip seems to provide a *catalyst* for individuals to talk and think about gossip in their own organizations and work settings in different ways. For example, a senior nurse commented, *'now, when my boss says 'you seem to spend a lot of time gossiping' I say 'I'm not gossiping I'm listening'—and I pick up a lot more issues and concerns this way.'* This is about changing the conversations that we have about gossip, and changing gossip into useable knowledge. It is what Ayim (1994, p. 87) terms 'investigative gossip,' referring to gossip's role in *eliciting*, rather than imparting or applying, information.

As the empirical materials presented in this book have demonstrated, gossip is deeply embedded in healthcare organizations. The organizational knowledge in question from this practice perspective 'emerges through experience, interpersonal relationships, conversations, and collaborative routines employed by these individuals as they struggle to cope with a turbulent organizational environment' (Murphy & Eisenberg, 2011, p. 266). Reflexive gossip also has the potential to reduce the gap between management knowledge and practitioner knowledge that so often foreshadows organizational failure and disaster. Finally, working with the concept of reflexive gossip as a form of 'investigative gossip' is a means of transforming gossip as 'soft' information into knowledge. In Reflection 9, I use the metaphorical concept of 'organizational alchemy' as one way of working towards achieving this transformation.

REFLECTION 9: GOSSIP AND ORGANIZATIONAL ALCHEMY

This reflection was inspired after a visit to an art gallery where Swiss artists Peter Fischli and David Weiss's film *The Way Things Go* (1987)was on display. The film shows a collection of everyday objects such as car tyres, chairs, rubbish bags, soap and petrol which are set off in a chain reaction with fire and fireworks. The point in this piece is that Fischli and Weiss remove things that surround us from their contexts in our daily lives, and then restructure their relationships to one another. Their aim is neither to glorify nor to alienate these common objects, but merely to create new references in which they might be considered. (http://icarusfilms.com/cat97/t-z/the_way_.html)

The Way Things Go got me thinking about alchemy, the medieval science and philosophical doctrine that sought to transform commonly found base metal such as iron or copper into gold. Metaphorically, organizational alchemy is the transformation of something commonly found—gossip—into something of value—knowledge. For alchemists, transformation was a process involving the interaction of elements within a closed, transparent container and heat. Its essence was the creation of potentially dangerous and destructive energies, but which could be used in a transformative way. Gossip surrounds us in our everday lives, it is social and shared with others and reactive—both in response to external events, and also as a catalyst to realize new insights and knowledge.

CONCLUSION

Ultimately, what are managers and leaders to do with gossip? They need to be able to work with the paradox of gossip articulated in this chapter. That is, gossip is both a hazardous and dangerous substance with the potential to harm, and also potentially useful practice-based knowledge that can warn of imminent danger. It is also potentially useful practice-based knowledge that can warn of imminent danger. Gossip is a slippery subject, and resistant to management control. Therefore, the following guiding principles are offered to help us differentiate sense from nonsense and non-trivia from trivia:

- Understand that gossip is potentially valuable and useable 'soft' information;
- Question information communicated as gossip and look for other sources for verification/refutation;
- Look out for emergent 'gossip-as-knowledge' arising in collaborative sensemaking conversations;
- Remember that the decision to gossip, or not, is always an ethical decision;
- Reflect upon what the content and emotions contained in gossip reveal about underlying organizational problems and issues.

This chapter was about the management of gossip and gossip as management. Kurtz and Snowden (2007, citing Williams, 1983) remind us that the English verb 'to manage' derived from the Italian *maneggiare*, meaning to to handle and train horses. This early meaning emphasized *learning with, abiding with, adapting to, respecting and working with another complex entity*. Around the early 18th century the original meaning merged with the French term *menage*, or household, resulting in the combined term *manage*, and associated meaning expressed in terms of controlling and directing. Kurtz and Snowden (2007) advocate a return to *manege*, and an unlearning of practices associated with *menage* and the directorial tradition of management theory. This chapter has gone some way towards this unlearning and has sought to challenge traditional approaches to the management of gossip. The management of gossip is less about managing and controlling 'the problem' of gossip, and more about working with, and learning from, the complex entity of gossip.

8 Future Directions

*Thus, the task is not so much to see what no one has yet seen;
but to think what nobody has yet thought, about that which everybody sees.*

—Erwin Schrödinger (1887–1961)

In this final chapter I draw together the main themes of the book and look to the future for gossip-related research, theorizing and organizational practice. A central task of the book has been to move gossip from being an invisible, neglected human interpersonal process, to becoming a visible, valued constitutive organizing process. Three claims are made. First, the empirical materials used to support the arguments and ideas developed in the book have shown how organizational gossip makes a contribution to extant theory with regard to emotion, identity, power and sensemaking. Second, gossip can be understood as a strand in the 'communicative constitution of organization' (CCO) perspective. Third, repositioning gossip as organizational communication and knowledge opens up new avenues of inquiry for future research and scholarship. This chapter highlights how gossip 'speaks to' these important trends in organization studies and work and organizational psychology.

My intention is not necessarily to outline a 'new theory' here. Rather, theoretical concepts are brought together in a framework for theorizing gossip. The pragmatist philosopher Charles Sanders Peirce's concept of abduction is used to develop a fuller account of the theorizing process. This is based on an understanding of abduction as concerned with the *generation of ideas* (Locke, Golden-Biddle, & Feldman, 2008; Van de Ven, 2007). The chapter revisits the 'dark side' of gossip because, in order to understand the better aspects of gossip, it is necessary to know the worst aspects as well. That is, we need to understand gossip as a kind of 'conceptual gestalt'—that is as a configuration or pattern, unified as a whole, which cannot be described (or measured) merely as a sum of its parts. This is followed by the articulation of a framework to guide future research, theoretical development and critical reflection. Aligned with this framework is an illustration from British artist Tacita Dean's 1997 work: *The Roaring Forties: Seven Boards in Seven Days*. The powerful imagery captured within this piece emphasizes the fluidity and movement within the theorizing framework and the theme of visual gossip advanced in the book. Premises of CCO scholarship are used to gauge the theoretical relevance of the framework. Practical relevance and application of the framework are addressed using critical incident technique and the notion of organizational alchemy introduced in the previous chapter. The chapter—and book—concludes by outlining potential areas future research and scholarship.

But first, I go right back to the beginning, and reflect upon research participants' 'first thoughts and impressions' when they were asked to participate in research exploring the role of gossip in nursing and healthcare organizations.

REFLECTION 10: GOSSIP? HOW INTERESTING!

At the end of data collection episodes I asked participants what had been their first thoughts and impressions when they were approached to take part in the research. 'How interesting' was by far the most frequent response, as shown in these short illustrative extracts from Clinical Nurse Specialist (CNS) interviews:

CNS 1: 'I thought it sounded extremely interesting because it is indicative in the subculture of nursing, as I'm sure it is in the subculture of all professions—and you do see it being there.'

CNS 5: 'Hmmm, I thought it was really interesting and it just got me thinking about the notion of gossip a little bit, I hadn't really thought about it before, it's a naturally occurring phenomenon, and there it is, it did actually trigger some thought.'

CNS 7: 'I suppose my first thought was [pause] . . . if I'm completely honest, I thought that's a fairly nebulous topic, so there was an element of that, and then there was an element of "that is actually quite interesting". And since then I've been occasionally thinking about talking about gossip—and my impression has changed.'

Reflecting upon Schrödinger's quotation at the start of the chapter leads me to conclude that (re)thinking about gossip as something which everybody sees, but which organizationally nobody has ever really noticed, helps us see other organizational phenomena, and organizations as constituted, in new ways.

The data extracts in Reflection 10 illustrate two important points. The first is CNS 1's reference to 'you do see it'–which foregrounds gossip as a visual phenomenon. The second is how thinking about gossip triggers further thought. Rather than dismissing gossip as trivia, being asked to think about it triggered interesting thoughts.

APPROACH TO THEORIZING GOSSIP

A key assertion of the book is that gossip is discourse worthy of serious theoretical attention—a form of 'non-trivial trivia' if you like. It is something which, on the surface, may appear unimportant but which can be quite precious and pertinent. Reactions of '*I thought it was really interesting*' epitomized in Reflection 10 are an important starting point for theorizing gossip. Weick's (1989, p. 516; 1995b; 1999) insights into the nature of theorizing and theory construction as 'disciplined imagination' have informed my approach to theorizing gossip:

> Whenever one reacts with the feeling *that's interesting,* that reaction is a clue that current experience has been tested against past experience, and the past understanding has been found inadequate. (Weick, 1989, p. 525, original emphasis).

The judgement *that's interesting* represents the selection of a conjecture for retention and further use, and is one of a number of criteria which are central to the notion of plausibility in the theorizing process. Weick (1989) continues:

> When theorists apply selection criteria to their conjectures, they ask whether the conjecture is interesting, obvious, connected, believable, beautiful, or real, in the context of the problem they are trying to solve. (p. 524).

According to Weick, the reaction *that's obvious* may be a clue to the significance as well as to the triviality of a conjecture. This is clearly an important consideration when theorizing gossip and discerning trivia from non-trivia, and sense from non-sense. The reaction *that's obvious* leads to the question, 'For whom might this not be obvious?' Answers to this question can help establish the boundary conditions inside which a conjecture will hold true (Van de Ven, 2007). Organizational communication and knowledge have been established as the boundary conditions within which the conjecture that *gossip is discourse worthy of serious theoretical attention* will hold true in future theorizing.

To recap, the essential aspects of the argument advanced in Chapter 2 are that knowledge is pluralistic phenomenon which embraces both explicit and implicit narrative forms. Both concepts need to be kept in mind simultaneously, 'at the edge so to speak, where knowledge is referred to as a discursive search' (Schneider, 2007, p. 615). The repositioning of gossip as organizational communication and knowledge is congruent with an understanding of knowledge as 'knowing-in-practice.' In this 'epistemology of practice' knowledge is no longer conceived as something that can be 'possessed.' Rather, it is conceptualized as a situated process which draws upon communication and reflection (Nicolini, 2011; Schreyögg & Geiger, 2007). A reflexive inquiry position has been embedded throughout the book, and reflection, as I argue more fully later in the chapter, is central to theorizing gossip.

Theorizing gossip is a hard task, and in this respect I am a novice theorist, in need of guiding 'rules' and principles. Peirce's concept of abduction is the starting point for developing a fuller and more explicit account of the creative theorizing process (see Anderson, 2010). Abduction suggests that something *may be*. It is 'an ampliative and conjectural model of inquiry through which we engender and entertain hunches, explanatory propositions, ideas, and theoretical elements' (Locke et al., 2008, pp. 907–908). In other words, abduction enlarges a conception by adding to that which is already known, and depends upon imagination to suggest the possible. The process of abduction is embodied, or sensory, in nature and requires reflexivity in order to challenge previously held assumptions (Hansen, 2007, cited in Locke et al., 2008). Adoption of Peirce's pragmatic philosophical approach to abductive reasoning usually begins with a surprising observation or experience. This was the surprising absence of gossip in the organizational literature when I unexpectedly encountered 'gossip as data' in research into a university's organizational culture (see Waddington, 2005a). Crucially, Peirce's ideas about science also support the repositioning of gossip as organizational communication and knowledge, as outlined below.

In Chapter 7 and in Waddington (2010, p. 313), I have used the term 'reflexive gossip' to describe mindful attention to evaluative talk in and about organizations that is spoken, written, or visual. Here I develop these ideas further, arguing that reflexive gossip is a mode of organizational inquiry which captures aspects of Peirce's notions of scientific inquiry:

> Peirce speaks specifically of the scientists' 'unreserved discussions with one another, . . .' . . . It is not just the prevalence of 'unreserved discussion' that links gossip to Peirce's notion of scientific inquiry. The nature of the initial hypothesis and the role of evidence in determining the ultimate status of the hypothesis are also analogous. The good scientist, as described in the work of Charles Sanders Peirce, will be likely to start with a hunch . . . The scientist's retroduction will be no more able to stand alone than the gossip's hunch, . . . The competent scientist, like the good investigative gossiper, will sift through the plethora of data generated in this listening stance and amend, embrace, or reject the hypothesis accordingly. (Ayim, 1994, pp. 87/89)

Peirce argues that a theory is not assembled inductively from observed phenomena, nor is it deduced from premises or axioms. Rather, it is an abductive process which makes it possible 'to observe phenomena as being of a certain sort, and as related to other phenomena' (Van de Ven, 2007, p. 104). The phenomenon of gossip is elusive. It can be everywhere and nowhere. Yet it also touches many other organizational processes and phenomena including sensemaking, emotion, identity and power. Understanding *context* is crucial to theorizing and understanding gossip. As Weick (1995b, p. 387) points out:

> It is tough to judge whether something is a theory or not when only the product itself is examined. What one needs to know, instead, is more about the context in which the product [theory] lives. This is the process of theorizing.

Mills's (2010) study of organizational communication during a chief executive officer (CEO) succession process exemplifies the relevance of context when locating and theorizing gossip. Evaluative talk about an absent third party by a selection panel is *not* gossip. Evaluative talk about the same absent third party in a different context, say a corridor, café or whilst waiting for a meeting to start, *is* gossip. Such talk may be complementary and/or critical, positive and/or negative; there is a dark side and a light side inherent in the process of theorizing gossip.

THE DARK SIDE AND LIGHT SIDE OF GOSSIP

The dark side of gossip is about collusive, dysfunctional processes, which are detrimental to healthy social and organizational relationships. It often has an emotional undertow of anger, frustration, resentment, and hatred. More generally, the term 'dark side' means different things to different disciplines, and has been described thus:

> In sum, the dark side is an appreciation, a perspective, a way of asking questions, that draws attention to the ambivalent, multivalent, and multifunctional nature of our needs, goals, dreams, nightmares, foibles, and courses of action. (Spitzberg & Cupach, 2007, p. 7)

Cognizance of a dark side perspective is integral to understanding gossip. When Thomas Hardy's novels were criticized for their portrayal of darkness and immorality in human relations, Hardy is alleged to have replied that 'to know the best, we must first regard the worst' (Blase & Blase, 2004, p. 245). Therefore, in order to know the best about organizational gossip and uncover its virtues, it is necessary to consider its worst aspects. Throughout this book I have argued that in advancing the scholarship of organizational gossip the intention is not to conceptually cleanse, nor uncouple, gossip from its dark side. Organizational gossip needs to be understood as a 'warts and all' phenomenon. The phrase 'warts and all' is attributed to Oliver Cromwell (1599–1658), who is alleged to have ordered the painter Sir Peter Lely (1618–1680) to 'not flatter me at all; but remark all these roughnesses, pimples, and warts and everything as you see' (Green, 1998, p. 1263). So it is with the scholarship of gossip, we need to see the 'whole picture' and not conceal its less attractive parts.

As discussed in Chapter 6, closer consideration of the power and politics of gossip, involves delving into some of the darker aspects of organizational life and organizational abuse such as bullying. These are the oppressive hegemonic practices that maintain the status quo and reinforce destructive and dysfunctional power relationships. Paradoxically, such practices are frequently found in organizations based on an ethic of caring, such as healthcare and educational institutions (Kahn, 2005; Obholzer & Roberts, 1994a). Rather than attending to and dealing with the dark side, the problems and conflicts contained therein are often avoided, brushed aside or individualized as a form of victim blaming and scapegoating.

Fitzgerald et al. (2010), writing in an appreciative inquiry context, draw attention to the associated concept of 'the shadow,' defined as 'censored emotional and/or cognitive content' (p. 220). At the intra- and interpersonal, group, and organizational levels 'the shadow' contains that which is feared, suppressed, considered inappropriate, shunned and censored. Notably 'the shadow' concept encompasses more than just the dark side of people and organizations, and embraces the full spectrum of censored feeling and cognition and suppressed strengths and qualities. Feelings and thoughts which are censored, suppressed or taboo emerge as gossip in unmanaged spaces and 'behind closed doors'. However it is unhelpful to polarize gossip as being *either* positive *or* negative. It is both. In order to better understand organizational gossip it is important that notions of darkness and lightness are held simultaneously. Although organizational gossip is undergoing a period of renaissance, it would be naïve to think that its darker side will disappear when issues have been recast in a new light. If anything, we may find that organizational harms such as backstabbing, mistrust, scapegoating, blame cultures, and bullying may be shown up in much sharper relief.

The empirical material presented throughout this book suggests that the light side of gossip can be conceptualized as three inter-related themes. The first theme relates to the 'light relief' that gossip can bring to day-to-day work, for example:

> I think the best gossip is usually about the kind of things that people try to hide about themselves, it's the other face of the person that they wouldn't normally present, so it might be a scandal, it might be a disclosure about somebody who has been on a pedestal maybe is knocked off that pedestal, that's probably sometimes the most interesting gossip I think that people like to hear.

> *KW*: Why is that the best gossip?

> Because it's unexpected, usually, and because it distracts you from the day to day mundane nature of work, and it usually is something that

you wouldn't expect, so it's shocking in a way, or somehow acts as a jolt to the everyday routine. (CNS 7)

Schön (1987, cited in Van de Ven, 2007) maintains that in situations of ambiguity and unexpected events our thinking turns back on the surprising phenomenon, whilst simultaneously turning thinking back on itself. Van de Ven (2007) describes this as 'abductive reflection-in-action' (p. 103). Rather than dismissing gossip as a trivial communicative event, pausing to think further about the 'unexpectedness' of gossip can trigger further thought, as outlined above in Reflection 10. Gossip is a form of abductive reflection-in-action. The second theme in the light side of gossip relates to the positive consequences of gossip, often expressed in terms of mutual support and pleasure. For instance:

> If I'm gossiping about someone it might be laughing about an idiosyncrasy that they have or something. Sometimes it's concern. . .gossip allows the release of feelings, discussion of the feelings, and also it allows other people to bolster up other people so they can feel supported, or vindicated or whatever. (CNS 4)

> It's often fun, it can be something that people do to make themselves feel better in a number of ways, to put somebody else down possibly, for support maybe—I think we all do it. (CNS 9)

Gossip plays a role in stress management and resilience, acting as an emotion and problem focussed coping strategy. This is a double edged sword. Firstly because of potential harm to the reputation and feelings of others, as reflected in CNS 7's and CNS 9's comments above about the *'best gossip'*, and *'to put somebody else down'*. This is gossip as a question of everyday ethics in practice—do the individual benefits to the gossiper outweigh the risks and harms to the gossipee/target of gossip? Secondly, in the short term people may feel better as a consequence of gossiping, but underlying organizational problems/issues which sparked the need to gossip may continue to fester unnoticed. Therefore, the longer term consequences of not attending to organizational knowledge embedded in gossip may be far-reaching. The third theme then, ironically perhaps, relates to the 'light' gossip can shine upon hidden or suppressed organizational concerns and blind spots which need to be surfaced and seen. The spookfish metaphor, introduced in Chapter 2, proves helpful here.

To recap, the spookfish has evolved a particular way of seeing in dark, deep sea environments and can 'make sense' of very low light emissions. The spookfish has—quite literally and physically—four eyes, and each eye is divided into two parts. One part has a conventional lens, pointing upwards, the other part of the eye points downwards, using mirrors to collect and focus light. I like to think of it as a fish with wing mirrors. Wing mirrors help drivers see areas outside of their peripheral vision and 'blind spots.' Organizations and their leaders also have blind spots, reinforced by self-legitimizing success narratives which are later revealed in public inquiries into organizational failure (e.g., Colin Thomé, 2009; Geiger & Antonacopoulou, 2009; Kennedy, 2001). The spookfish metaphor, I suggest, prompts us to think differently about ways of detecting glimmers of gossip which may be early warning signs of failure.

DEVELOPING THE THEORIZING FRAMEWORK

The framework for theorizing gossip was guided by the following questions:

1. Why is it necessary to develop a framework for theorizing gossip?
2. What are the historical contexts and theoretical antecedents?
3. How useful is the theorizing framework with regard to its ability to guide future research?
4. What tangible difference might theorizing gossip make to organizational practices in the 'real world?'

The first question, *why is it necessary to develop a framework for theorizing gossip* was partially addressed in Chapter 1. Spaces for face-to-face communication and gossip have moved and mutated. One of the consequences of electronic technologies and globalized, networked communities and organizations is that the importance of gossip has now been thrown into sharp relief. As has its theoretical neglect. There is an ongoing torrent of organizational and business failures and financial scandals where warning signs expressed in gossip may have gone unheeded or unnoticed. The analyses and discussion of public inquiries presented in Chapter 7 indicate the need for *prescience* in theorizing. Prescience draws attention to areas of organization and organizing that need deeper understanding from a theoretical standpoint. These are areas which represent significant social and organizational issues and problems, and prescience involves:

> sensitivity towards developing trends but acting to influence those trends via prospective sensemaking . . . in other words, giving meaning to ambiguous informational cues and articulating viable interpretations and actions to cope with coming organizational and environmental demands. (Corley & Gioia, 2011, p. 24)

Articulation of a framework for the process of theorizing and understanding organizational gossip helps give meaning to ambiguous informational cues, and provides a means of offering some interpretations. However, as a subject of inquiry, organizational gossip is a contested, stigmatized, taboo topic, and tainted talk, as illustrated in Chapter 3. It is an ethically challenging and young field of inquiry. Some researchers may choose to stay out of the field altogether. Others might observe from the sidelines, with varying degrees of interest, scepticism and critique. And there are those, both now and in the future, who make a deliberate choice to come into this field of inquiry. Scholars may be more likely to stay if there are opportunities to contribute to imaginative and creative theoretical developments in the field. Creation of a robust yet flexible theorizing framework will enhance cumulative development of inter-disciplinary knowledge in organizational gossip and related domains of inquiry.

The second question, *what are the historical contexts and theoretical antecedents* was informed by Peirce's philosophical position:

> What I would recommend is that every person who wishes to form an opinion concerning fundamental problems should first make a complete survey of human knowledge, should take note of all the valuable ideas in each branch of science, should observe in just what respect each has been successful, and where it has failed. (Peirce, cited in Anderson, 2010, p. 2)

The historical contexts and theoretical antecedents of gossip were addressed in Chapters 2 and 3. Gossip has been variously trivialized, demonized and sensationalized, and from a philosophical standpoint it has been vilified as inauthentic discourse. The rehabilitation of gossip as a noteworthy topic of inquiry and organizational process challenges the assumptions, stereotypes and myths which have historically contributed to its neglect. There is nothing necessarily wrong with gossip; it *may* be wrong, but it is also acceptable and beneficial. Westacott (2012) argues that we should be 'suspicious of the censorious attitude that moralists have traditionally taken toward gossip' (p. 99). Efforts of philosophers like Heidegger and Kierkegaard to define the 'appropriateness' of dialogical discourse/s erases and hides the power relationships embedded within them (Leach, 2000). Inclusion of theoretical concepts and frameworks of ethics, power and politics into the theorizing framework are critical in this regard, allowing fuller exploration of the positive and negative attributes and consequences of gossip (see Clegg, 1989; Gotsis & Kortezi, 2010; Walker & Ivanhoe, 2009).

It is important at this juncture differentiate between contributions *from theory*, such as Clegg's (1989) circuits of power theory, and what is being proposed here, which is a framework for new *theorizing*. With regard to the former, the scholarship of gossip is informed by extant theory in domains of power, emotion, identity and sensemaking. Closer analysis of gossip can, in turn, breathe new life into our understanding of these important themes in studies of organizations and work. With regard to the latter—*new theorizing*—the framework needs to illustrate the complexity of organizational gossip, and also tell a good story. It must possess a quality of flow and structure that enables the reader to make sense of it, remember it and communicate it to others (Fiske, 2004). A guiding principle has been to aim for vividness and interconnectedness, and metaphor has been important device in imaginative theorizing.

A multiplicity of metaphors has been used throughout the book. A veritable smörgåsbord in fact. Smörgåsbord is a Swedish term meaning an assortment of hot and cold foods from appetizers to desserts laid out together on a table and served as a buffet meal (http://www.websters-online-dictionary.org). The 'collective' metaphor of smörgåsbord is used deliberately to recall Difonzo et al.'s (1994) metaphorical comparison between gossip and rumour:

> [Rumours] are speculations that arise to fill knowledge gaps or discrepancies. This function differentiates rumor from gossip, which is meant primarily to entertain or convey mores. Gossip is a tasty hors d'oeuvre savoured at a cocktail party; rumor is a morsel hungrily eaten amid an information famine. (p. 52)

Metaphor has been an important device in the early stages of imaginative theorizing. Metaphor creates semantic domains whereby connections between terms and concepts are '*constructed* rather than deciphered and where the resulting image and meaning is *creative*' (Cornelissen 2005, p.751, original emphasis). Furthermore, as Brewer and Hunter (2006, p. 56) assert:

> Mixed metaphors, crossover of theories, or applications of a theory developed in one subfield to another may provoke new questions, provide useful insights, and suggest new ways of looking at phenomena.

In summary, the previous three sections have sketched out stages in the theorizing process thus far, based on three underpinning principles:

- An understanding of abduction as concerned with the generation of ideas;
- The abductive process, which makes it possible see phenomena in a certain way, and as related to other phenomena; and
- Imaginative theorizing, which involves working with empirical materials to imagine new processes, structures and characterizations (Alvesson & Sköldberg, 2009; Locke et al., 2008; Locke, Golden-Biddle, & Feldman, 2004; Van de Ven, 2007; Weick, 1989; 1995b).

The next section draws further upon the use of metaphor and visual imagery to present a framework for new ways of theorizing and understanding gossip and organizations.

ARTICULATING THE FRAMEWORK

This is an ambitious framework with two primary aims. The first is to stimulate future research, and guide further thinking and theorizing; the second is provide a model to promote critical reflection and reflexive inquiry which can be used by researchers and practitioners alike. The framework *articulates* new characterizations and processes of organizational gossip. Semantically, the term 'articulated' comes from the Latin *articulus* meaning small joint. A key feature of the framework is the notion of inter-related 'moving joints' which provide strength and flexibility. For example, consider the human spine or backbone as modelling a particular type of articulated skeletal structure. The human spine is made up of irregularly shaped bones (vertebrae), divided into discernable regions such as thoracic (chest) and lumbar (lower back). Each region has different characteristics and functions. The small joints *between* individual vertebrae are facet joints. Individually, they are not very flexible, but working together in an inter-related manner they give the spine a wide range of forward, backward, arching and twisting movements.

The components of the inter-disciplinary theoretical 'backbone' of the theorizing framework have been set out in previous chapters. In Chapter 4, I argued that the emerging field of organizational gossip could learn much from more established, fields such as organizational emotion. The explosion of emotion research over the last twenty years or so has been both a boon and a mess. A key issue in that field has been clarification of conceptual boundaries because 'for emotion to mean anything, it cannot mean everything' (Elfenbein, 2007, p.316). To avoid falling in to the trap of gossip being 'everything and nothing,' organizational communication and knowledge provide plausible boundary conditions within which to theorize and understand gossip and organizations. The framework for theorizing gossip presented in Figure 8.1 comprises five concepts, ethics, emotion, sensemaking, identity, and power, located within the aforesaid boundary conditions.

The framework presented in Figure 8.1 is deliberately presented without any upward or downward arrows as I am not implying causal relationships between and among concepts. Rather, they are presented as inter-related, inter-disciplinary perspectives with which to theorize and better understand gossip and organizations. Figure 8.1 is also aligned with an image from British artist Tacita Dean in Figure 8.2, which powerfully captures and underscores the intended fluidity and movement of the theorizing framework. Dean's work explores the boundaries between fact and fiction, perception and reality—features which are conceptually significant to theorizing gossip.

Figure 8.2 constructs a narrative of sailors battling storms in an area of the Atlantic known for strong winds. The image is also, like gossip, a little ambiguous, but can be seen as a 'spine of men'. As discussed above, the framework can be seen as an inter-disciplinary theoretical 'backbone'

Figure 8.1 Framework for theorizing gossip and organizations.

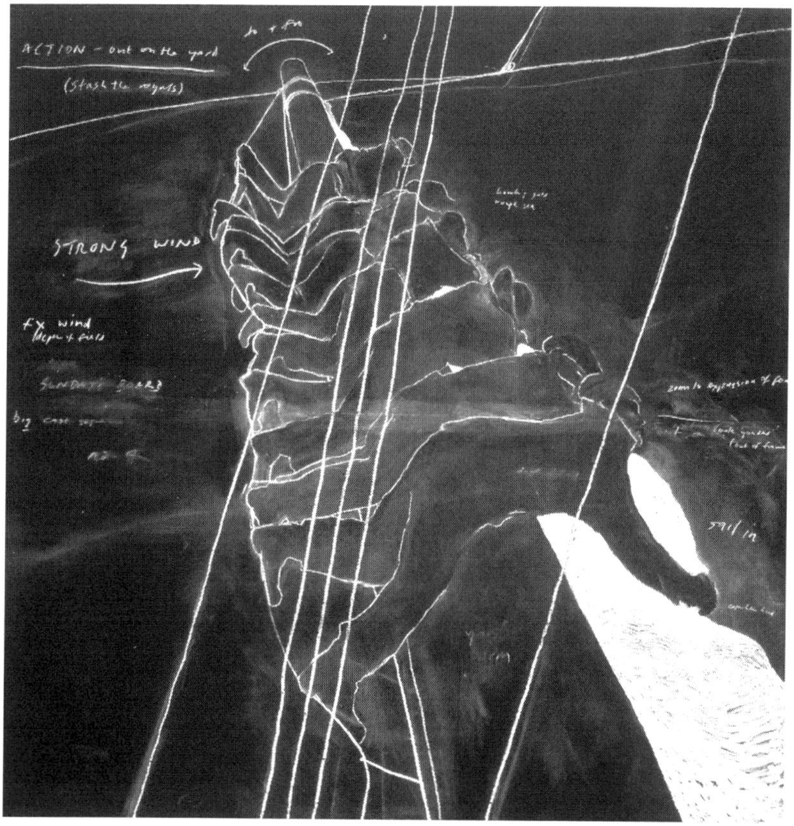

Figure 8.2 *The Roaring Forties: Seven Boards in Seven Days.* © Tacita Dean, 1997, Frith Street Gallery, London and Marian Goodman Gallery, New York/ Paris. Reproduced with permission.

which is both strong and flexible. The framework and imagery captured jointly in Figures 8.1 and 8.2 represent imaginative theorizing, a visual perspective, flexibility and the importance of contextual factors in understanding gossip and organizations.

The Roaring Forties: Seven Boards in Seven Days (Figure 8.2) was created on chalkboard, evoking the aesthetic of black and white cinema and contains diagrammatic arrows and notes that specify atmospheric conditions, camera angles and details of narrative incident. The image is of seven sailors hauled over a mast gathering in the sails. Instructions signal various actions and effects: 'ACTION—out on the yard.' 'Zoom in expression of fear.' 'fx wind.' A curved arrow with the words 'to and fro' indicates the movement of the mast as it sways in the wind. These written cues invite the viewer's imagination to animate the image, which also portrays a sense of ambiguity and impermanence (http://www.tate.org.uk/research/tateresearch/tatepapers/10autumn/krcma.shtm).

Canary and McPhee's (2011a) theoretical template for developing a communicative perspective on organizational knowledge used Glaser's (1978) grounded theory model of the 'six Cs' (context, conditions, causes, covariances, contingencies, and consequences). It is not my intention to invoke grounded theory per se into the theorizing framework, although this may be a very valuable approach for future research and theory development. Rather, I am locating the framework within a contemporary context of theory and practice in the field of communication and organizational knowledge. Thus the imagery in Tacita Dean's work evokes organizational *contexts* and *conditions* of gossip. The stormy seas imagery also evokes environmental *causes* of gossip via the 'perfect storm' metaphor.

The 'perfect storm' refers to the storm which hit the north east coast of the United States in October 1991. The storm was the result of the collision of three weather systems, and resulted in deaths and billions of dollars in damage. Organizationally, the metaphor of the perfect storm signifies the simultaneous occurrence of events which had they occurred individually would be less powerful than their combination (Rousseau & Batt, 2007). The relevance of this popular metaphor lies in its potential to illuminate the environmental and organizational conditions, climate and 'atmospherics' that are the precursors of gossip and predictors of organizational downfall. There is scope for further empirical work here.

Theoretical Concepts within the Framework

The framework represented in Figures 8.1 and 8.2 embodies an engaged scholarship model of theorizing as a set of concepts located within boundary conditions (Van de Ven, 2007). Ethics is an integral philosophical, organizational, managerial and practical dimension of the framework, quite simply because gossip has the potential to both harm and help. This is congruent with the message throughout the book that gossip is everday ethics in practice. The other conceptual domains of emotion, identity, power and sensemaking are data driven, derived from empirical materials presented and discussed in Chapters 4 to 7. The framework also aligns with the constitutive view of communication and organization, which has evolved as scholars confront power and the politics of meaning (Ashcraft et al., 2009; Leclercq-Vandelannoitte, 2011). Furthermore, as Cooren et al. (2011) note, organizational sensemaking and identity are areas where CCO scholarship has started to make a significant contribution.

An overlooked area in CCO scholarship however is that of emotion. Gossip is a means of expressing and managing emotion, and as illustrated in Chapter 6, emotions associated with McPhee and Zaug's (2000; 2009) flows of communication act as triggers for gossip. For example, the murmurs of discontent circulating as gossip characterize reaction and resistance to formal rules, roles and organizational policies and procedures—the flow of 'organizational self-structuring.' Strong emotions about colleagues, such as envy or hatred, are constitutive of the 'dark side' of gossip, and can impede and sabotage the communication flow of 'activity coordination.' The theorizing framework thus has scope to influence the future direction of CCO theorizing and scholarship.

The utility of the framework is addressed by asking the question *how useful is the theorizing framework with regard to its ability to guide future research*. Principles and premises drawn from the communicative constitution of organization perspective provide a partial answer.

THEORIZING GOSSIP AS THE COMMUNICATIVE CONSTITUTION OF ORGANIZATIONS

The idea that organizations can no longer be seen as objects or entities inside which communication happens is a fundamental aspect of the CCO perspective. Putnam and Nicotera (2010) assert that is important to clarify and distinguish the senses in which the term *organization* refers to process, entity, and/or entity from a process view. The approach I have taken is one of organization as grounded in actions and events of gossip, that is, entity from process. Cooren et al. (2011, pp. 1151–1153) identify six premises to help define more precisely what the CCO perspective entails in terms of an evolving research agenda, methodologies, and epistemologies. These premises are not intended to be 'checklist for assessing scholarship' (p. 1151), and nor do they necessarily dictate the future research agenda. However in the absence of prior substantive scholarship in the field of organizational gossip, they are a starting point with which to think about the relevance of gossip in future CCO research.

Premise 1: *CCO scholarship studies communicational events*. An 'event,' is 'a segment of an ongoing and situated stream of socio-discursive practice' (Schatzki, 2001, 2006, cited in Cooren et al., 2011, p. 1151).

Gossip is clearly a stream of socio-discursive practice, which may trickle or surge through organizations. Communication events also include any turn of talk, metaphor, artefact or narrative, and as I have argued, and demonstrated, gossip is visual and present in material objects and technologies. Furthermore gossip blends and blurs with other communicative events such as rumour and storytelling as part of a wider family of communicative practices.

Premise 2: CCO scholarship should be as inclusive as possible about what we mean by (organizational) communication. The majority of work on organizational communication and discourse has ignored gossip, and focused almost exclusively on the *textual* aspects of communication such as documents and conversations. It is as if gossip has been an embarrassing relative in the family of (organizational) communication, who might 'spoil the party' and therefore has not, in the past, been invited. If CCO scholarship is serious about being as inclusive as possible, gossip can no longer be ignored.

Premise 3: CCO scholarship acknowledges the co-constructed or co-oriented nature of (organizational) communication. A constitutive view of organizations needs to take into account how the meaning and action of policies, decisions or job descriptions 'are negotiated, translated and/or debated' (Mumby, 1987, cited in Cooren et al., 2011, p. 1152). The four flows model was used to re-visit and re-analyze empirical materials in Chapter 5. This showed how communication of formal organization strategy, for example, fails to flow in disconnected organizations. Chapter 6 illustrated how organizational policies, and the way in which they are written and communicated, act as triggers for gossip. As unofficial discourse, gossip produces in an 'inverted' constitution of organization than was originally intended in (organizational) communication.

Premise 4: CCO scholarship holds that who or what is acting always is an open question. This premise advocates inclusivity regarding *who* or *what* is taking part in the constitution of organizational processes. Again, this includes strategies, visions, organizational mission statements and such like, which can often evoke strong emotional responses. In this sense then, it could be argued that emotions are also 'constitutive of organizations.' Premise 4 could be extended to include *how* organizational strategies and visions also constitute *emotional* undercurrents and contexts. Speaking, acting and *feeling* in the name of strategies or visions and other material elements of organization is, I argue, another way to speak of their agency.

Premise 5: CCO scholarship never leaves the realm of communicational events. Contemporary communicative thinking broadens its explanatory reach to consider how material aspects such as strategies, bodies, conversations, art, photographs, and documents are co-implicated and co-constituted in organizing. Organizations are thus constituted by what buildings, for example, say about them, and by what

people say about the buildings. Evaluative talk (i.e. gossip) about buildings might be about unreliable lifts or the colour schemes and ambiance
of reception areas.

Premise 6: CCO *scholarship favours neither organizing nor organization.* Cooren et al. (2011) argue that 'CCO scholarship refuses to choose
between studying how people get organized and how organizations come
to be re-enacted and reproduced through these [organizing] activities'
(p. 1153). Knowledge, rules, processes, markets, and organizations are all
produced from situated interactions (Ashcraft et al., 2009). Thinking about
gossip as organizational communication and knowledge, and as a process
and a product, is, in essence, CCO thinking and theorizing.

The above premises of CCO scholarship have the potential to shape a
future research agenda for organizational gossip, and gossip also has the
potential to inform CCO thinking. However as discussed in Chapter 2, the
claim that organizations are communicatively constituted has been criticized as analytically ambitious and ontologically audacious (Reed, 2010).
CCO scholarship is clearly not the only way forward; other psychological, sociological, narrative and discursive analyses and approaches all have
much to offer. Theorizing gossip is in its infancy, and the field of organizational gossip is currently 'theory-lite'. As discussed earlier in the chapter I
have been, to some extent, a 'novice theorist' in a sparsely populated area of
organizational scholarship. I look to more expert theorists and scholars in
fields such as CCO, organizational discourse, and storytelling to develop
the thinking in the book yet further.

Methodological Considerations

I hope that the framework represented in Figures 8.1 and 8.2 will provide
a stimulus for innovative research questions and future theoretical development. The framework helps to identify *what* aspects of gossip should be
studied in order to ascertain *how* and *why* they relate to each other, and to
other domains of inquiry in organization studies. Flexibility is a core element
of the framework, and the inter-disciplinary scholarship of gossip needs to be
tolerant and accepting of different approaches and paradigms, but this is not
unproblematic. There is a risk of conceptual drift and clarity of definition is
an issue. I have approached the problematic issue of defining organizational
gossip by describing it in terms of constituent attributes with coalescent
properties. Put differently, gossip has a number of inherent characteristics
which unite to form a whole. To recap, gossip is informal evaluative talk
about individuals/issues/groups in and about organizations between at least
two people which may be spoken (most common), written (less common) or
visual. Importantly, informal talk can, and does, occur in and around formal organization. Although a little cumbersome, this composite definition
includes constitutive components of gossip drawn from different disciplinary
perspectives (see also Michelson et al., 2010 for more detailed discussion).

Methodologically, in Chapter 4 I argued that a mixed-methods approach to researching gossip was justified, underpinned by philosophical principles of pragmatism. However writing about mixed-methods research can be difficult. There are well-established approaches to writing—and publishing—qualitative and quantitative research, but fewer such guidelines for researchers using mixed-methods research. Bryman (2011) therefore suggests researchers using mixed-methods in organizational research 'use *visual* and other aids to display and help the reader to follow the components of a mixed-methods study and their *interconnections*' (p. 527, emphasis added). The framework for theorizing gossip illustrated in the combined concepts and imagery of Figures 8.1 and 8.2 is a novel visual representation of the components and contexts of organizational gossip.

Visual methods, organizational ethnography and case studies are particularly promising approaches for future researchers to explore (see Carmel, 2011; Clegg, 2011; Cresswell & Plano Clark, 2011; Fine et al., 2011; Hurdley, 2010b). Methods such as these offer great potential for developing richer understanding of organizational and organizing processes and dynamics of gossip. For instance how its materialities, communicative attributes, and linkages with other flows of communication, knowledge and power can be seen as a whole. From a CCO perspective, visual methods offer a tangible way of *really seeing* how gossip as organizational communication constitutes organization.

The final question, *what tangible difference might theorizing gossip make to organizational practices in the 'real world'* is now addressed by considering the relevance of the framework as a model for critical reflection and reflexive inquiry. The empirically based framework represented in Figures 8.1 and 8.2 can thus be used as a field guide by researchers and practitioners alike to undertake detailed analyses of the communicative contexts of gossip as practice-based organizational knowledge.

A MODEL FOR CRITICAL REFLECTION AND REFLEXIVE INQUIRY

The concepts and imagery in Figures 8.1 and 8.2 can be integrated and used as a model to promote critical reflection and reflexive inquiry. In this section I develop the organizational alchemy metaphor (see Reflection 9 in the previous chapter) further, and outline practical ways of transforming gossip into organizational knowledge. Alchemy sought to transform commonly found base metal such as iron or copper into gold. It involved the creation of potentially dangerous and destructive energies, but which could be used in a transformative way. Alchemy was a 'search for understanding how the deepest meaning of life could be derived from quotidian experience' (Case & Phillipson, 2004, p. 482).

Metaphorically, organizational alchemy is the creation of something commonly found (gossip) into something of value (knowledge).

Tacita Dean's image of sailors in stormy seas working together in harsh environmental conditions (Figure 8.2) provides a contextual focus for creative critical reflection and reflexivity in an organizational context. We can ask questions such as: Is the organizational context stormy or calm? What are the emotional undertows and currents? What dangers lie ahead and below the surface? How might reflexive gossip, in other words mindful attention to everyday evaluative talk, help to transform gossip into organizational knowledge? What instructions and cues signalling various actions, effects, and emotions might be inscribed? Crucially, critical reflection and reflexivity in an organizational context transcend individual reflective practice. Co-creation of knowledge from gossip occurs through collective, contextualized, critical interpretive practices and techniques. Critical incident technique, which was used in the empirical research upon which this book is based, is now used an example of the *practical application* of the theorizing framework.

Critical Incident Technique

Critical incident technique (CIT) has a long history in work and organizational psychology, and can be used to explore the context of critical communicative events of gossip (Bradley, 1992; Chell, 2004). I have refrained from suggesting what might make an event 'critical', as this will depend upon subjectivities, consequences, organizational context, climate and culture. However events which provoke strong emotions are one place to start (Molloy & Waddington, 2011). CIT can be used in a workshop or meeting format, with the aim of producing or eliciting new knowledge drawn from:

- Contextualized communicative incidents of gossip; and/or
- Gossip *surrounding* a contextualized critical organizational incident.

Table 8.1 suggests questions and probes which could be used to by researchers and practitioners alike to explore contextual critical incidents of gossip. It is not intended to be prescriptive or definitive; it is simply intended as guide for organizational inquiry and critical reflective practice.

The realization of organizational knowledge from critical incidents requires collective, critical interpretive practices and techniques (e.g., see Fook & Gardner, 2007). The realization of knowledge from critical incidents is not a linear process. It differs radically from the 'marching up a hill' of Ackoff's (1989) concepts of data →information →knowledge→ understanding →wisdom traditionally found the mainstream field of

Table 8.1   Exploring Contextualized Critical Incidents of Gossip

Suggested Probes	Identifying
What organizational issues lie beneath the incident/ event? What is already known about these issues? What are the underlying emotions? What are the risks of not attending to gossip?	**Underlying issues** Clarifying, focussing, and reviewing the evolving issues
What are the organizational triggers? How and where is power manifest? Where are the 'pockets' of gossip? Who are the key gatekeepers and stakeholders?	**Context** Exploring, discovering, and revealing the context
Is the gossip toxic or harmless? How do we judge the credibility of the content/ source? What needs further verification from other sources? What/where are gaps between knowledge sources?	**Ethical issues** Revealing and clarifying the nature of knowledge from gossip
How practical is it to use this knowledge from gossip? What are the risks and benefits associated with its use? What are the ethical implications of acting/not acting? How can this knowledge be integrated with other sources?	**Actions** Disseminating and integrating with other sources of knowledge

knowledge management. I contend that re-positioning gossip as organizational communication and knowledge represents the 'other side' of knowledge management and knowledge work. Ackoff's concepts are important to conceptualizing gossip as organizational knowledge. However I argue (and have tried to demonstrate here) that this conceptual and theoretical re-positioning is a critical, creative and imaginative process. It is an iterative, recursive dialogue which involves sensing and selecting, being open to surprise, and looking for patterns and gaps. The framework for combining and integrating different types of data presented in Appendix A (Figure A.2) may also be helpful in this regard.

I am proposing that close and careful scrutiny of gossip in its many guises is a means of picking up and honouring what might be seen as discarded trivia and trifles, and turning them into something useful. However the true relevance of snippets or glimmers of gossip can only be fully appreciated when debated with others and coalesced into the wholes that we call organizations, and revealing the knowledge 'holes' therein.

THE FUTURE

In thinking about the future it is necessary to consider first of all what has been achieved in *Gossip and Organizations*. In addition to offering scholars and practitioners what I hope has been a contemporary, challenging, lively and empirically grounded book on gossip, its primary contribution is fourfold. First, the empirical materials used to support the arguments and ideas developed in the book have shown how organizational gossip makes a contribution to extant theory with regard to emotion, identity, power, and sensemaking. These ideas and arguments are relevant to those who view informal, hidden and subterranean elements of organizational life as particularly salient to understanding organizing and organizations. Second, the book has demonstrated that gossip can be understood as a strand in the 'communicative constitution of organization' perspective. Notably, if CCO scholarship is to be as inclusive as possible in its study of communicative events and materialities as it claims to be, gossip can no longer be ignored. Importantly, the book has also revealed an 'emotional gap' in CCO thinking and theorizing. Third, repositioning gossip as organizational communication and knowledge opens up new avenues of inquiry for future research and scholarship, particularly with regard to contemporary ideas about practice as the site of knowing. A practice perspective gives prominence and explanatory power to materiality, spaces, emotion, time, interests and preoccupations. Infusion of gossip into this perspective can contribute to a richer picture of knowing and organizing. Fourth, the book has provided some practical tools and techniques for thinking differently about gossip and organizations.

The book has sought to foreground a more positive side to organizational gossip, whilst simultaneously holding its dark side. The dark side of gossip is an ever present shadow which needs to be acknowledged, and not forgotten, neglected or ignored. Clearly, a judgement as to what is seen as positive or negative depends to some extent on the perspectives, prejudices and position of those who are making the judgement. The important point is that new ways need to be found to draw out the positive, and this involves reflexively challenging assumptions and transforming thinking. In highlighting the virtues and positive side of gossip, there may be a place for gossip in the growing field of 'positive organizational scholarship' (POS) (Bakker & Schaufeli, 2008; Caza & Caza, 2008). POS includes the also growing field of positive psychology but draws upon a broader range of perspectives and theories. At the core of POS is the invitation for researchers to 'to imagine another world in which almost all organizations are typified by appreciation, collaboration, virtuousness, vitality, and meaningfulness' (Cameron, Dutton,

& Quinn, 2003, cited in Caza & Caza, 2008, p. 24). Despite its negative 'dark side' and potential to harm—bad and toxic gossip—there is a good, virtuous, side to gossip which, in moderation, is pleasurable and fun. POS is a potentially fruitful area for future scholarship of gossip.

As we have seen in Chapter 5, gossip and emotion are closely intertwined. People feel better after 'letting off steam' through gossip. Gossip is a way of expressing and managing emotion, and this can make a positive contribution to how we understand employee resilience, well-being and emotion work. However a word of caution is needed. There is a risk that without further rigorous, conceptually sound research and theorizing, gossip might become popularized. There is a need to guard against gossip being everywhere and nowhere in organization studies. The emergent field of organizational gossip can learn a great deal from the emerged field of organizational emotion.

Conceptually, this book has outlined a framework for understanding gossip as constitutive organizational communication and knowledge. Uniquely, it has included a *visual* element to theorizing, thinking and understanding gossip and organizations. Gossip has been conceptualized more widely and imaginatively than has previously been the case, and this has paved the way for future research. The big research priorities in the first instance, I would suggest, are twofold. The first is with regard to the role of gossip as an early warning signal of systemic failures, which would potentially avert much human suffering (and costly public inquiries). Second, and relatedly, as a consequence of global financial and business failures, there is increasing scholarly interest in the relationship between trust and organizational processes and performance (e.g., Gillespie & Dietz, 2009; Searle & Skinner, 2011). Therefore there is promising scope for future research into the role of gossip in organizational- and institutional-level trust failures and repair.

There are some limitations in the book which also point to the need for further thinking and research. The mixed-methods employed to gather empirical materials used in the book did not necessarily reveal the full extent of 'visual talk' and the nonhuman materialities of gossip as organizational communication, constitutive or otherwise. Nor did they address different cultural understandings and manifestations of organizational gossip. The primary research upon which this monograph is based was doctoral research in psychology, conducted in a professional and organizational context of UK nursing and healthcare at the turn of the twentieth and twenty first centuries. While the book has adopted an inter-disciplinary perspective, there is a need for future work in different business and organizational settings, and from different disciplinary perpsectives. There is no doubt that the corporate scandals and organizational failures that have marked, or marred, the first decade of the twenty first century indicate a pressing need for further research. At conceptual, theoretical and societal levels there is more work to be done to bring gossip into full view.

However this call for future research and theorizing raises further questions surrounding the wider implications of repositioning gossip as organizational communication and knowledge. In other words, as 'formal' or 'approved' knowledge and theory generated using empirical materials and systematic methods. Referring back to Foucault's (1979) neologism of power/knowledge, 'approved knowledge' is a tool for the exercise of power over those considered deviant within the discourse that knowledge creates. What are the implications of shifting gossip as 'deviant discourse' and 'tainted talk' to gossip as 'approved knowledge?' Who and what might become the 'new deviants'? And what happens when that which has been previously been 'disappeared' becomes visible? A focus on hidden or repressed elements of gossip in organizational life will inevitably change discursive practices— what are the implications for discursive and communication studies scholars? How do we ensure that gossip does not become conceptually cleansed and uncoupled from its dark side as a result of greater theoretical attention and research? These are all important questions for the future.

Final Reflections

Reflexivity and reflexive inquiry are core to the scholarship of gossip, and I have engaged with these concepts by interweaving reflective material throughout the book, and the use of metaphor. Metaphor has also been a core concept in imaginative theory construction and creation of the theorizing framework. As Alvesson and Sköldberg (2009) note, choice of metaphor 'will depend on what has personal significance for the individual' (p. 311). I am mindful that my choice of metaphors has been diverse, and has included, amongst others, the spookfish, gossamer walls, border-runners and alchemy. For me, metaphor has facilitated thoughts and insights about detecting and describing organizational gossip as a volatile, uncertain, complex and ambiguous phenomenon. There is more work to be done here, particularly with regard to use of metaphor and future theorizing.

Refexively, my early career background as a nurse and my experience as academic, working in hospitals and universities, have all influenced and shaped my practice-based view of gossip as organizational communication and knowledge. Notably, Corley and Gioia (2011) assert:

> The two key notions arising from adopting a practice view of knowledge then are (1) that knowledge should be treated as process, and (2) that the production of knowledge should be treated as a recursive dialogue between theorists *and* reflective practitioners. (p. 23, emphasis added)

I would argue that theorists *are also* (or should be) reflective practitioners (e.g., see Yanow, 2009). I therefore suggest that organizational scholars as reflective, reflexive practitioners should re-think about the role and place of gossip in their own research and organizational practice. As Carmel

(2011) observes, gossip is closely linked with social access to participants in ethnographic research. I suggest this is also often the case with access to participants in many other types of organizational research, but this is not always talked or written about. Furthermore, scholars as reflective and reflexive practitioners, can be recast as participant observers, listeners and interpreters of gossip in and around their own institutions and disciplines. This may feel a little uncomfortable, and there are potentially some difficult ethical issues to confront, but arguably there is much scope here for future ethnographic research.

The topic of organizational gossip has given me much 'food for thought,' which I have shared here with readers. I'm curious as to what the future might hold now that gossip has been brought into the foreground. What iterative insights and knowledge might 'gossip about gossip' generate in academic and practitioner communities? Will current and future scholars of gossip be treated with suspicion as writers enmeshed in a morally contentious discourse? Or will we be seen as trustworthy colleagues with whom 'off the record' comments can be shared at conferences and in corridors? I hope that this book will provide a platform for further exploration of organizational gossip and critically reflective evidence-based management practice. There is, I think, plenty of work yet to be done.

Appendix A

Summary of PhD Thesis: The Characteristics and Function of Gossip in Nursing and Healthcare Organizations

This was exploratory research into the charactersistics and function of gossip in nursing and healthcare organizations. The research drew upon theory and research from work and organizational psychology, sociology, and anthropology. A mixed-methods approach was adopted, combining qualitative and quantitative methods of data collection, analysis, and inference. The sample comprised 96 participants, who were all qualified nurses working in a range of National Health Service (NHS) and non-NHS settings in London and South East England. The study comprised three phases. The initial phase of the research used Repertory Grids and a Twenty Statements Test to explore the characteristics and constructs of gossip and compared individual differences in the constructs of gossip with regard to gender and position in the organization. This was followed by in-depth qualitative interviews exploring the role of gossip in relation to organizational socialization, sensemaking, and the expression and management of emotion. The final phase used paper-and-pencil diary records and telephone interviews to explore further the emotional and organizational factors. Critical incident technique was used in the second and third phases to explore contextualized communicative events and incidents of gossip. The findings revealed that gossip is a process through which people construct meaning and communicate emotion. Gossip is a means of 'doing' the emotional labour of nursing work, and is also a problem-solving and emotion-focused coping strategy for dealing with stress. Gossip may also function as both an individual and an organizational defence mechanism. It is the individual who gossips, whereas the organization provides the context, triggers, and opportunities. The research was limited in its exploration of organizational factors relating to size, formal communication, and levels of uncertainty and change, representing potential areas for future research. Postmodernism was advanced as a potentially relevant, but not unproblematic position, within which to understand gossip as discursive practice in nursing and healthcare organizations. Acknowledging the tensions, scepticism, and ambivalence associated with postmodern epistemology, postmodernism was used as a reflexive device to question and reinterpret research findings, disciplinary traditions and practices (Waddington, 2005a).

Table A.1 illustrates the qualitative interview guide; Figure A.1 is an example of structured diary record sheets; Figure A.2 illustrates the framework for data analysis.

Table A.1   Summary of Interview Guide

Dimensions of gossip:
- gossip is informal talk
- occurring between small groups of 2 or more people and
- concerns the verbal exchange of information
- about work related issues

Key words: Perceptions and experience of gossip at work re:
- sensemaking
- socialization
- stress
- emotion – expression/management

Other issues:
- reminder re confidentiality/consent/right to withdraw from study
- will send copy of cognitive map for feedback/comment

Key questions:
1. Background information – how long in post/organization/nursing?
2. How would you define gossip?
3. Please give some examples of times recently when you/others have been engaged in work-related gossip
4. What emotions are being expressed when people gossip?
5. What role does gossip play in the management of emotion?
6. Is there a relationship between gossip and stress?
7. What role does gossip play when someone new starts in the organization?

Date.........Time......am/pm   Length of time of incident approx.........minutes

No of people involved...........Females.........Males

Where the incident took place:..

I disclosed	very little	1	2	3	4	5	6	7	a great deal
Others disclosed	very little	1	2	3	4	5	6	7	a great deal
Social integration	I didn't feel part of the group	1	2	3	4	5	6	7	I felt part of the group
Quality	unpleasant	1	2	3	4	5	6	7	very pleasant
Initiation	I initiated	1	2	3	4	5	6	7	others

What did you gossip about?

How did you feel at the time the above incident took place?

Figure A.1   Example of diary record sheet.

TEXTUAL DATA

Styles of Analysis   **Levels of Analysis**

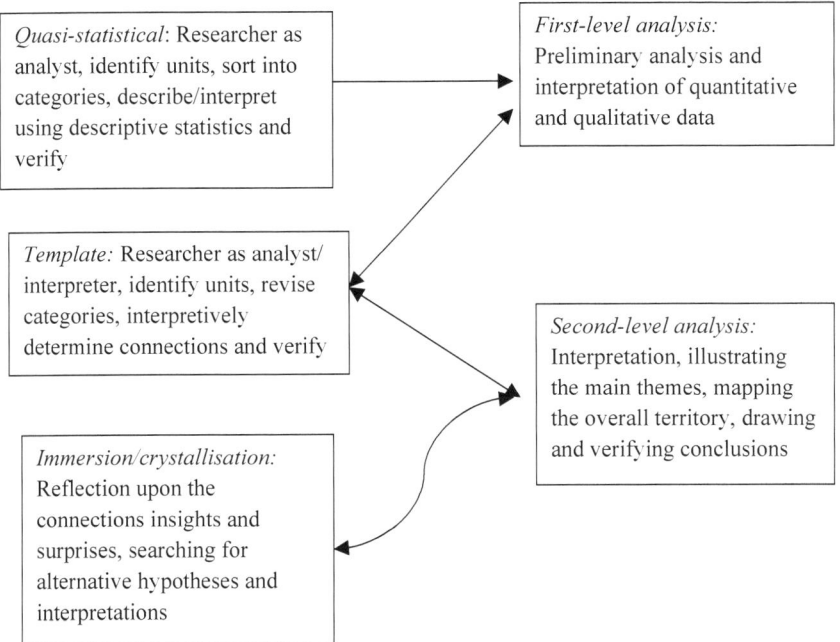

Figure A.2   Framework for combining and integrating qualitative and quantitative data. Adapted from Waddington (2005c).

Appendix B
Summary of HRM Strategies and Academic Engagement Project

BACKGROUND AND AIMS

This was a small-scale mixed-methods research study in six universities in England. The aims were to explore the degree of engagement of academic staff with universities' Human Resource Management (HRM) strategies and associated HR-driven initiatives, and to ascertain reasons for the levels of engagement reported. For the purposes of the research, we defined engagement as the alignment and 'connectivity' of the HR function and academic functions relating to leadership, staff development, recognition, and reward. The project was also located within a broader theoretical and conceptual context of employee engagement, which is defined in terms of being positively present during the performance of work, willingly contributing intellectual effort, experiencing positive emotions and meaningful connections to others (Leiter & Bakker, 2010). The original thinking behind the project arose from Guest and Clinton's (2007) research into HRM and university performance, which had shown that there was no direct association between HR activities and key performance indicators (KPIs) in universities in the UK.

RESEARCH DESIGN

A collaborative academic-practitioner model of research was adopted with the explicit intention of generating research findings of interest and value to HR practitioners, managers of academics, and researchers. Data collection methods were individual interviews with Human Resources Directors (HRDs) and Pro Vice Chancellors (PVCs); an online survey of Heads of Academic Departments; and focus groups with academic staff. Template analysis guided the integration of qualitative and quantitative data. Data collection took place from a sample of six Higher Education Institutions (HEIs) in England. This included pre-and post-1992 universities (so called 'old' and 'new' universities), a Russell Group university (representing one of twenty leading UK universities), and a relatively newly constituted university.

MAIN FINDINGS

Academic staff perceived HR as part of management armoury—the means by which some unpopular initiatives are implemented, rather than as the driving force. HR was generally most valued for its advisory/support role, but valuing HR does not necessarily translate into strong engagement with the HR *strategy.* Where engagement with HR strategy did occur this was characterised by evidence of: (i) unequivocal support for HR at most senior levels of the institution, manifested as familiarity with and 'buy-in' to the content of the HR strategy at PVC level; and (ii) clear organization-wide articulation of the role of the HEI's HR strategy in supporting the institution's wider objectives engenders academic engagement. Academic staff who feel valued and supported are engaged and are more likely to create a more positive student experience. Academics gain advancement by 'movement' within a field/discipline and development of external profile so are less likely to defer to their employing institution for career management and development.

Full report available at: http://www.lfhe.ac.uk/research/smallprojects/research/smallprojects/finalreportcity.pdf

Bibliography

Ackoff, R. L. (1989). From data to wisdom. *Journal of Applied Systems Analysis, 16*(1), 3–9.

Adkins, K. C. (2002). The real dirt: Gossip and feminist epistemology. *Social Epistemology, 16*(3), 215–232.

Alaszewski, A. (2002). The impact of the Bristol Royal Infirmary disaster and inquiry on public services in the UK. *Journal of Interprofessional Care, 16*(4), 371–378.

Alvesson, M., & Ashcraft, K. (2011). Critical methodology in management and organization research. In D. A. Buchanan & A. Bryman (Eds.), *The SAGE handbook of organizational research methods* (pp. 61–77). London: Sage.

Alvesson, M., & Sköldberg, K. (2009). *Reflexive methodology: New vistas for qualitative research,* 2nd ed. London: Sage.

American Psychological Association, (APA). (2010). *Publication manual of the American Psychological Association,* 6th ed. Washington, DC: APA.

Anderson, D. A. (2010). *Creativity and the philosophy of C. S. Peirce.* Dordrecht: Martinus Nijhoff Publishers.

Anderson, E., Seigel, E. H., Bliss–Moreau, E., & Barrett, L. F. (2011). The visual impact of gossip. *Science, 332*(6036), 1446–1448).

Arjoon, S. (2008). Reconciling situational social psychology with virtue ethics. *International Journal of Management Reviews, 10*(3), 221–243.

Armstrong, D. (2004). Emotions in organizations: Disturbance or intelligence? In C. Huffington, D. Armstrong, W. Halton, L. Hoyle, & J. Pooley (Eds.), *Working below the surface: The emotional life of contemporary organizations* (pp. 11–30). London: Karnac.

Armstrong, D., & Huffington, C. (2004). Introduction. In C. Huffington, D.Armstrong, W. Halton, L. Hoyle, & J. Pooley (Eds.), *Working below the surface: The emotional life of contemporary organizations* (pp. 1–10). London: Karnac.

Ashcraft, K. L., Kuhn, T. R., & Cooren, F. (2009). Constitutional amendments: "Materializing" organizational communication. *The Academy of Management Annals, 3*(1), 1–64.

Ashkanasy, N. M. (2003). Emotions in organizations: A multilevel perspective. In F. Dansereau & F. J. Yammarino (Eds.), *Research in multi–level issues, vol. 2: Multi–level issues in organizational behavior and strategy* (pp. 9–54). Oxford: Elsevier Science.

Ashkanasy, N. M. (2011). International happiness: A multilevel perspective. *Academy of Management Perspectives, 25*(1), 23–29.

Ashkanasy, N. M., & Cooper, C. L. (Eds.). (2008). *Research companion to emotion in organizations.* Cheltenham: Edward Elgar Publishing.

Ashkanasy, N. M., Wilderom, C. P. M., & Peterson, M. F. (Eds.). (2011a). *The handbook of organizational culture and climate*, 2nd ed. Thousand Oaks, CA: Sage.

Ashkanasy, N. M., Wilderom, C. P. M., & Peterson, M. F. (2011b). Introduction. In N. M. Ashkanasy, C. P. M. Wilderom, & M. F. Peterson (Eds.), *The handbook of organizational culture and climate*, 2nd ed. (pp.3–10). Thousand Oaks, CA: Sage.

Audi, R. (2012). Virtue ethics as a resource in business. *Business Ethics Quarterly, 22*(2): 273–291.

Ayim, M. (1994). Knowledge through the grapevine: Gossip as inquiry. In R. F. Goodman & A. Ben-Ze'ev (Eds.), *Good gossip* (pp. 85–99). Lawrence, KS: University Press of Kansas.

Aziz, Z. (Ed.). (2010). *English translation of the holy Quran*. Wembley: Ahmadiyya Anjuman Lahore Publications.

Bakker, A. B., & Daniels, K. (Eds.). (2012). *A day in the life of a happy worker*. Hove/New York: Psychology Press.

Bakker, A. B., & Schaufeli, W. B. (2008). Positive organizational behavior: Engaged employees in flourishing organizations. *Journal of Organizational Behavior, 29*(2), 147–154.

Banks-Wallace, J. (2002). Talk that talk: Storytelling and analysis rooted in African American oral tradition. *Qualitative Health Research, 12*(3), 410–426.

Bartlett, II, J. E., & Bartlett, M. E. (2011). Workplace bullying: An integrative literature review. *Advances in Developing Human Resources, 13*(1), 69–84.

Baumeister, R. F., Zhang, L., & Vohs, K. D. (2004). Gossip as cultural learning. *Review of General Psychology, 8*(2), 111–121.

Becker, F. (2007). Nursing unit design and communication patterns: What is "real" work? *Health Environments Research & Design Journal, 1*(1), 58–62.

Becker, W. J., Cropanzano, R., & Sanfey, A. G. (2011). Organizational neuroscience: Taking organizational theory inside the neural black box. *Journal of Management, 37*(4), 933–961.

Beersma, B., &Van Kleef, G. A. (2011). How the grapevine keeps you in line: Gossip increases contributions to the group. *Social Psychological and Personality Science, 2*(6), 642–649.

Bell, E., & Wray–Bliss, E. (2011). Research ethics: Regulations and responsibilities. In D. A. Buchanan & A. Bryman (Eds.), *The SAGE handbook of organizational research methods* (pp. 78–92). London: Sage.

Ben-Ze'ev, A. (1994). The vindication of gossip. In R. F. Goodman & A. Ben-Ze'ev (Eds.), *Good gossip* (pp. 11–24). Lawrence, KS : University Press of Kansas.

Bergmann, J. R. (1993). *Discreet indiscretions: The social organization of gossip*. New York: Aldine de Gruyter.

Beswick, J., Gore, J., & Palferman, D. (2006) *Bullying at work: A review of the literature WPS/06/04*. Health & Science Laboratory. Retrieved from http://www.hse.gov.uk/research/hsl_pdf/2006/hsl0630.pdf

Bisel, R. S. (2010). A communicative ontology of organization? A description, history, and critique of CCO theories for organization science. *Management Communication Quarterly, 24*(1), 124–131.

Blackler, F. (1995). Knowledge, knowledge work and organizations: An overview and interpretation. *Organization Studies, 16*(6), 1021–1046.

Blase, J., & Blase, J. (2004). The dark side of school leadership: implications for administrator preparation. *Leadership and Policy in Schools, 3*(4), 245–273.

Bloom, P. (2004). Postscript to the special issue on gossip. *Review of General Psychology, 8*(2), 138–140.

Boddy, C. R. (2011). Corporate psychopaths, bullying and unfair supervision in the workplace. *Journal of Business Ethics, 100*(3), 367–379.

Boden, D. (1994). *The business of talk: Organizations in action*. Cambridge: Polity Press.

Boje, D. M. (2008). *Storytelling organizations*. London: Sage.

Bolton, S. C. (2005). *Emotion management in the workplace*. Houndmills: Palgrave Macmillan.

Borodzicz, E. P. (2005). *Risk, crisis and security management*. Chichester: John Wiley & Sons.

Bordia, P., Jones, E., Gallois, C., Callan, V. J., & DiFonzo, N. (2006).Management are aliens! Rumors and stress during organizational change. *Group & Organization Management, 31*(5), 601–621.

Borkan, J. (1999). Immersion/crystallization. In B. F. Crabtree & W. L. Miller (Eds.), *Doing qualitative research*, 2nd ed. (pp. 179–194). Thousand Oaks, CA: Sage.

Bosson, J. K., Johnson, A. B., Niederhoffer, K., & Swann Jr., W. B. (2006). Interpersonal chemistry through negativity: Bonding by sharing negative attitudes about others. *Personal Relationships, 13*(2), 135–150.

Bradley, C. P. (1992). Turning anecdotes into data: The critical incident technique. *Family Practice, 9*(1), 98–103.

Bradshaw, K. M., & Saha, S. (2011). Academic administrators and the challenge of social-networking websites. In S. Levmore & M. C. Nussbaum (Eds.), *The offensive internet: Speech, privacy and reputation* (pp. 140–154). Cambridge, MA/London: Harvard University Press.

Bratianu, C. (2011). Changing paradigm for knowledge metaphors from dynamics to thermodynamics. *Systems Research and Behavioral Science, 28*(2), 160–169.

Brenkert, G. G. (2010). The limits and prospects of business ethics. *Business Ethics Quarterly, 20*(4), 703–709.

Briner, R. B., & Kiefer, T. (2005). Psychological research into the experience of emotion at work: Definitely older, but are we any wiser? In N. M. Ashkanasy, C. E. J., Härtel, & W. J. Zerbe (Eds.), *Research on emotion in organizations: The effects of affect in organizational settings, volume 1* (pp. 289–315). Oxford: Elsevier.

Briner, R. B., & Kiefer, T. (2009). Whither psychological research into emotion at work? Feeling for the future. *International Journal of Work Organisation and Emotion, 3*(2), 161–173.

Brown, J. S., Denning, S., Groh, K. & Prusak, L. (2005). *Storytelling in organizations*. Burlington, MA: Elsevier Butterworth-Heinemann.

Brown, J. S., & Duguid, P. (2001). Knowledge and organization: A social-practice perspective. *Organization Science, 12*(2), 198–213.

Browning, L. D., Greene, R. W., Sitkin, S. B., Sutcliffe, K., & Obstfeld, D. (2009). Constitutive complexity: Military entrepreneurs and the synthetic character of communication flows. In L. L. Putnam & M. A. Nicotera (Eds.), *Building theories of organization: The constitutive role of communication* (pp. 89–116). New York/Abingdon: Routledge.

Brummans, B. H. J. M. (2006). The Montréal School and the question of agency. In F. Cooren, J. R. Taylor, & E. J. Van Every (Eds.), *Communication as organizing* (pp. 197–212). Mawah, NJ: Lawrence Erlbaum Associates.

Bryman, A. (2006). Paradigm peace and the implications for quality. *International Journal of Social Research Methodology, 9*(2), 111–126.

Bryman, A. (2011). Mixed methods in organizational research. In D. A. Buchanan & A. Bryman (Eds.), *The SAGE handbook of organizational research methods* (pp. 516–531). London: Sage.

Buchanan, D. (2001). The role of photography in organization research. A reeingeneering case illustration. *Journal of Management Inquiry, 10*(2), 151–164.

Buchanan, D. A. (2008). You stab my back, I'll stab yours: Management experience and perceptions of organization political behaviour. *British Journal of Management, 19*(1), 49–64.

Buchanan, D. A., & Badham, R. J. (2008). *Power, politics and organizational change*, 2nd ed. London: Sage.

Buchanan, D. A., & Bryman, A. (2007). Contextualizing methods choice in organizational research. *Organizational Research Methods, 10*(3), 483–501.

Canary, H. E. (2011). Knowledge types in cross–system policy knowledge construction. In H. E. Canary & R. D. McPhee (Eds.), *Communication and organizational knowledge: Contemporary issues for theory and practice* (pp. 224–263). New York/Abingdon: Routledge.

Canary, H. E., & McPhee, R. D. (Eds.). (2011a). *Communication and organizational knowledge: Contemporary issues for theory and practice*. New York/Abingdon: Routledge.

Canary, H. E., & McPhee, R. D. (2011b). Introduction: Toward a communicative perspective on organizational knowledge. In H. E. Canary & R. D. McPhee (Eds.), *Communication and organizational knowledge: Contemporary issues for theory and practice* (pp. 1–14). New York/Abingdon: Routledge.

Capp, B. (2003). *When gossips meet: Women, family and neighbourhood in early modern England*. Oxford: Oxford University Press.

Carmel, S. (2011). Social access in the workplace: Are ethnographers gossips? *Work, Employment and Society, 25*(3), 551–560.

Case, P., & Phillipson, G. (2004). Astrology, alchemy and retro-organization theory: An astro-genealogical critique of the Myers–Briggs Type Indicator®. *Organization, 11*(4), 473–495.

Cassell, C., & Walsh, S. (2004). Repertory grids. In C. Cassell & G. Symon (Eds.), *Essential guide to qualitative methods in organizational research* (pp. 61–72). London: Sage.

Caza, B. B., & Caza, A. (2008). Positive organizational scholarship: A critical theory perspective. *Journal of Management Inquiry, 17*(1), 21–33.

Chapman, S., with Sharkey, B. (2009). *The no-gossip zone*. Naperville, IL: Sourcebooks.

Chell, E. (2004). Critical incident technique. In C. Cassell & G. Symon (Eds.), *Essential guide to qualitative methods in organizational research* (pp. 45–60). London: Sage.

Chia, R. (2004). Re-educating attention: What is foresight and how is it cultivated? In H. Touskas & J. Shepherd (Eds.), *Managing the future: Foresight in the knowledge economy* (pp. 21–31). Oxford: Blackwell.

Chia, R. (2005). The aim of management education: Reflections on Mintzberg's 'Managers not MBAs'. *Organization Studies, 26*(7), 1090–1092.

Chong, P. (2009). Servitude with a smile: A re-examination of emotional labour. *Just Labour: A Canadian Journal of Work and Society, 14*, 177–185. Retrieved from http://www.justlabour.yorku.ca/volume14/pdfs/ss_06_chong_press.pdf

Christensen, L. T., & Cornelissen, J. (2011). Bridging corporate and organizational communication: Review, development and a look to the future. *Management Communication Quarterly, 25*(3), 383–414.

Clegg, S. R. (1989). *Frameworks of power*. London: Sage.

Clegg, S. (2011). Doing power work. In D. A. Buchanan & A. Bryman (Eds.), *The SAGE handbook of organizational research methods* (pp. 141–159). London: Sage.

Clegg, S. R., & van Iterson, A. (2009). Dishing the dirt: Gossiping in organizations. *Culture and Organization, 15*(3–4), 275–289.

Code, L. (1994). Gossip, or in praise of chaos. In R. F. Goodman & A. Ben-Ze'ev (Eds.), *Good gossip* (pp. 100–105). Lawrence, KS : University Press of Kansas.

Colin Thomé, D. (2009). *Mid Staffordshire NHS Foundation Trust: A review of lessons learnt for commissioners and performance managers following the Healthcare Commission investigation.* Retrieved from http://www.midstaff-spublicinquiry.com/sites/default/files/David_Colin-Thome_report_on_Mid_Staffs.pdf

Collins, G. (2007). *Scorpion tongues.* New York: Harper Perennial.

Connolly, T. H. (2010). Business ritual studies: Corporate ceremony and sacred space. *International Journal of Business Anthropology, 1*(2), 32–47.

Contandriopoulos, D., Lemire, M., Denis, J.-L., & Tremblay, É. (2010). Knowledge exchange processes in organizations and policy arenas: A narrative systematic review of the literature. *The Milbank Quarterly, 88*(4), 444–483.

Conte, J. M. (2005). A review and critique of emotional intelligence measures. *Journal of Organizational Behavior, 26*(4), 433–440.

Cooper-Thomas, H. D., & Anderson, N. (2006). Organizational socialization: A new theoretical model and recommendations for future research and HRM practices in organizations. *Journal of Managerial Psychology, 21*(5), 492–516.

Cooren, F. (2000). *The organizing property of communication.* Amsterdam/Philadelphia: John Benjamins.

Cooren, F., & Fairhurst, G. T. (2009). Dislocation and stabilization: How to scale up from interactions to organization. In L. L. Putnam & M. A. Nicotera (Eds.), *Building theories of organization: The constitutive role of communication* (pp.117–152). New York/Abingdon: Routledge.

Cooren, F., Kuhn, T., Cornelissen, J. P., & Clark, T. (2011). Communication, organizing and organization: An overview and introduction to the special issue. *Organization Studies, 32*(9), 1149–1170.

Cooren, F., Taylor, J. T., & Van Every, E. J. (2006). Introduction. In F. Cooren, J. R. Taylor, & E. J. Van Every (Eds.), *Communication as organizing* (pp. 1–18). Mawah, NJ: Lawrence Erlbaum Associates.

Corley, K. G., & Gioia, D. A. (2011). Building theory about theory building: What constitutes a theoretical contribution? *Academy of Management Review, 36*(1), 12–32.

Cornelissen, J. P. (2005). Beyond compare: Metaphor in organization theory. *Academy of Management Review, 30*(4), 751–764.

Cornelissen, J. P. (2006a). Making sense of theory construction: Metaphor and disciplined imagination. *Organization Studies, 27*(11), 1579–1597.

Cornelissen, J. P. (2006b). Metaphor and the dynamics of knowledge in organization theory: A case study of the organizational identity metaphor. *Journal of Management Studies, 43*(4), 683–709.

Cornelissen, J. P. (2007). The metaphorical construction of organizational identity. In A. Pullen, N. Beech, & D. Sims (Eds.), *Exploring identity: Concepts and methods* (pp. 44–60). Houndmills/New York: Palgrave Macmillan.

Cornelissen, J. P., Oswick, C., Christensen, L. T., & Phillips, N. (2008). Metaphor in organizational research: Context, modalities and implications for research—introduction. *Organization Studies, 29*(1), 7–22.

Côté, S., & Hideg, I. (2011). The ability to influence others via emotion displays: A new dimension of emotional intelligence. *Organizational Psychology Review, 1*(1), 53–71.

Cresswell, J. W., & Plano Clark, V. L. (2011). *Designing and conducting mixed methods research,* 2nd ed. Thousand Oaks, CA: Sage.

Cunliffe, A. L. (2003). Reflexive inquiry in organizational research: Questions and possibilities. *Human Relations, 56*(8), 983–1003.

Cupach, W. R., & Spitzberg, B. H. (Eds.). (2011). *The dark side of close relationships,* 2nd ed. New York/Abingdon: Routledge.

Dale, K., & Burrell, G. (2008). *The spaces of organization and the organization of space: Power, identity and materiality at work*. Basingstoke: Palgrave Macmillan.

Danaher, G., Schirato, T., & Webb, J. (2000). *Understanding Foucault*. St Leonards, NSW: Allen & Unwin.

Dane, E., & Pratt, M. G. (2007). Exploring intuition and its role in managerial decision making. *Academy of Management Review, 32*(1), 33–54.

Davey, K. M. (2008). Women's accounts of organizational politics as a gendering process. *Gender, Work and Organization, 15*(6), 650–671.

Denzin, N. K., & Lincoln, Y. S. (2005). Introduction: The discipline and practice of qualitative research. In N. K. Denzin & Y. S. Lincoln (Eds.), *The SAGE handbook of qualitative research*, 3rd ed. (pp. 1–32). Thousand Oaks, CA: Sage.

Department of Health (DH). (2005). *The Kerr/Haslam inquiry*. London: The Stationery Office.

DiFonzo, N. (2008). *The watercooler effect*. New York: Avery.

DiFonzo, N., & Bordia, P. (2007). *Rumor psychology: Social and organizational approaches*. Washington, DC: American Psychological Association.

DiFonzo, N., Bordia, P., & Rosnow, R. (1994). Reining in rumors. *Organizational Dynamics, 23*(1), 47–62.

Doucet, A. (2008)."From her side of the gossamer wall(s)": Reflexivity and relational knowing. *Qualitative Sociology, 31*(1), 73–87.

Douglas, M. (1966). *Purity and danger: An analysis of concepts of pollution and taboo*. London: Routledge & Kegan Paul.

Doyle, J. (2000). *New community or new slavery? The emotional divison of labour*. London: The Industrial Society.

Draft Defamation Bill. (2011). London: The Stationary Office. Retrieved from http://www.justice.gov.uk/downloads/consultations/draft-defamation-bill-consultation.pdf

Dreyfus, H. L., & Rabinow, P. (1983). *Michel Foucault: Beyond structuralism and hermeneutics*, 2nd ed. Chicago: The University of Chicago Press.

du Gay, P. (2007). *Organizing identity*. London: Sage.

Dunbar, R. (1992). Why gossip is good for you. *New Scientist, 136*(1848), 28–31.

Dunbar, R. (1996). *Grooming, gossip and the evolution of language*. London: Faber & Faber.

Dunbar, R. (2004). Gossip in evolutionary perspective. *Review of General Psychology, 8*(2), 100–110.

Dunbar, R., Duncan, N., & Marriott, A. (1997). Human conversational behaviour. *Human Nature, 8*(3), 231–246.

Eder, D., & Enke, J. L. (1991). The structure of gossip: Opportunities and constraints on collective expression among adolescents. *American Sociological Review, 56*(4), 494–508.

Einarsen, S., Hoel, H., Zapf, D. & Cooper, C. L. (Eds.). (2003). *Bullying and emotional abuse in the workplace*. London/New York: Taylor & Francis.

Elfenbein, H. A. (2007). Emotion in organizations: A review and theoretical integration. *Academy of Management Annals, 1*(1), 315–386.

Elias, N., & Scotson, J. L. (1965). *The established and the outsiders: A sociological enquiry into community problems*. London: Cass & Co.

Emler, N. (1994). Gossip, reputation, and social adaptation. In R.F. Goodman & A. Ben-Ze'ev (Eds.), *Good gossip* (pp. 117–138). Lawrence, KS : University Press of Kansas.

Ernst, S. (2003). From blame gossip to praise gossip? Gender, leadership and organizational change. *European Journal of Women's Studies, 10*(3), 277–299.

Ervin-Tripp, S. (1964). An analysis of the interaction of language, topic and listener. *American Anthropologist, 66*(6), 86–102.

Escartín, J., Zapf, D., Arrieta, C., & Rodríguez–Carballeira, A. (2011). Workers' perception of workplace bullying: A cross-cultural study. *European Journal of Work and Organizational Psychology, 20*(2), 178–205.

Esser, J. K., & Lindoerfer, J. S. (1989). Groupthink and the space shuttle Challenger accident: Toward a quantitative case analysis. *Journal of Behavioral Decision Making, 2*(3), 167–177.

Farley, S. D. (2011). Is gossip power? The inverse relationships between gossip, power, and likability. *European Journal of Social Psychology, 41*(5), 574–579.

Fayard, A-L., & Weeks, J. (2007). Photocopiers and watercoolers: Affordances of informal interaction. *Organization Studies, 28*(5), 605–634.

Ferris, G. R., Treadway, D. C., Kolodinsky, R. W., Hochwarter, W. A., Kacmar, C. J., Douglas, C., & Frink, D. D. (2005). Development and validation of the Political Skills Inventory. *Journal of Management, 31*(1), 126–152.

Fine, G., & Rosnow, R. (1978). Gossip, gossipers, gossiping. *Personality and Social Psychology Bulletin, 4*(1), 161–168.

Fine, G. A., Morrill, C., & Surianarain, S. (2011). Ethnography in organizational settings. In D. A. Buchanan & A. Bryman (Eds.), *The SAGE handbook of organizational research methods* (pp. 602–619). London: Sage.

Fineman, S. (Ed.). (1993). *Emotion in organizations*. London: Sage.

Fineman, S. (Ed.). (2000). *Emotion in organizations*, 2nd ed. London: Sage.

Fineman, S. (2003). *Understanding emotion at work*. London: Sage.

Fineman, S. (2005). Appreciating emotion at work: Paradigm tensions. *International Journal of Work Organisation and Emotion, 1*(1), 4–19.

Fisher, C. D. (2010). Happiness at work. *International Journal of Management Reviews, 12*(4), 384–412.

Fiske, S. T. (2004) Mind the gap: In praise of informal sources of formal theory. *Personality and Social Psychology Review, 8*(2), 132–137.

Fitzgerald, S. P., Oliver, C., & Hoxsey, J. C. (2010). Appreciative inquiry as a shadow process. *Journal of Management Inquiry, 19*(3), 220–233.

Flanagin, A. J., & Bator, M. (2011). The utility of information and communication technologies in organizational knowledge management. In H. E. Canary & R. D. McPhee (Eds.), *Communication and organizational knowledge: Contemporary issues for theory and practice* (pp. 173–190). New York/Abingdon: Routledge.

Fletcher, Joyce K. (2009). *Disappearing acts: Gender, power and relational practice at work*. Cambridge, MA: The MIT Press.

Fletcher, Pamela. (2009). Narrative painting and visual gossip at the early-twentieth-century Royal Academy. *Oxford Art Journal, 32*(2), 243–262.

Fook, J., & Gardner, F. (2007). *Practising critical reflection: A resource handbook*. Maidenhead: Open University Press.

Foster, E. K. (2004). Research on gossip: Taxonomy, methods and future directions. *Review of General Psychology, 8*(2), 78–99.

Foucault, M. (1979). *Discipline and punish: The birth of the prison*. Translated by Alan Sheridan. New York: Vintage/Random House.

Fox, K. (2001). *Evolution, alienation and gossip*. Oxford: Social Issues Research Centre.

Frost, P. J. (2003). *Toxic emotions at work*. Boston MA: Harvard Business School Press.

Gabriel, Y. (1995). The unmanaged organization: Stories, fantasies and subjectivity. *Organization Studies, 16*(3), 477–501.

Gabriel, Y. (1999). *Organizations in depth*. London: Sage.

Gabriel, Y. (2000). *Storytelling in organizations: Facts, fictions and fantasies*. Oxford: Oxford University Press.

Gabriel, Y., with Schwartz, H. S. (1999). Introduction: Psychoanalysis and organization. In Y. Gabriel, *Organizations in depth* (pp. 1–12). London: Sage.

Gallos, J. (2008). Learning from the toxic trenches. *Journal of Management Inquiry, 17*(4), 354–367.

Geiger, D., & Antonacopoulou, E. (2009). Narratives and organizational dynamics: Exploring blind spots and organizational inertia. *The Journal of Applied Behavioral Science, 45*(3), 411–436.

Gelade, G. A. (2006). But what does it mean in practice? The Journal of Occupational and Organizational Psychology from a practitioner perspective. *Journal of Occupational and Organizational Psychology, 79*(2), 153–160.

Gillespie, N., & Dietz, G. (2009). Trust repair after an organizational-level failure. *Academy of Management Review, 34* (1), 127–145.

Gillis, T. L. (Ed.). (2006). *The IABC handbook of organizational communication.* San Francisco: Jossey-Bass.

Gilmore, D. (1978). Varieties of gossip in a Spanish rural community. *Ethnology, 17*(1), 89–99.

Glaser, B. G. (1978) *Theoretical sensitivity.* Mill Vallery, CA: Sociology Press.

Glinert, L., Loewenthal, K. M., & Goldblatt, V. (2003). Guarding the tongue: A thematic analysis of gossip control strategies among orthodox Jewish women in London. *Journal of Multilingual and Multicultural Development, 24*(6), 513–524.

Gluckman, M. (1963). Gossip and scandal. *Current Anthropology, 4*(3), 307–316.

Goffman, E. (1959). *The presentation of self in everyday life.* New York: Doubleday.

Goodman, R. F., & Ben-Ze'ev, A. (Eds.). (1994). *Good gossip.* Lawrence, KS : University Press of Kansas.

Gorard, S. (2005). Current contexts for research in educational leadership and management. *Educational Management Administration and Leadership, 33*(2), 155–164.

Gotsis, G. N., & Kortezi, Z. (2010). Ethical considerations in organizational politics: Expanding the perspective. *Journal of Business Ethics. 93*(4), 497–517.

Graham, J. W., & Van Dyne, L. (2006). Gathering information and exercising influence: Two forms of civic virtue organizational citizenship behavior. *Employee Responsibilities and Rights Journal, 18*(2), 89–109.

Grandey, A. A. (2008). Emotions at work: a review and research agenda. In J. Barling & C. L. Cooper (Eds.), *Handbook of organizational behaviour* (pp. 235–261). London: Sage.

Grant, D., Hardy, C., Oswick, C., & Putnam, L. L. (Eds.). (2004). *The SAGE handbook of organizational discourse.* London: Sage.

Grant, D., Hardy, C., & Putnam, L. L. (Eds.). (2011). *Organizational discourse studies.* Thousand Oaks, CA: Sage.

Green, J. (1998). *The Cassell dictionary of slang.* London: Cassell.

Greene, J. C. (2008). Is mixed methods social inquiry a distinctive methodology? *Journal of Mixed Methods Research, 2*(1), 7–22.

Greenfield, S. (2009). *ID: The quest for meaning in the 21st century.* London: Sceptre.

Greengard, S. (2001). Gossip poisons business: HR can stop it. *Workforce, 80*(7), 24–28.

Greenhalgh, T. (2010). What is this thing knowledge that we seek to "exchange"? *Milbank Quarterly, 88*(4), 492–499.

Grey, C., & Sinclair, A. (2006). Writing differently. *Organization, 13*(3), 443–453.

Grosser, T. J., Lopez–Kidwell, V., & Labianca, G. (2010). A social network analysis of positive and negative gossip in organizational life. *Group & Organization Management, 35*(2), 177–212.

Guest, D. E., & Clinton, M. (2007). *Human resource management and university performance*. London: Leadership Foundation for Higher Education.

Guillemin, M., & Gillam, L. (2004). Ethics, reflexivity, and "ethically important moments" in research. *Qualitative Inquiry, 10*(2), 261–280.

Hallam Moorhouse, E. (1909/2008). *Samuel Pepys: Administrator, observer, gossip*. London: Leonard Parsons.

Hallett, T., Harger, B., & Eder, D. (2009). Gossip at work: Unsanctioned evaluative talk in formal school meetings. *Journal of Contemporary Ethnography, 38*(5), 584–618.

Harrington, C. L., & Bielby, D. D. (1995). Where did you hear that? Technology and the social organization of gossip. *Sociological Quarterly, 36*(3), 607–628.

Hartley, J., Fletcher, C., Wilton, P., Woodman, P., & Ungemach, C. (2007). *Leading with political awareness*. London: Chartered Management Institute.

Hartman, E. M. (2008). Socratic questions and Aristotelian answers: A virtue–based approach to business ethics. *Journal of Business Ethics, 78*,(3), 313–328.

Harvey, J. B. (1974). The Abilene paradox: The management of agreement. *Organizational Dynamics, 3*(1), 63–80.

Haslam, Michael (2006). *Sailing close to the wind*. Durham: The Memoir Club.

Haslam, S. Alexander (2004). *Psychology in organizations: The social identity approach*, 2nd ed. London: Sage.

Haslam, S. Alexander, & Ellemers, N. (2005). Social identity in industrial and organizational psychology: Concepts, controversies and contributions. In G. P. Hodgkinson & J. K. Ford (Eds.), *International review of industrial and organizational psychology 2005, volume 20* (pp. 39–118). Chichester: John Wiley & Sons.

Haslam, S. Alexander, Reicher, S. D, & Platow, M. J. (2011). *The new psychology of leadership: Identity, influence and power*. Psychology Press: Hove/New York.

Heidegger, M. (1962). *Being and time*. New York: Harper & Row.

Henriksen, K., & Dayton, E. (2006). Organizational silence and hidden threats to patient safety. *HSR: Health Services Research 41*(4, Part 2), 1539–1554.

Heracleous, L., & Jacobs, C. D. (2008). Understanding organizations through embodied metaphors. *Organization Studies, 29*(1), 45–78.

Hinshelwood, R.D., & Skogstad, W. (Eds.). (2000). *Observing organisations: Anxiety, defence and culture in health and social care*. London/Philadelphia: Routledge.

Ho, J. A. (2010). Ethical perception: Are differences between ethnic groups situation dependent? *Business Ethics: A European Review, 19*(2), 154–182.

Hochschild, A. R. (1979). Emotion work, feeling rules and social structure. *American Journal of Sociology, 85*(3), 551–575.

Hochschild, A. R (1983). *The managed heart: Commercialization of human feeling*. Berkeley: University of California Press.

Hodgkinson, G. P., Langan-Fox, J., & Sadler-Smith, E. (2008). Intuition: A fundamental bridging concept in the behavioural sciences. *British Journal of Psychology, 99*(1), 1–27.

Hofstede, G., Hofstede, G. J., & Minkov, M. (2010). *Cultures and organizations: Software of the mind*. New York: McGraw–Hill.

Holland, J. (2007). Emotions and research. *International Journal of Social Research Methodology, Theory and Practice, 10*(3), 195–209.

Hurdley, R. (2010a). The power of corridors: Connecting doors, mobilising materials, plotting openness. *The Sociological Review, 58*(1), 45–64.

Hurdley, R. (2010b). In the picture or off the wall? Ethical regulation, research habitus, and unpeopled ethnography. *Qualitative Inquiry, 16*(6), 517–528.

Hutchinson, M., Vickers, M. H., Jackson, D., & Wilkes, L. (2010). Bullying as circuits of power. *Administrative Theory & Praxis, 32*(1), 25–47.

Huy, Q. N. (2011). How middle managers' group–focus emotions and social identities influence strategy implementation. *Strategic Management Journal, 32*(13), 1387–1410.

Hyde, D. (2008). *Vagueness, logic and ontology.* Aldershot: Ashgate.

Ivester, M. (2011). *Lol. . .OMG!* Reno, NV: Serra Knight Publishing.

Jablin, F. M., & Putnam, L. L. (Eds.). (2001). *The new handbook of organizational communication.* Thousand Oaks, CA: Sage.

Jaeger, M. E., Skleder, A. A., & Rosnow, R. (1998). Who's up on the low down? Gossip in interpersonal relationships. In B.H. Spitzberg and W.R. Cupach (Eds.), *The dark side of close relationships* (pp. 103–117). Mahwah, NJ: Lawrence Erlbaum Associates.

Janis, I. (1972). *Victims of groupthink: A psychological study of foreign–policy decisions and fiascoes.* Boston: Houghton Mifflin.

Johnson, R. B., Onwuegbuzie, A. J., & Turner, L. A. (2007). Toward a definition of mixed methods research. *Journal of Mixed Methods Research, 1*(2), 112–133.

Jones, Candace, & Volpe, E. H. (2011). Organizational identification: Extending our understanding of social identities through social networks. *Journal of Organizational Behavior, 32*(3), 413–434.

Jones, Deborah. (1980). Gossip: Notes on women's oral culture. *Women's Studies International Quarterly, 3*(2/3), 193–198.

Jones, Elizabeth, Watson, B., Gardner, J. and Gallois, C. (2004). Organizational communication: challenges for the new century, Journal of Communication, 54(4), 722–750.

Kahn, W. A. (2005).*Holding fast: The struggle to create resilient caregiving organizations.* Hove/New York: Routledge.

Kellerman, B. (2004). *Bad leadership: What it is, how it happens, why it matters.* Boston, MA: Harvard Buisiness School Press.

Kelly, G. A. (1955). *The psychology of personal constructs, volumes 1 and 2.* New York: Norton.

Kennedy, I. (2001). *Learning from Bristol: The report of the public inquiry into children's heart surgery at Bristol Royal Infirmary 1984–1995.* The Stationary Office: London.

King, N. (1994). The qualitative research interview. In C. Cassell & G. Symon (Eds.), *Qualitative methods in organizational research* (pp.14–36). London: Sage.

Klaes, M. (2004). Evolutionary economics: In defence of 'vagueness'. *Journal of Economic Methodology, 11*(3), 359–376 .

Kniffin, K. M., & Wilson, D. S. (2005). Utilities of gossip across organizational levels: Multilevel selection, free-riders, and teams. *Human Nature, 16*(3), 278–292.

Kniffin, K. M., & Wilson, D. S. (2010). Evolutionary perspectives on workplace gossip: Why and how gossip can serve groups. *Group & Organization Management, 35*(2), 150–176.

Kolb, D. G. (2008). Exploring the metaphor of connectivity: Attributes, dimensions and duality. *Organization Studies, 29*(1), 127–144.

Kruml, S. M., & Geddes, D. (2000). Catching fire without burning out: Is there an ideal way to perform emotional labor? In N. M. Ashkanasy, C. E. J. Härtel, & W. J. Zerbe (Eds.), *Emotions in the workplace: Research, theory, and practice* (pp. 177–88). Westport: Quorum Books.

Kuhn, T., & Jackson, M. H. (2008). Accomplishing knowledge: A framework for investigating knowing in organizations. *Management Communication Quarterly, 21*(4), 454–485.

Kurland, N .B., & Pelled, L. H. (2000). Passing the word: Toward a model of gossip and power in the workplace. *Academy of Management Review, 25*(2), 428–438.

Kurtz, C. F., & Snowden, D. J. (2007). Bramble bushes in a thicket: Narrative and the intangibles of learning networks. In M. Gibbert & T. Durand (Eds.), *Strategic networks: Learning to compete* (pp. 121–150). Malden, MA: Blackwell Publishing Ltd.

Laing, M. (1993). Gossip: Does it play a role in the socialization of nurses? *IMAGE: Journal of Nursing Scholarship, 25*(1), 37–43.

Lakoff. G., & Johnson, M. (1980). *Metaphors we live by.* Chicago: University of Chicago Press.

Latour, B. (2007). *Reassembling the social: An introduction to actor-network-theory.* Oxford: Oxford University Press.

Leach, M. (1995). (Re)searching Dewey for feminist imaginaries: Linguistic continuity, discourse and gossip. In J. W. Garrison (Ed.), *The new scholarship on Dewey* (pp. 123–138). Dordrecht: Kluwer Academic Publishers.

Leach, M. (2000). Feminist figurations: Gossip as counterdiscourse. In E. A. St. Pierre & W.S. Pillow (Eds.), *Working the ruins: Poststructural theory and methods in education* (pp. 223–236). New York/London: Routledge.

Leclercq-Vandelannoitte, A. (2011). Organizations as discursive constructions: A Foucauldian approach. *Organization Studies, 32*(9), 1247–1271.

Lee, R. M. (1993). *Doing research on sensitive topics.* London: Sage.

Lee, R. M. (1995). *Dangerous fieldwork: Qualitative research methods series 34.* London: Sage.

Leiter, M. P., & Bakker, A. B. (2010). Introduction. In A. B. Bakker & M. P. Leiter (Eds.), *Work engagement: A handbook of essential theory and research* (pp. 1–9). Hove/New York: Psychology Press.

Leonardi, P. M. (2011). Information, technology, and knowledge sharing in global organizations. In H. E. Canary & R. D. McPhee (Eds.), *Communication and organizational knowledge: Contemporary issues for theory and practice* (pp. 89–112). New York/Abingdon: Routledge.

Levin, J., & Arluke, A. (1985). An exploratory analysis of sex differences in gossip. *Sex Roles, 12*(3/4), 281–286.

Levmore, S., & Nussbaum, M. C. (2011). Introduction. In S. Levmore, & M. C. Nussbaum (Eds), *The offensive internet: Speech, privacy and reputation* (pp. 1–14). Cambridge MA/London: Harvard University Press.

Lewis, M., Haviland-Jones, J. M., & Barrett, J. F. (Eds.). (2008). *Handbook of emotions*, 3rd ed. New York: The Guildford Press.

Lipman-Blumen, J. (2005). *The allure of toxic leaders: Why we follow destructive bosses and corrupt politicians—and how we can survive them.* New York: Oxford University Press.

Locke, K., Golden-Biddle, K., & Feldman, M. S. (2004). Imaginative theorizing in interpretive organizational research. *Academy of Management Best Conference Paper RM*, B1–B6. Retrieved from http://daviddenyer.info/wp-content/uploads/2011/10/Locke-Golden-Biddle-Feldman-IMAGINATIVE-THEORIZING-IN-INTERPRETIVE-ORGANIZATIONAL-RESEARCH.pdf

Locke, K., Golden-Biddle, K., & Feldman, M. S. (2008). Making doubt generative: Rethinking the role of doubt in the research process. *Organization Science,19*(6), 907–918.

Luhmann, N. (1995). *Social systems.* Stanford, CA: Stanford University Press.

Lyon, A., & Chesebro, J. L. (2011). The politics of knowledge. In H. E. Canary & R. D. McPhee (Eds.), *Communication and organizational knowledge: Contemporary issues for theory and practice* (pp. 69–86). New York/Abingdon: Routledge.

MacLean, T., Anteby, M., Hudson, B. & Rudolph, J.W. (2006). Talking tainted topics: Insights and ideas on researching socially disapproved organizational behaviour. *Journal of Management Inquiry, 15*(1), 59–68.

Mark, A. (2005). Organizing emotions in health care. *Journal of Health Organization and Management, 19*(4/5), 277–289.

Martin, J. (1990). Deconstructing organizational taboos: The suppression of gender conflict in organizations. *Organization Science, 1*(4), 339–359.

Marzano, M. (2007). Informed consent, deception, and research freedom in qualitative research. *Qualitative Inquiry, 13*(3), 417–436.

May, Steve, & Mumby, D. K. (Eds.). (2005a). *Engaging organizational communication theory and research.* Thousand Oaks, CA: Sage.

May, Steve, & Mumby, D. K. (2005b). Conclusion: Engaging the future of organizational communication theory and research. In S. May & D. K. Mumby (Eds.), *Engaging organizational communication theory and research* (pp. 263–281). Thousand Oaks, CA: Sage.

May, Tim, with Perry, B. (2011). *Social research and reflexivity: Content, consequence and context.* London: Sage.

Mayer, J. D., & Salovey, P. (1997). What is emotional intelligence? In P. Salovey, & D. Sluyter (Eds.), *Emotional development and emotional intelligence: Educational implications* (pp. 3–31). New York: Basic Books.

Mayer, J. D., Roberts, R. D. & Barsade, S. G. (2008). Human abilities: Emotional intelligence. *Annual Review of Psychology, 59*, 507–536.

Maxwell, J. A., & Mittapalli, K. (2010). Realism as a stance for mixed methods research. In A. Tashakkori & C. Teddlie (Eds.), *SAGE handbook of mixed methods in social & behavioural research* (pp. 145–168). Thousand Oaks, CA: Sage.

McGowan, R. A. (2009). Managerial discourses of work and eldercare: (Re)producing, resisting and negotiating boundaries between private and public. *Culture and Organization, 15*(3–4), 307–329.

McPhee, R. D. (2004). Clegg and Giddens on power and (post)modernity. *Management Communication Quarterly, 18*(1), 129–145.

McPhee, R. D., & Zaug, P. (2000). The communicative constitution of organization: A framework for explanation. *Electronic Journal of Communication, 10*(1/2). Retrieved from http://www.cios.org/www/ejc/v10n1200.htm

McPhee, R. D., & Zaug, P. (2009). The communicative constitution of organization: A framework for explanation. In L. M. Putnam & A. M. Nicotera (Eds.), *Building theories of organization: The constitutive role of communication* (pp. 21–47). New York/Abingdon: Routledge.

McPhee, R. D., & Iverson, J. (2009). Agents of constitution in Communidad: Constitutive processes of communication in organizations. In L. L. Putnam & A. M. Nicotera (Eds.), *Building theories of organization: The constitutive role of communication* (pp. 49–88). New York/Abingdon: Routledge.

McPhee, R. D., Canary, H. E., & Iverson, J. O. (2011). Conclusion: Moving forward with communicative perspectives on organizational knowledge. In H. E. Canary & R. D. McPhee (Eds.), *Communication and organizational knowledge: Contemporary issues for theory and practice* (pp. 304–313). New York/Abingdon: Routledge.

Medini, G., & Rosenberg, E.H. (1976). Gossip and psychotherapy. *American Journal of Psychotherapy, 30*(3), 452–462.

Menzies, I. E. P. (1989). *The functioning of social systems as a defence against anxiety.* London: Tavistock Institute of Human Relations.

Michelson, G., & Mouly, S. (2000). Rumour and gossip in organisations: A conceptual study. *Management Decision, 38*(5), 339–346.

Michelson, G., & Mouly, S. (2002). "You didn't hear it from us but. . .": Towards an understanding of rumour and gossip in organisations. *Australian Journal of Management,* Special Issue, *27*(1), 57–65.

Michelson, G., & Mouly, S. (2004). Do loose lips sink ships? The meaning, antecedents and consequences of rumour and gossip in organisations. *Corporate Communications: An International Journal, 9*(3), 189–201.

Michelson, G., van Iterson, A., & Waddington, K. (2010). Gossip in organizations: Contexts, consequences and controversies. *Group & Organization Management, 35*(4), 371–390.

Miettinen, R., Samra-Fredericks, D., & Yanow, D. (2009). Re-turn to practice: An introductory essay. *Organization Studies, 30*(12), 1309–1327.

Miller, B. K., Rutherford, M. A., & Kolodinsky, R. W. (2008). Perceptions of organizational politics: A meta-analysis of outcomes. *Journal of Business and Psychology, 22*(3), 209–222.

Milliken, F. J., Morrison, E. W., & Hewlin, P. F. (2003). An exploratory study of employee silence: Issues that employees don't communicate upward and why. *Journal of Management Studies, 40*(6), 1453–1476.

Mills, C. (2010). Experiencing gossip: The foundations for a theory of embedded organizational gossip. *Group & Organization Management, 35*(2), 213–240.

Mirchandani, K. (2003). Challenging racial silences in studies of emotion work: Contributions from antiracist feminist theory. *Organization Studies, 24*(5), 721–742.

Moeller, S., & Brady, C. (2007). *Intelligent M & A: Navigating the mergers and acquisitions minefield*. Chichester: John Wiley & Sons.

Molloy, K., & Waddington, K. (2011). Learning about leadership through critical reflection and practitioner-academic co-inquiry. *European Work and Organizational Psychology in Practice, 4*, 18–39.

Morrison, E. W., & Milliken, F. J. (2000). Organizational silence: A barrier to change and development in a pluralistic world. *Academy of Management Review, 25*(4), 706–725.

Moser, K. S. (2007). Metaphors as symbolic environment of the self: How self-knowledge is expressed verbally. *Current Research in Social Psychology, 12*(11), 151–178.

Mumby, D. K. (2001). Power and politics. In F. M. Jablin & L. L. Putnam (Eds.), *The new handbook of organizational communication* (pp. 585–623). Thousand Oaks, CA: Sage.

Mumby, D. K. (2004). Nomadic theorizing with a power compass: Clegg, interstitiality, and critical organizational communication studies. *Management Communication Quarterly, 18*(1), 115–128.

Murphy, A. G., & Eisenberg, E. M. (2011). Knowledge in health care organizations. In H. E. Canary & R. D. McPhee (Eds.), *Communication and organizational knowledge: Contemporary issues for theory and practice* (pp. 264–284). New York/Abingdon: Routledge.

Myers, K. K. (2011). Socialization through workgroup interaction. In H. E. Canary & R. D. McPhee (Eds.), *Communication and organizational knowledge: Contemporary issues for theory and practice* (pp. 285–303). New York/Abingdon: Routledge.

Nevo, O., Nevo, B., & Derech-Zehavi, A. (1994). The tendency to gossip as a psychological disposition: Constructing a measure and validating it. In R.F. Goodman & A. Ben-Ze'ev (Eds.), *Good gossip* (pp. 180–192). Lawrence, KS : University Press of Kansas.

Nicholson, N. (2001). The new word on gossip. *Psychology Today, 34*(3), 40–45.

Nicolini, D. (2011). Practice as the site of knowing: Insights from the field of telemedicine. *Organization Science, 22*(3), 602–620.

Nilan, P. (2002). 'Dangerous fieldwork' re-examined: The question of researcher subject position. *Qualitative Research, 2*(3), 363–386.

Nonaka, I. (1994). A dynamic theory of organizational knowledge creation. *Organization Science, 5*(1), 14–37.

Nonaka, I., & von Krogh, G. (2009). Tacit knowledge and knowledge conversion: Controversy and advancement in organizational knowledge creation theory. *Organization Science, 20*(3), 635–652.

Noon, M. (2001). Suggested revisions to Kurland and Pelled's model of gossip and power. *Academy of Management Review, 26*(2), 173–174.

Noon, M., & Blyton, P. (2007). *The realities of work*, 3rd ed. Houndmills: Palgrave Macmillan.

Noon, M., & Delbridge, R. (1993). News from behind my hand: Gossip in organizations. *Organization Studies, 14*(1), 23–36.

Obholzer, A. (2005). The impact of agency and setting. *Journal of Health Organization and Management, 19*(4/5), 297–303.

Obholzer, A., & Roberts, V. Z. (Eds.). (1994a). *The unconscious at work: Individual and organizational stress in the human services*. London/New York: Routledge.

Obholzer, A., & Roberts, V. Z. (1994b). The troublesome individual and the troubled institution. In A. Obholzer & V. Z. Roberts (Eds.), *The unconscious at work: Individual and organizational stress in the human services* (pp. 129–138). London/New York: Routledge.

O'Farrell, C. (2005). *Michel Foucault*. London: Sage.

Oliver, C. (2005). *Reflexive inquiry: A framework for consultancy practice*. London: Karnac (Books).

Palmer, S. E. (1999). *Vision science: From photons to phenomenology*. Cambridge, MA: Bradford Books/MIT Press.

Pfeffer, J. (1992). *Managing with power: Politics and influence in organizations*. Boston, MA: Harvard Business School Press.

Pfeffer, J., & Fong, C. T. (2005). Building organization theory from first principles: The self-enhancement motive and understanding power and influence. *Organization Science, 16*(4), 372–388.

Pless, N. M. (2007). Understanding responsible leadership: Role identity and motivational drivers. *Journal of Business Ethics, 74*(4), 437–456.

Polanyi, M. (1966). *The tacit dimension*. New York: Doubleday.

Prasad, A. (2008). Towards a system of global ethics in international business: A Rawlsian manifesto. *Management Decision, 46*(8), 1166–1174.

Pratt, M. G., Rockmann, K,. & Kaufmann, J. (2006). Constructing professional identity: The role of work and identity learning cycles in the customization of identity among medical residents. *Academy of Management Journal, 49*(2), 235–262.

Prins, S. (2006). The psychodynamic perspective in organizational research: Making sense of the dynamics of direction setting in emergent collaborative processes. *Journal of Occupational and Organizational Psychology, 79*(3), 335–356.

Provis, C. (2005). Dirty hands and loyalty in organisational politics. *Business Ethics Quarterly 15*(2), 283–298.

Putnam, L. L., & Nicotera, A. M. (2009). Preface. In L. L. Putnam & A. M. Nicotera (Eds.), *Building theories of organization: The constitutive role of communication* (pp. ix–xi). New York/Abingdon: Routledge.

Putnam, L. L., & Nicotera, A. M. (2010). Communicative constitution of organization is a question: Critical issues for addressing it. *Management Communication Quarterly, 24*(1), 158–165.

Putnam, L. L., Nicotera, A. M., & McPhee, R., (2009). Introduction: Communication constitutes organization. In L. L. Putnam & A. M. Nicotera (Eds.), *Building theories of organization: The constitutive role of communication* (pp. 1–20). New York/Abingdon: Routledge.

Reed, M. (2010). Is communication *constitutive* of organization? *Management Communication Quarterly, 24*(1), 151–157.

Reed, M. I. (2011). Critical realism: Philosophy, method, or philosophy in search of a method? In D. A. Buchanan & A Bryman (Eds.), *The SAGE handbook of organizational research methods* (pp. 430–448). Thousand Oaks, CA: Sage.

Rees, A., & Nicholson, N. (2004). The twenty statements test. In C. Cassell & G. Symon (Eds.), *Essential guide to qualitative methods in organizational research* (pp. 86–97). London: Sage.

Richardson, R. C. (2010). *Household servants in early modern England*. Manchester/New York: Manchester University Press.

Richardson, B. K., & McGlynn, J. (2011). Rabid fans, death threats, and dysfunctional stakeholders: The influence of organizational and industry contexts on whistle-blowing cases. *Management Communication Quarterly, 25*(1), 121–150.

Richardson, L., & St Pierre, E. A. (2005). Writing: A method of inquiry. In N. K. Denzin & Y. S. Lincoln (Eds.), *The SAGE handbook of qualitative research*, 3rd ed. (pp. 959–978). Thousand Oaks, CA: Sage.

Roberts, V. Z. (1994). Caring and uncaring in work with the elderly. In A. Obholzer & V. Z. Roberts (Eds.), *The unconscious at work: Individual and organizational stress in the human services* (pp. 75–83). London/New York: Routledge.

Robertson, C. J., Crittenden, W. F., Brady, M. K., & Hoffman, J. J. (2002). Situational ethics across borders: A multicultural examination. *Journal of Business Ethics, 38*(4), 327–338.

Robichaud, D. (2006). Steps towards a relational view of agency. In F. Cooren, J. R. Taylor, & E. J. Van Every (Eds.), *Communication as Organizing* (pp. 101–114). Mawah, NJ: Lawrence Erlbaum Associates.

Rogoff, I. (2003). Gossip as testimony: A postmodern signature, In A. Jones (Ed.), *The feminism and visual culture reader* (pp. 268–276). London/New York: Routledge.

Rosnow, R., & Fine, G. A. (1976). *Rumor and gossip: The social psychology of hearsay*. New York: Elsevier.

Rousseau, D. M., & Batt, R. (2007). Global competition's perfect storm: Why business and labor cannot solve their problems alone. *Academy of Management Perspectives, 21*(2), 16–23.

Rousseau, D. M., Manning, J., & Denyer, D. (2008). Evidence in management and organizational science: Assembling the field's full weight of scientific knowledge through syntheses. *The Academy of Management Annals, 2*(1), 475–515.

Rowe, D. (2005). The meaning of emotion. *Journal of Health Organization and Management, 19*(4/5), 290–296.

Rowe, M. M., & Sherlock, H. (2005). Stress and verbal abuse in nursing: Do burned out nurses eat their young? *Journal of Nursing Management, 13*(3), 242–248.

Rubin, R. S., & Dierdorff, E. C. (2011). On the road to Abilene: Time to manage agreement about MBA curricular relevance. *Academy of Management Learning & Education, 10*(1), 148–161.

Schein, S. (1994). Used and abused in medieval society. In R. F. Goodman & A. Ben-Ze'ev (Eds.), *Good gossip* (pp. 139–153). Lawrence, KS : University Press of Kansas.

Schneider, U. (2007). Coping with the concept of knowledge. *Management Learning, 38*(5), 613–633.

Schreyögg, G., & Geiger, D. (2007). The significance of distinctiveness: A proposal for rethinking organizational knowledge. *Organization, 14*(1), 77–100.

Schoeneborn, D. (2011). Organization as communication: A Luhmannian perspective. *Management Communication Quarterly, 25*(4), 663–689.

Searle, R. H., & Skinner, D. (Eds.) (2011). *Trust and human resource management*. Cheltenham: Edward Elgar Publishing Limited.

Shotter, J. (1989). Rhetoric and the recovery of civil society. *Economy and Society, 18*(2), 149–166.

Shotter, J. (2008). *Conversational realities revisited: Life, language, body and world*. Chagrin Falls, OH: Taos Institute Publications.

Shumate, M. (2011). Knowledge management systems and work teams. In H. E. Canary & R. D. McPhee (Eds.), *Communication and organizational knowledge: Contemporary issues for theory and practice* (pp. 191–208). New York/Abingdon: Routledge.

Sieben, B., & Wettergren, A. (Eds.). (2010). *Emotionalizing organizations and organizing emotions*. Houndmills: Palgrave Macmillan.

Sillince, J. A. A. (2010). Can CCO theory tell us how organizing is distinct from markets, networking, belonging to a community, or supporting a social movement? *Management Communication Quarterly, 24*(1), 132–138.

Silverman, D. (2006). *Interpreting qualitative data: Methods for analyzing talk, text and interaction*, 3rd ed. London: Sage.

Silvester, J. (2008). The good, the bad, and the ugly: Politics and politicians at work. In G. P. Hodgkinson and J. K. Ford (Eds.), *International Review of Industrial and Organizational Psychology 2008, volume 23* (pp. 107–148). Chichester: John Wiley & Sons.

Sims, D. (2004). Management learning as a critical process: The practice of storying. In P. Jeffcutt (Ed.), *The foundations of management knowledge* (pp. 152–166). London/New York: Routledge.

Sinclair M., & Ashkanasy N. M. (2005). Intuition: Myth or a decision-making tool? *Management Learning, 36*(3), 353–370.

Skakon, J., Nielsen, K., Borg, V., & Guzman, J. (2010). Are leaders' well-being, behaviours and style associated with the affective well–being of their employees? A systematic review of three decades of research. *Work & Stress, 24*(2), 107–139.

Soeters, J., & van Iterson, A. (2002). Blame and praise gossip in organizations: Established, outsiders and the civilising process. In A. van Iterson, W. Mastenbroek, T. Newton, and D. Smith (Eds.), *The civilised organization: Norbert Elias and the future of organization studies* (pp. 25–40). Amsterdam/Philadelphia: John Benjamins.

Sonenshein, S. (2007). The role of construction, intuition, and justification in responding to ethical issues at work: The sensemaking-intuition model. *Academy of Management Review, 32*(4), 1022–1040.

Spacks, P. M. (1985). *Gossip*. New York: Alfred A. Knopf.

Spitzberg, B. H., & Cupach, W. R. (Eds.). (2007). *The dark side of interpersonal communication*, 2nd ed. Mawah, NJ: Lawrence Erlbaum Associates.

Stacey, R. D. (2001). *Complex responsive processes in organizations: Learning and knowledge creation*. London/New York: Routledge.

Stacey, R. D. (2010). *Complexity and organizational reality*, 2nd ed. Abingdon/New York: Routledge.

Stein, M. (2003). Unbounded irrationality: Risk and organizational narcissism at Long Term Capital Management. *Human Relations, 56*(5), 523–540.

Stein, M. (2004). The critical period of disasters: Insights from sense–making and psychoanalytic theory. *Human Relations, 57*(10), 1243–1261.

Stein, M. (2007). Toxicity and the unconscious experience of the body at the employee—customer interface. *Organization Studies, 28*(8),1223–1241.

Stewart, P. J., & Strathern, A. (2004). *Witchcraft, sorcery, rumors and gossip*. New York: Cambridge University Press.

Stiles, D. (2004). Pictorial representation. In C. Cassell & G. Symon (Eds.), *Essential guide to qualitative methods in organizational research* (pp. 127–139). London: Sage.

Stohl, C., & Stohl. M. (2011). Secret agencies: The communicative constitution of a clandestine organization. *Organization Studies, 32*(9), 1197–1215.

Sturdy, A., Clark, T., Fincham, R., & Handley, K., (2008). Management consultancy and humor in action and context. In S. Fineman (Ed.), *The emotional organization: Passions and power* (pp. 134–152). Malden, MA: Blackwell.

Subotsky, F. (2010). Psychiatry: Responding to the Kerr/Haslam Inquiry. In F. Subotsky, S. Bewley, & M. Crowe (Eds.), *Abuse of the doctor-patient relationship* (pp. 64–77). London: RCPsych Publications.

Sunstein, C. R. (2009). *On rumours*. London: Allen Lane.

Sussman, L., Adams, A. J., Kuzmits, F. E. & Raho, L. E. (2002). Organizational politics: Tactics, channels and hierarchical roles. *Journal of Business Ethics*, 40(4), 313–329.

Sutcliffe, K., Brown, A. D., & Putnam, L. L. (2006). Introduction to the special issue 'making sense of organizing': In honor of Karl Weick'. *Organization Studies*, 27(11), 1573–1578.

Svensson, G., Wood, G. & Callaghan, M. (2010). A comparison of business ethics commitment in private and public sector organizations in Sweden. *Business Ethics: A European Review*, 19(2), 213–232.

Symonds, J. E., & Gorard, S. (2010). Death of mixed methods? Or the rebirth of research as a craft. *Evaluation & Research in Education*, 23(2), 121–136.

Talbot, M. (2010). *Language and gender*, 2nd ed. Cambridge: Polity Press.

Taminiau, Y., Smit, W., & de Lange, A. (2009) Innovation in management consulting firms through informal knowledge sharing. *Journal of Knowledge Management*, 13(1), 42–55.

Taylor, Gabriele (1994). Gossip as moral talk. In R. F. Goodman & A. Ben-Ze'ev (Eds.), *Good gossip* (pp. 34–46). Lawrence, KS : University Press of Kansas.

Taylor, James R. (2009). Organizing from the bottom up? Reflections on the constitution of organization in communication. In L. M. Putnam & A. M. Nicotera (Eds.), *Building theories of organization: The constitutive role of communication* (pp. 153–186). New York/Abingdon: Routledge.

Taylor, James R. (2011). Organization as an (imbricated) configuring of transactions. *Organization Studies*, 32(9), 1273–1294.

Taylor, Scott, Bell, E., Grugulis, I., Storey, J., & Taylor, L. (2010). Politics and power in training and learning: The rise and fall of the NHS university. *Management Learning*, 41(1), 87–99.

Tebbutt, M. (1995). *Women's talk? A social history of 'gossip' in working-class neighbourhoods, 1880–1960*. Aldershot: Scolar Press.

Tehrani, N. (2004). Bullying: A source of chronic post traumatic stress? *British Journal of Guidance and Counselling*, 32(3), 357–366.

The Mid Staffordshire NHS Foundation Trust Inquiry. (2010). *Independent inquiry into care provided by Mid Staffordshire NHS Foundation Trust January 2005–March 2009*. London: The Stationery Office.

Thomas, S. A., & Rozell, E. J. (2007). Gossip and nurses: Malady or remedy? *Health Care Manager*, 26(2), 111–115.

Tourish, D., & Robson, P. (2006). Sensemaking and the distortion of critical upward communication in organizations. *Journal of Management Studies*, 43(4), 711–730.

Traynor, M. (1999). *Managerialism and nursing: Beyond profession and oppression*, London/New York: Routledge.

Tschan, F., Rochat, S. & Zapf, D. (2005). It's not only clients: Studying emotion work with clients and co-workers with an event sampling approach. *Journal of Occupational and Organizational Psychology*, 78(2), 195–220.

Tsoukas, H. (2005). New times, fresh challenges: Reflections on the past and the future of organization theory. In H. Tsoukas & C. Knudsen (Eds.), *The Oxford handbook of organization theory* (pp. 607–622). Oxford: Oxford University Press.

Tufecki, Z. (2008). Grooming, gossip, Facebook and MySpace. *Information, Communication and Society, 11*(4), 544–564.

Van de Ven, A. H. (2007). *Engaged scholarship: A guide for organizational and social research.* Oxford: Oxford University Press.

van Dick, R., Ullrich, J., & Tissington, P. A. (2006). Working under a black cloud: How to sustain organizational identification after a merger. *British Journal of Management, 17*(S1), S69–S79.

Van Fleet, D. D., & Griffin, R. W. (2006). Dysfunctional organization culture: The role of leadership in motivating dysfunctional work behaviors. *Journal of Managerial Psychology, 21*(8), 698–708.

Van Fleet, D. D., & Van Fleet, E. W. (2006). Internal terrorists: The terrorists inside organizations. *Journal of Managerial Psychology, 21*(8), 763–774.

van Iterson, A., & Clegg, S. R. (2008). The politics of gossip and denial in interorganizational relations'. *Human Relations, 61*(8), 1117–1137.

van Iterson, A., Waddington, K., & Michelson, G. (2011). Breaking the silence: The role of gossip in organizational culture. In N. M. Ashkanasy, C. P. M. Wilderom, & M. F. Petersen (Eds.), *Handbook of organizational culture and climate,* 2nd ed. (pp. 375–392). Thousand Oaks, CA: Sage.

van Knippenberg, D. (2011). Advancing theory in organizational psychology. *Organizational Psychology Review, 1*(1), 3–8.

Van Maanen, J. (1988). *Tales of the field.* Chicago: Chicago University Press.

Vickers, D. (2008). Beyond the hegemonic narrative—A study of managers. *Journal of Organizational Change Management, 21*(5), 560–573.

Vidal, J. B. I., & Möller, M. (2007). When should leaders share information with their subordinates? *Journal of Economics & Management Strategy, 16*(2), 251–283.

von Scheve, C., & von Luede, R. (2005). Emotion and social structures: Towards an interdisciplinary approach. *Journal for the Theory of Social Behaviour, 35*(3), 303–328.

Waddington, K. (2005a). *The characteristics and function of gossip in nursing and health care organisations* (unpublished doctoral dissertation). University of London. Retrieved from http://ethos.bl.uk:8080/OrderDetails.do?did=1&uin=uk.bl.ethos.425359

Waddington, K. (2005b). Behind closed doors: The role of gossip in the emotion work of nursing. *International Journal of Work, Organisation and Emotion, 1*(1), 35–47.

Waddington, K. (2005c). Using diaries to explore the characteristics of work-related gossip: Methodological considerations from exploratory, multimethod research. *Journal of Occupational and Organizational Psychology, 78*(2), 221–236.

Waddington, K. (2010). Organisational gossip, sense-making and the spookfish: A reflexive account. *International Journal of Management Concepts and Philosophy, 4*(2), 311–325.

Waddington, K. (2011). Watch this space: Working between disciplines and paradigms in the scholarship of organizational gossip. *International Journal of Interdisciplinary Social Sciences, 5*(9), 323–330.

Waddington, K. (2012). Using qualitative diary research to understand emotion at work. In A. B. Bakker & K. Daniels (Eds.), *A day in the life of a happy worker.* Hove/New York: Psychology Press.

Waddington, K., & Fletcher C. (2005). Gossip and emotion in nursing and healthcare organisations. *Journal of Health, Organisation and Management, 19*(4/5), 378–394.

Waddington, K., & Lister, J. (2010). *HRM strategies and academic engagement.* Retrieved from http://www.lfhe.ac.uk/research/smallprojects/research/smallprojects/finalreportcity.pdf

Waddington, K., & Michelson, G. (2007). Analysing gossip to reveal and understand power relationships, political action and reaction to change inside organisations. *Electronic Journal of Radical Organisation Theory*. Retrieved from http://www.management.ac.nz/ejrot/cmsconference/2007/proceedings/talkpowerandorganisational/waddington.pdf

Walker, R. L., & Ivanhoe, P. J. (2009). Introduction. In R. L. Walker & P. J. Ivanhoe (Eds.), *Working virtue: Virtue ethics and contemporary moral problems* (pp. 1–40). Oxford: Oxford University Press.

Watson, David. (2009). *The question of morale*. Maidenhead: Open University Press.

Watson, Tony. (2007). Identity work, managing and researching. In A. Pullen, N. Beech, & D. Sims (Eds.), *Exploring identity: Concepts and methods* (pp. 135–150). Houndmills/New York: Palgrave Macmillan.

Webley, S., & Werner, A. (2009). *Employee views of ethics at work: The 2008 national survey*. London: Institute of Business Ethics.

Weick, K. E. (1979). *The social psychology of organizing*, 2nd ed. Reading, MA: Harvard University Press.

Weick, K. E. (1989). Theory construction as disciplined imagination. *Academy of Management Review, 14*(4), 516–531.

Weick, K. E. (1995a). *Sensemaking in organizations*. Thousand Oaks, CA: Sage.

Weick, K. E. (1995b). What theory is *not*, theorizing *is*. *Administrative Science Quarterly, 40*(3), 385–390.

Weick, K. E. (1999). Theory construction as disciplined reflexivity: Tradeoffs in the 1990s. *Academy of Management Review, 24*(4), 797–808.

Weick, K. E., & Putnam, T. (2006). Organizing for mindfulness: Eastern wisdom and Western knowledge. *Journal of Management Inquiry, 15*(3), 275–287.

Weick, K. E., & Sutcliffe, K. M. (2007). *Managing the unexpected: Resilient performance in an age of uncertainty*. San Francisco: Jossey-Bass.

Weick, K. E., & Sutcliffe, K. M., & Obstfeld, D. (2005). Organizing and the process of sensemaking. *Organization Science, 16*(4), 409–421.

Weir, H., & Waddington, K. (2008). Continuities in caring? Emotion work in a NHS Direct call centre. *Nursing Inquiry, 16*(1), 67–77.

West, M. A. (2000). Reflexivity, revolution and innovation in work teams. In M. M. Beyerlein, D.A. Johnson, & S.T. Beyerlein (Eds.), *Product development teams* (pp. 1–29). Stamford, CT: JAI Press.

Westacott, E. (2000). The ethics of gossiping. *International Journal of Applied Philosophy, 14*(1), 65–90.

Westacott, E. (2012). *The virtues of our vices: A modest defense of gossip, rudeness, and other bad habits*. Princeton, NJ: Princeton University Press.

Wilkes, R. (2002). *Scandal: A scurrilous history of gossip*. London: Atlantic Books.

Wolf, R. (1997). *Andy Warhol, poetry and gossip in the 1960s*. Chicago: University of Chicago.

Woolford, J. (2002). *The Central Estate and the Hartlepools (1800–2000)*. Hartlepool: Printability Publishing.

Yanow, D. (2009). Ways of knowing: Passionate humility and reflective practice in research and management. *The American Review of Public Administration, 39*(6), 579–601.

Ybema, S., Keenoy, T., Oswick, C., Beverungen, A., Ellis, N., & Sabelis, I. (2009). Articulating identities. *Human Relations, 62*(3), 299–322.

Zapf, D., & Holz, M. (2006). On the positive and negative effects of emotion work in organizations. *European Journal of Work and Organizational Psychology, 15*(1), 1–28.

Zerbe, W.J. (2000). Emotional dissonance and employee well–being. In N. M. Ashkanasy, C. E. J. Härtel, & W. J. Zerbe (Eds.), *Emotions in the workplace: Research, theory, and practice* (pp. 189–214). Westport: Quorum Books.

Zinko, R., Ferris, G. R., Humphrey, S. E., Meyer, C. J., & Aime, F., (2012). Personal reputation in organizations: Two-study constuctive replication and extension of antecedents and consequences. *Journal of Occupational and Organizational Psychology, 85*(1), 156–180.

Author Index

Note: Page numbers ending in "f" refer to figures. Page numbers ending in "t" refer to tables.

Subject Index

Note: Page numbers ending in "f" refer to figures. Page numbers ending in "t" refer to tables.

An environmentally friendly book printed and bound in England by www.printondemand-worldwide.com

This book is made entirely of sustainable materials; FSC paper for the cover and PEFC paper for the text pages.

#0247 - 200214 - C0 - 229/152/11 - PB